The Miracle of Lourdes

Books by Ruth Cranston

THE STORY OF WOODROW WILSON
WORLD FAITH
THE MIRACLE OF LOURDES

The Miracle of

LOURDES

by

RUTH CRANSTON

McGraw-Hill Book Company, Inc.

NEW YORK   TORONTO   LONDON

Published by the McGraw-Hill Book Company, Inc.
PRINTED IN THE UNITED STATES OF AMERICA

The Episcopal Residence,
Lourdes
August 16, 1955

*The Bishop of Tarbes and Lourdes wishes to congratulate
and to thank Mrs. Ruth Cranston for her beautiful book*
The Miracle of Lourdes. *He hopes for it a very wide circulation.*

(signed) *Pietro Maria Théas*
BISHOP OF TARBES AND LOURDES

*The accounts of cures in this book are medically correct
and in accordance with the records and findings of the Medical Bureau and the Medical Commission of Lourdes.*

(signed) Dr. S. Oberlin
SURGEON OF THE PARIS HOSPITALS;
MEMBER OF THE INTERNATIONAL
MEDICAL COMMISSION OF LOURDES

Contents

PART THREE: *Recent Cures: Causes and Conclusions*

List of Illustrations

To the Valiant and Devoted Men
Who Have Established, Developed, and Maintained
the Medical Study of the Cures at Lourdes,
Thus Performing an Inestimable Service
to Science, to Religion, and to All Mankind

Foreword

I n the southwest corner of France, near the Spanish border, is one of the most beautiful little towns in the world—and one of the most famous: the town of Lourdes.

Famous because hundreds of people have been reported cured there—cured instantly, permanently, completely: cured of practically every known disease. And this without treatment of any kind. They have been cured at the Shrine of Lourdes—many people believe—miraculously.

Two million persons visit the Shrine each year. They are from every faith and nation, for this is a universal shrine of all the world. They come with one common longing: to be healed of their miseries; there, at that simple altar in the rock, to be made whole.

The cures are not, as is commonly supposed, of hysterical or neurotic patients. They are cures of diabetes, tuberculosis, blindness, tumors, bone disease, cancer.

The day is past when professional men could scoff at such things. Five thousand doctors have banded together in an international medical association for the scientific study of the cures at Lourdes. They are from many countries: Australia, Argentina, India, Egypt, Turkey, Spain, Sweden, England, the United States, and many others. Investigations of the cures are as precise and methodical as the analyses at any first-class hospital. A Medical Commission of twenty distinguished physicians and surgeons of various countries passes upon these records before a cure is finally and officially declared. When it *is* declared, you may be sure it is authentic and rests on unimpeachable evidence.

Why should the everyday active person take time to read about such a place? Because it has an answer not only for the physically sick and suffering but for the ills and problems of us all. It has an answer for the world sickness, and for our individual sickness also.

Come and take a look at it. Whatever your special burden or secret malady, you may find a solution here. You may find that you, too, if you will, can be cured at Lourdes.

Part One

EARLY CURES AND ORGANIZATION

1

We Go on Pilgrimage

I went to Lourdes out of an irrepressible curiosity.

For years I had been interested in the power of religious faith in the relief of human ills, and had made a special study of it. I had visited a good many healing centers in America and other countries, inquiring into different methods and philosophies.

But until recently I knew very little about Lourdes, although I had spent a good part of my earlier life in France. At that time I was not interested in such things.

Then came that bright morning when my eye fell on an item in a newspaper lent me by a French friend:

IDIOT CHILD CURED AT LOURDES. BOY OF SEVEN REGAINS FULL INTELLIGENCE AFTER THREE YEARS LIVING LIKE AN ANIMAL.

Accounts of other cures followed: cancer of the stomach, peritonitis, ununited bone fracture, lung tumor. I read them, every word. They stirred my imagination. I wanted to know more about them. I wanted to know more about Lourdes.

I asked the Sisters at a nearby convent. They lent me books. I sent to France for other books. The more I read, the more interested I became. There was something in this place and in these stories—between the lines as well as within—that drew me; as it draws hundreds and thousands of people from all over the earth.

"Nonsense!" says the "rational" everyday mind. "A lot of pious exaggerations. Don't be carried away. It's probably

nothing but our old friend autosuggestion—nervous emotionalism at a beautiful spot and an historic shrine."

But that wasn't enough. As I got deeper into it, I found the
facts so impressive, and the whole picture so challenging, I began to want to see and study Lourdes for myself.

Now of course there are many books on Lourdes. However,
most of them are either stories about Bernadette and her
visions—volumes keyed especially to religious devotions, or they
are early histories written in the romantic style of the nineteenth
century: books that would strike the modern reader as old-
fashioned and outdated. Or they are written in French. Recent
fine accounts such as those that stirred my interest—Dr. Leuret's
Guérisons Miraculeuses Modernes, Dr. Vallet's *La Vérité sur
Lourdes*; Dr. Molinery's *Le Fait de Lourdes*, and several other
excellent volumes—are all in French. There seemed to be no
up-to-date factual story in English of this astonishing place and
the prodigious things going on there. I wanted to write that
story.

I talked it over with my friends. I told them the tremendous
impression accounts of this place had made on me. I mentioned
my years of residence in France and my knowledge of French
and the French people, which should prove useful.

"But you are not a Catholic!" was the immediate objection—
Lourdes being of course a celebrated Catholic shrine.

I asked whether that might not be an advantage rather than
a limitation. Catholic leaders whom I consulted seemed to
think it might not be a bad idea to have a book on Lourdes
written by a Protestant.

"A modern book on Lourdes by a Protestant—excellent!"
said a genial Catholic professor. "Go ahead. We'll help in any
way we can."

The idea kept tugging at me; I kept turning it over in my
mind. The main point that roused my curiosity was the change
in attitude of many physicians. I knew that in times past, even
as late as the early part of this century, Lourdes was considered

a place for crackpots and hysterical women who were "cured" of a lot of imaginary nervous troubles through a sort of religious mass-suggestion. Most reputable medical men refused to get involved with it. What had happened to change this viewpoint (as I found it had, radically, changed)—to make not merely a few hundred but thousands of first-rate doctors today take a different stand, and study Lourdes cures with interest and respect?

No one can read Alexis Carrel's case history of Marie Bailly in *Voyage to Lourdes*—one doctor's unforgettable experience—without being brought up sharp before the tremendous implications for all doctors of this extraordinary place.

There were the astounding physical cures; there was also the dramatic and moving human-interest side of the story: the joining together of many nations and classes in simple human helpfulness—hundreds of thousands of volunteer workers coming here year after year to devote their time and services to the sick. There was the colorful pictorial side; continual pilgrimages from all over the world, the great Eucharistic processions, the vast torchlight processions by night; the quaint costumes, the fraternizing among different peoples—Buddhist and Moslem peoples, as well as Bretons and Dutch, Indians and Argentines; the unceasing prayers in every language under the sun; the many vivid human incidents.

It was all too much—for a person with any imagination. I decided I must have a first-hand look at the place.

I met with plenty of opposition from friends and associates. "Lourdes, eh? Why on earth should anybody want to go to Lourdes? Mediaeval superstition . . . ecclesiastical trumpery . . . old wives' tales!"

"Most depressing spot I ever visited," said one. "All that pomp and mummery, all those rows and rows of sick people lying about. . . . Why in the world do you want to go there?"

"Eyewash," said another. "Obvious charlatanism. . . . Big piece of smart Catholic propaganda. Don't waste your time on it."

The more they talked, the firmer I became—the more determined to go and see for myself. Was this truly, as the French authors presented it, a place of simple sincerity and wonderful deeds? Or was it a gigantic hoax, a marvelously planned propaganda piece, cleverly conceived by astute ecclesiastics to lead erring followers back into the fold? Was it a mass delusion, an hallucination as great, though as sincere, as that of which Bernadette herself was accused? Or was it an amazing and extraordinary fact—as it has been called now for a hundred years, the Fact of Lourdes: a challenge to medical men and to all men and women of this skeptical twentieth century?

I intended to go there and find out. I had no ax to grind. I belonged to no organization—religious, medical, or metaphysical. I was just an ordinary citizen with an inquiring mind and a friendly (if wary) spirit, out on my own special quest and pilgrimage.

In the spring of 1953 I started out. Catholic friends, instead of creating opposition, had given sympathetic encouragement. Cardinal McIntyre, Archbishop of my own region of Los Angeles; Father Bunn, President of Georgetown University; Father Gardner and Father Lafarge of the magazine *America*; and in England, Father Martindale and the Lourdes Association of Great Britain helped me most generously with letters, long talks, good counsel. When I reached Lourdes, the kindness and active, practical help of Monseigneur Théas, the Bishop of Lourdes, and of Dr. Leuret, President of the Medical Bureau, opened every door—made this book possible. Nurses, Cures, and the sick themselves cooperated wholeheartedly.

Protestant physicians and friends of Lourdes also made valuable contributions. So this book, created with so much friendly assistance and goodwill from so many sources, has been written —in the hope that the story of Lourdes may become a little better known, and the Fact of Lourdes better appreciated by people generally.

The question may be asked: Why this special, strong attraction to Lourdes above all other healing centers? Why go six thousand miles, when many remarkable cures are claimed around the corner, so to speak, right here at home? How does Lourdes differ from other healing places? What are its peculiar characteristics in relation to unusual cures?

The outstanding characteristic of the healing center at Lourdes, and the one that made it of particular interest to me, is the medical *controle* or checking of alleged cures through an elaborate and rigorous scientific machinery involving large numbers of doctors, some of them religious, some not. Second, the powerful influence of the organized group work—the Hospitallers and nurses—in relation to the large numbers of sick; the comradeship and extraordinary sense of unity of these masses of sick for each other.

Then there is the special atmosphere in which the cures take place: the beauty of the surroundings, the pageantry and ritual of a great Church bringing dignitaries and endless caravans of common folk from all over the world. But above all, the perpetual prayer, going on day and night, on the part of vast numbers of people—so that the very air is charged and vibrant with it.

These are some of the things that characterize Lourdes; that give it, in my opinion, a special appeal. The reader can, if he chooses, take it as the study of one healing center among many, and can compare it with others he may have investigated. But I hope that he will study it impartially and fairly, making it for the time being a personal pilgrimage of his own.

2

How the Shrine Began

There it lies, a shining jewel of a town, slipped into the velvet pocket of the Pyrenees—spires, towers, green trees and gleaming gardens, dazzling in the brilliant southern sunlight. Smiling country—lush fields, flashing streams; crisp keen air resounding all day long with the songs of pilgrims, the tramp of hurrying feet.

In this town of sturdy Bearn mountain folk, about the middle of the nineteenth century, something extraordinary happened. The story goes that one day (February 11, 1858) the Virgin appeared to the child of a poor peasant family in the region—a girl of fourteen named Bernadette Soubirous—while she was out gathering firewood. Bernadette saw "The Lady" in a sort of radiant mist, high up on a rock in a grotto above the river. She was a young and very beautiful lady, in a white robe with a blue sash. The girl saw her so vividly that she could not understand why everyone else did not see her too.

After the first day The Lady came to Bernadette in a series of visions, or Apparitions, as they have traditionally been called. She spoke to the child in the Lourdes dialect, saying: "Please come here every day for a fortnight. Go and tell the priests to build a chapel on this spot. I want people to come here in procession . . . Pray—tell them to pray! Prayer and penitence! (The Lady stressed this over and again.) . . . Go and drink in the spring and wash in it," she commanded. "I am the Immaculate Conception. I desire a chapel here."

8

The Spring was invisible and unknown till The Lady pointed it out to Bernadette and led her to dig in the earth and make it gush forth. At first it was a mere trickle, no thicker than a finger. Soon it became a powerful stream, made famous by the cures which took place there.

From the first, the country people believed in Bernadette. She communicated her intense faith to them and they followed her implicitly, praying with her at the grotto at each of the "apparitions" of The Lady. They gathered in small bands at first, then in crowds from all over the surrounding country. They set up a rude little shrine and brought candles and flowers and small gifts. Local clergy at first were cool and aloof. Civic authorities scorned the visions, threatened Bernadette and her family, closed the grotto, confiscated the shrine.

But then the miracles began. A blind man who washed his eyes in the spring water regained his sight. A mother, neighbor of the Soubirous, dipped her dying child in the waters, and the child not only lived but became well and robust for the first time. People began to bring their sick from all over the land. It was reported that the son of the Emperor Napoleon III had been cured by the application of Lourdes water. The grotto, which had been closed by police order, was declared by the Emperor open to the public. After the first cures the crowd trebled. Hotels sprang up, churches were built—all the fanfare of a tourist and pilgrimage center quickly developed.

Finally the Bishop of the diocese set up a commission of investigation to look into the matter. The commission—hardheaded and skeptical men—after four years' study came through with a complete vindication of Bernadette and a declaration that certain cures that had occurred at the shrine definitely must be considered miraculous—i.e., contrary to all known biological laws and medical science.

In January, 1862, the Bishop of Tarbes and Lourdes issued a decree: "We declare that Mary the Immaculate, Mother of God, did in reality appear to Bernadette Soubirous on February

11, 1858, and on certain subsequent occasions, to the number of eighteen in all, in the Grotto of Massabieille near the town of Lourdes . . . and that the faithful are justified in believing it certain."

Bernadette was canonized (1933) in a magnificent ceremony at St. Peter's, the Pope and all the College of Cardinals participating. She had died years before (1879), in her convent at Nevers—a person remarkable for her independence of spirit, absolute honesty and courage, who had stood by her visions and her convictions despite threats of prison and insane asylums, persecutions and humiliations of all sorts. The transformation of her life and character, under the influence of her visions and alleged contact with the heavenly Lady, her change from an ignorant, undeveloped little peasant girl into a woman of extraordinary strength and reserve, is one of the amazing facets of this altogether amazing story.

⊷§ *The Church capitulated;* the medical profession did not. Doctors pronounced Bernadette "hallucinated"—some said demented. Any physician who dared speak a believing word for the cures at Lourdes was himself considered hallucinated and undeserving of a scientific reputation. Professor Pitrès, Dean of the Faculty of Medicine at the University of Bordeaux, told his students: "If ever people talk to you about the so-called miraculous cases of Lourdes, know that it is mere exploitation of human stupidity."

The Spring was called "fixed," the patients "sentimental neurasthenics." "Hysteria" . . . "self-hypnosis" . . . "autosuggestion" . . . "false diagnosis" . . . these were some of the explanations given for the remarkable things going on there. Lourdes became a focal point for the bitter battle between freethinkers and believers raging in Europe during the latter half of the nineteenth century. Doctors scorned the idea of any real cure coming out of the place. They considered it a resort for dupes and charlatans and called its defenders quacks and fakers.

In 1905 a young doctor was turned out of the University of Lyons Medical Faculty because he stated that a case of tuberculous disease in which he was interested had been miraculously cured at Lourdes.

"With such views, sir," said the Dean coldly, "you can hardly expect to be received as a member of our Faculty!"

"In that case," said the young physician, "I must look elsewhere."

He came to New York, to the Rockefeller Institute, and in 1912, as result of his researches there, received the Nobel Prize. His name is Alexis Carrel.

In 1912, another medical student at Lyons, Madame Jeanne Bon, was rejected on her thesis for her doctorate—"not for lack of merit, but because it dealt with the cures at Lourdes, with the miraculous." Eighteen years later, 1930, Henri Monnier received his doctorate (and very honorable mention) from the University of Paris with a thesis on the same subject. What had happened during those eighteen years?

To go back a little: After the vindication of Bernadette and the Church's recognition of the miracles, the Spring of the Grotto by order of the Bishop was channeled to fill the reservoir with twelve taps and five piscines, or pools, to receive the sick for bathing. This of course greatly increased the number of pilgrims and declared cures.

In 1872, the first National Pilgrimage was organized; and in 1884, the first "Hospitality" Association for the transportation and care of the sick. In 1885 came the establishment of the Medical Bureau—for professional study and verification of alleged cures. This gave the place a much more serious atmosphere, from the medical point of view. Curiosity brought to the Bureau doctors of all beliefs, and the number of visitors for a while doubled each year.

In 1893, the celebrated French neurologist Charcot gave his interpretation of the cures at Lourdes under the title: "The Faith Which Heals." In 1894, Zola published his novel *Lourdes* in which he deliberately falsified accounts of certain famous cures, but which again focused public attention on the place.

In 1906, Paris editor Bonnefon launched a bitter press campaign to close Lourdes in the name of hygiene. He met with an unexpected and thunderous reply. Dr. Vincent of Lyons got together the signatures of three thousand doctors testifying to the invaluable services rendered by Lourdes to the sick "whom we doctors have been powerless to save," and insisting that nothing be done to interfere with them.

A number of books appeared, by medical men of high reputation, discussing the phenomena of Lourdes and giving well-documented accounts of some of the outstanding cures: *Medical History of Lourdes*, by Dr. Boissarie; *The Facts of Lourdes*, by Dr. Marchand; *Medical Proof of the Miraculous*, by Dr. Le Bec; and various others.

All these things gradually—one might say painfully, and with slow and stubborn impact—wore away the early absolute resistance and broke down bit by bit the implacable professional prejudice against Lourdes.

But the most powerful force in this gradual transformation of public and professional opinion was that of the Cures themselves. They constituted a living argument difficult to explain away.

3

Early Cures

One of those to be shaken out of his early skepticism was Bernadette's own physician, Dr. Dozous.

This Dozous was an unusual fellow to be found in a little French mountain town in the middle of the nineteenth century. When the strange goings-on were first reported about his young patient, the Soubirous girl, he was as incredulous as other good citizens. But Dozous was a real scientist. Instead of turning his back, with a flat denial, he took the trouble to investigate and see for himself.

He went to the Grotto with his chronometer—the only scientific instrument available to him then—to observe Bernadette in her "visions." The unearthly beauty of her face during her trances made a deep impression on him. After the first experience he went every day and watched her intently, clocked her psychological states, and made careful notes of his observations.

His devotion was rewarded. For, while watching, he witnessed one of the first important Lourdes cures. And this happened to another of his patients—a little neighbor of Bernadette's, Louis-Justin Bouhohorts.

Louis-Justin was eighteen months old. Bernadette's mother was often called in by his frantic mother to help, during the child's terrifying seizures. The little boy had a disease which resulted in complete paralysis of his legs. Dr. Dozous in his notes on the case wrote: "Diagnosis hesitates between meningitis and poliomyelitis." The child could not walk, stand, or sit up. He had violent convulsions and high fever, with increasingly serious attacks. Finally the doctor said, "It is only a matter of hours."

The child moaned and gasped in his crib, and his father said to the mother, who was trying to help him, "Let him alone. Can't you see he is very nearly dead?"

He went to get a neighbor to assist with the burial arrangements. She soon arrived, with linens to make the shroud. But the mother would not give up.

She snatched the child from the cradle, rolled him in her apron, and ran to the Grotto. She found the piscine that the workmen had dug a few days before; and in that icy pool she plunged her baby up to the neck, for fifteen whole minutes. Neighbors looked on, aghast. Dr. Dozous, who was there with his chronometer watching Bernadette, counted the minutes for Mother Bouhohorts, too. When she took the baby out, the little body was all stiff and blue.

His mother carried him home and put him in his crib again. When his father saw him, he said harshly: "Well, are you happy now? Have you finished killing him?"

The mother knelt and prayed beside the cradle. At the end of a few minutes she pulled her husband's sleeve. "Look—he is breathing!" And the child *was* breathing—quietly and normally. He went to sleep and had a very good night. The next morning, his mother said, he ate a good breakfast. She put him back in his crib while she did her housework.

Some minutes later she heard a slight noise. She looked around. It was Louis-Justin. He had climbed out of his crib and was *walking*—toddling toward her like any normal child.

Later in the day Dr. Dozous and Dr. Lecrampe examined him, the former producing his notes on the case. "I examined this child three days ago," he said. "No change at that time. I wrote here: 'Still paralysis of the thighs.' I gave him twelve hours to live. And here he is—*walking!*"

"Yes, yes, go to Lourdes," said Professor Pitrès. "You will see there some fine cases of autosuggestion, with all the flowers and candles and incense, the collective prayers and so on."

But for Louis-Justin Bouhohorts there were neither flowers, nor chants, nor prayers, nor incense—just a few curious people standing about, more or less skeptical, and an observing physician definitely distrustful. And then—eighteen months old! Is it possible that at eighteen months one can make an act of faith and be subject to autosuggestion?

The case of the Bouhohorts child made a profound impression on Dr. Dozous. He was one of the first medical witnesses of the acts at Lourdes, and has been called the first operator in the medical verification work there.

An interesting sequel to the story: Louis-Justin Bouhohorts, aged seventy-seven, was one of the honored guests at the great ceremony of the canonization of St. Bernadette at Rome in 1933. He owed her a long and healthy life.

◄§ *Also in the early days* came the sensational cure of Joachime Dehant. Joachime, twenty-nine years old, had suffered for twelve years from a frightful ulcer on her right leg. She came from Gesves, Belgium. Dr. Marique and Dr. Froidebise, who attended her there, furnished precise details in their certificates describing her condition when she left for Lourdes.

They stated that the right leg showed an ulcer 12 inches long by 6 inches broad, extending to the bone. During the years, the muscles of the leg had been partly destroyed, the bone deadened. Foul-smelling pus discharged constantly from the wound. The foot, lacking all support, was inverted, the knee joint rigid —the whole limb could be represented by the figure 4. On the train the odor from the wound revolted everybody.

But Joachime was so sure she would be cured at Lourdes that she took a pair of boots with her to wear on her way home. On reaching Lourdes, she was carried to the Grotto and her leg was immersed in the waters of the pool for some thirty minutes. Nothing happened. Without losing heart she returned some hours later, bathed the leg for another thirty minutes. Agonizing pain followed—but then a feeling of great ease and the disappearance of all suffering. The wound was completely cured, the skin re-formed, and a perfect scar developed.

Mademoiselle Dorval, who had accompanied Joachime to the baths, the Abbé Devos who had cared for her in the train, and many pilgrims who had shrunk from her previously, all verified her sudden and radical change. The right leg had resumed its normal straightness and shape, and functioned naturally. When Joachime alighted at Gesves on the return journey, she was wearing her boots and could walk as well as anybody. She has made forty-five pilgrimages of thanksgiving to Lourdes since her cure, and always in the best of health. The Church lists Joachime Dehant as one of its fifty-one recognized Miraculous Cures.

◄§ *When French pension offices* start paying out money—and big money—you can be sure they believe an injury is genuine. That's what they did in the case of Gabriel Gargam, a railway post-office clerk.

On a cold evening in December, the Orleans Southwest Express was racing through the night on the run between Bordeaux and Angoulême. In the postal car, up near the engine, the clerks worked swiftly and silently, sorting the mail. Gargam worked quietly and expertly with the rest. In a few hours he'd be home, stomping into his own house hungry and tired, sitting down to the excellent soup his mother always kept for him in the big iron pot on the back of the stove. Off with his boots, on with his slippers—a good pipe, a nip of cognac, a glance at the papers, and then to bed. So he dreamed contentedly, sorting his letters, humming a little tune.

Suddenly, a deafening shriek. The train buckled. Cracking

timber—lamps smashing—people screaming—a bridge crashing into the ravine. Gargam felt a searing pain in his back. Then—blackness.

He woke up in a hospital, bandaged from head to foot, paralyzed from the waist down. He had been crushed almost to death—his spine injured beyond any hope of recovery. The least movement produced vomiting. They had to feed him through a tube, which caused terrible suffering. The tube could be inserted only once a day. Not eating, he became very weak and emaciated. Gangrenous sores formed on both feet. His physician, Dr. Decressac, declared in his certificate that the spinal disease would inevitably result in death.

The doctors of the Orleans Railroad and the Postal Administration placed exhaustive reports before the court that judged the case. The patient was awarded the then substantial amount of 6,000 francs annuity—the court pronouncing him "a human wreck who would henceforth need at least two persons to care for him day and night."

After twenty months in the hospital he was growing weaker every day. He could no longer swallow. The sores on his feet grew worse, and the doctors warned his family that death was near.

Gargam was completely unreligious and had not set foot in a church for fifteen years. But his mother was a deeply religious woman. Because of her entreaties he agreed to enroll for the pilgrimage to Lourdes. The journey was accomplished with great suffering, on a stretcher.

On his first afternoon at Lourdes he lay on the route of the Procession of the Blessed Sacrament—very weak, and soon entirely unconscious; his features relaxed, cold and blue. But at the moment when his nurse thought him dying, suddenly he opened his eyes, raised himself on his elbow, fell back again—but made another effort. Now he was up. He took several steps after the Blessed Sacrament, but he had no clothes or shoes. He was stopped and put back on his stretcher.

Never mind. Nothing they could do to him mattered now. He was cured! His paralysis was gone. He had recovered complete freedom of movement.

His entrance into the Medical Bureau was dramatic. Sixty doctors, many newspaper correspondents, believers and unbelievers, surrounded him. "Gargam arrived on his plank," says the record, "wrapped in a long bathrobe. He stood before us, a specter. Big, staring eyes alone were living in his emaciated, colorless face." Emotion ran so high, and the crowds were so great, they had to defer his examination till the next day.

Now Gargam came no longer on his plank, but in a new suit, and walking. The sores on his feet, yesterday open and suppurating, were closing perceptibly. He walked without much difficulty. The doctors examined and questioned him for two hours.

X-rays showed the compression of the lumbar vertebrae where spinal-cord injury had caused the paralysis of the lower part of the body. Now he was able to put aside his feeding tube and to eat normally. In a few days he gained 20 pounds in weight, four inches in the circumference of his leg. From the first, his endurance was astonishing. The crowd and the reporters besieged him. He answered them all calmly and never wearied.

Gargam's return home was a stirring event. The news of his cure had spread through all the stations of the Orleans road. It was verified by the physician of the Post-Office Department who told him he should immediately resume his post.

This case created a sensation. The sixty physicians who examined him at Lourdes all agreed: this cure was scientifically inexplicable. One might have expected the railroad to make some effort to recover the annuity. Instead, Gargam had great difficulty in persuading the incredulous railroad officers to take back their money.

He came to Lourdes each year for many years and served as stretcher-bearer, sturdily carrying other patients on his once gangrenous feet.*

* He was there in 1951—but died in 1952, at the ripe old age of eighty-three.

❧ A *cure of blindness* is especially moving.

Madame Biré of Lucon, hard-working country woman and mother of six children, woke up one morning not to the light but to total darkness. For a long time she had been having violent headaches, hemorrhages from the stomach, queer confused dizzy feelings. She knew she was seriously ill. But she never dreamed of this. *Blind!*

The doctor tried to comfort her in her terror. Maybe it was only temporary. These things happened sometimes—"nervous blindness," it was called . . . "The delicate mechanism of the eye, susceptible to inner strains, tensions"—and so on.

After the examination the doctor's voice was grave, compassionate. "I hate to tell you, madame, but there has been a complete wasting of the optic nerves—on both sides. I'm afraid there's no cure for that, and no recovery." In his notes Dr. Hibert put down: "Luminous reflexes entirely destroyed. Blindness from double papillary atrophy."

The papillae are the optic discs at the end of the optic nerves; normally a beautiful, bright orange-red, a network of strong, fine fibers; in Madame Biré's case they were grayish white and wasted away to a mere thread.

Her doctor told her, in effect, that the mechanism of vision itself had been destroyed.

How would you feel? How would anybody feel? Working people—the children—so little money—and *blind!*

Madame Biré grew rapidly worse. The emotional disturbance brought on more serious hemorrhages. She couldn't eat—continuous vomiting and lack of food produced dangerous weakness. And this went on for six months. Her family and Dr. Hibert were deeply concerned.

Finally she decided to join the Vendée Pilgrimage to Lourdes. Her doctor and her eldest daughter accompanied her. In the train during the night she had prolonged fainting spells, and arrived at Lourdes in a nearly dying condition.

In the morning she was taken to the baths, but the crowd was so great she had to return to the Grotto, where she remained for some time, lying back in her little carriage and praying with the other sick.

Mass ended at 10:15 and the Sacred Host was taken back into the Church of the Rosary. As the priest passed beside her, Madame Biré suddenly stood up and said in a weak voice: "Ah, I see the Blessed Virgin!" She fell back into her carriage, fainting. A little blood oozed from her lips. Her daughter thought she was dying.

But Madame Biré soon came to her senses. She saw the statue of the Virgin there in the niche—"less white and brilliant than the first time," she said. But—she could see!

Crowds flocked around her. She was taken to the Medical Bureau with her certificate from Dr. Hibert, stating the fact of her complete blindness for months past. Several doctors at the Bureau examined her, among them Dr. Lainey, an oculist from Rouen. He entered his report in the Bureau record:

Examination of the eyes with the ophthalmoscope showed on both sides a white pearly papilla, devoid of all color. The veins and the arteries, thrown to one side, were thin and threadlike. The diagnosis was forced upon me: here was white atrophy of the optic nerve, of cerebral cause. This, one of the gravest affections, is recognized by all authorities as incurable. But Madame Biré had recovered her sight that morning. She could read the finest print, and her distant vision was just as good.

She had recovered her sight but the lesions remained, to disappear shortly afterward.

Ten doctors made a second examination next day, with the findings: the organ still atrophied and lifeless, the sight clear and perfect. Questions followed thick and fast, with many scientific words the patient did not understand.

"How *can* you see, madame, when you have no papillae?" one doctor asked impatiently.

"I beg your pardon—the Blessed Virgin has given me some!" Madame Biré replied with spirit. "Listen, gentlemen, I am not familiar with your long, learned words. I have just one thing to say"—and she said it in nearly Biblical terms: "For nearly six months I could not see; I could not see even yesterday morning; and now I *can* see. That is enough for me!"

It had to be enough for her questioners also. They acknowledged that the cure appeared complete. The future would tell whether it was permanent.

A month after her return home the Medical Bureau asked Madame Biré to go to Poitiers where three specialists, among them Dr. Rubbrecht, a Belgian oculist, examined her. The Bureau wished to know whether she was still seeing with "dead" eyes. Dr. Rubbrecht found that the phenomena had ceased. "All traces of papillary atrophy," he wrote, "have disappeared. There are no longer any lesions, and the cure is complete."

From the hour of her cure Madame Biré could eat normally; she recovered her strength at once. During the following year she gained fifty pounds, could do all her housework, and was perfectly well.

The next year she came back to Lourdes. Dr. Lainey again examined her. He found the back of the eye normal, and the sight perfect. The register stated: "Madame Biré is now in splendid health." The President of the Bureau, Dr. Vallet, saw her twenty years later. Her sight was still excellent. And a Canonical Commission, after lengthy investigation, had pronounced her one of the Miraculous Cures of the Church.

Dr. Mariaux of Belgium, discussing this case at the Medical Bureau, said: "The instantaneous return of sight and the restoration of the sclerosed optic nerve is a fact absolutely inexplicable from a clinical point of view." All the doctors who studied the case unanimously set down the same opinion.

In two fine drawings, afterward photographed (see illustrations), Dr. Lainey showed Madame Biré's eyes as they were the first year he examined her, and again the second year. An American physician, Dr. J. Arthur Reed, of Pasadena, California, who recently operated on my own eyes, declared on reading the Medical Bureau record and seeing the drawings:

"Such a case is medically impossible. By all means publish it. Any eye doctor would be dumfounded before such a cure. Cases of optic atrophy, such as the one in the photograph, just don't recover."

� *Other extraordinary cures* baffled the doctors during those early years of the Shrine. Little Yvonne Aumaitre, daughter of a Nantes physician, was cured at the age of two of double club-foot. Her father recorded the case for the Medical Bureau files. Constance Piquet was cured of cancer of the breast—an advanced case pronounced inoperable by Doctors Laverne and Morlet, of Paris. Madame Pecantet was healed of cancer of the lower lip. For two years she could feed herself only liquids, through a small pipe. After several days' washing with Lourdes water, the hideous sore disappeared and the lip became completely normal.

Marie Le Marchand, her face half eaten away by a tuberculous skin disease, came out of the piscine with only a long red scar to remind her of her former malady. Dr. d'Hombres gives a vivid account of the Before and After appearance of this case.

With such impressive evidence it was not surprising that public interest steadily increased, and that even doctors who were most antagonistic had to shift their position somewhat. A place where such things happened could no longer be dismissed as merely a resort for charlatans and crackpots.

The early 1900s saw the spectacular cures of Madame Biré, Gargam, Adele Gofette (another sensational accident case), Marie Borel, Henriette Hauton, Marie Bailly of whom Carrel wrote, and many others. The cures were studied with increasing interest by physicians in France and other countries.

In 1930, a British doctor wrote: "The attitude of the medical profession as a whole toward Lourdes has changed very considerably of late years. The change is from skepticism and incredulity to an acknowledgment, not necessarily of the supernatural, but that cures in connection with Lourdes do occur which cannot be explained by any known biological laws."

In December, 1931, at the very same university where Professor Pitrès had pronounced his scathing indictment of Lourdes, a meeting was held by the Society of Medicine and Surgery of Bordeaux for the serious and very respectful study of Lourdes cures.

Dr. Pierre Mauriac, brother of the famous academician and dean of the Faculty of Medicine of Bordeaux, presented the history of a severe rheumatic case, with resulting deformities, which had progressed steadily for three years and which was cured suddenly after a pilgrimage to Lourdes. At the same meeting Professor Portman reported the cure of a cancer of the upper jaw; Professor Duverguey, that of a large varicose ulcer; Dr. Moulinier, the sudden amelioration of a young girl suffering from tuberculosis—the cure still in effect after nine years; while Dr. Gourdon told of a nurse who fell from an elevator on the third floor, sustaining concussion, fracture of the pelvis and both legs—the fractured bones failed to unite and a fatal end appeared certain. The patient went to Lourdes, against strong objections from her doctor. On the fourth day there, all pain ceased, and two days later she could stand. She resumed her work and was still working—active and in the best of health—several years after her accident.

All this may sound like a medical fairy tale, but the telling of fairy tales within such a hardheaded and first-rate organization as the Society of Medicine and Surgery of Bordeaux—narrated also in the *Fortnightly Gazette of Medical Science of Bordeaux* —seems very unlikely.

The truth was that forty years of steady, conscientious plugging away by the doctors of the Medical Bureau had had their effect. In 1927 came the founding of the International Medical Association of Lourdes, an organization for the scientific study of Lourdes cures, with a membership that rapidly spread to include physicians of many lands. A large correspondence developed, with letters of inquiry pouring in from all parts of the world. The President of the Medical Bureau was invited to hold conferences in Ireland, Holland, Belgium, Luxembourg, Switzerland, Italy, Algeria, Morocco, and Egypt, and but for the war would have continued to South America and the Antilles.

Requests came from Japan for an account of Lourdes cures to be submitted to a celebrated physician of that country, who desired to study the subject before coming to Lourdes himself. There were pilgrimages to Lourdes from Ceylon, from Dakar, from the United States, from Trinidad, from Denmark, from Lithuania, and many other countries.

In 1950, Dr. Vallet, the retiring President of the Medical Bureau, was made an officer of the Legion of Honor.

All this does not mean that there was no longer any opposition or hostility. There was plenty—and still is to this day. It takes courage (as several American doctors have assured me) to introduce the subject of Lourdes at a medical meeting or doctors' dinner party. One is still met with looks of pity, astonishment, or downright impatience in some quarters.

"But," as Dr. Marchand wrote, "the time of systematic contempt has passed. Many doctors have visited Lourdes, arriving there as absolute skeptics and irreconcilable adversaries of the miraculous. They have left convinced by the evidence, not ashamed to avow that they have witnessed facts accomplished before their eyes which they were totally unable to explain."

4

Lourdes Today

*M*odern *Lourdes is* a thriving town of some 13,000 residents, busy and prosperous with its huge tourist and pilgrimage trade.

If you are lucky, you arrive there as I did—in the radiant early morning: the sun just rolling up into a dazzling sky, birds singing, silver streams rushing along between rows of swaying willows; the mountains soft and hazy, still shrouded in their morning mist; and in the distance a slender spire, just visible against the rounded hills.

For an hour the train had been speeding through rich, waving cornfields dotted with red-roofed farmhouses and clumps of dark-green cypress trees. Nearing Lourdes, we saw that a pilgrimage train was arriving just ahead of us—a train evidently with a large number of sick patients. As it pulled into the station, from every window faces looked out, filled with hope and expectation, greeting their promised land: the dear land where their miseries were to be left behind—or at least forgotten for a few blissful days; for which they had endured the bitter sufferings and hardships of the long journey, most of them on the hard wooden benches during a night of "sitting up" in third-class.

But they seemed amazingly cheerful. Someone started a hymn—the "Song of Bernadette." It caught fire. Car after car took it up, till the whole long train rang with it:

"Avé, Avé—Ave, Mariá
Avé, Avé—Ave, Mari-ia!"

The train swung forward, and on this wave of joyous praise and hope we moved into the Lourdes station.

Groups of leather-harnessed stretcher-bearers hurry along the platform to the compartments reserved for the very sick. Blue-caped nurses appear at the car doors. The pilgrims who are well line up with their Director to show their tickets and to see their invalids safely established in the hospital ambulances.

I show my own ticket and pass through the station along with the rest. I rattle up to my hotel in the hotel bus, and find the usual French hotel room with its brass bed and red carpet and walnut wardrobe. I deposit my belongings, then go down and out into the street to see the town.

From that moment on, nothing is usual—or like any place I ever saw before. For this is a city of pilgrims, and they are everywhere; people who have come from the four corners of the earth with but one purpose: prayer, and healing—for them-selves or for their loved ones. The city exists for them. One is surrounded by them, and steeped in their atmosphere every moment of existence in Lourdes. A great block of them closes in on me the minute I step outside my hotel.

Out into the thronged streets and hot summer sunshine, blinking up at the high white plaster houses, the old stone walls, the crowds and the banners and the weaving cars and *chara-bancs*. Masses of people everywhere: peasants, many of them, in their Sunday clothes, looking a bit dazed and uncomfortable; flocks of little girls and boys in provincial costume—lots of young people; Sisters and priests of many different Orders.

It is a town of steep hills and sudden, dramatic vistas—a town rich in history. On the hill to the right is the square old fortress, built by the Romans two thousand years ago, and claimed by many different rulers. The Moors took it around the year 800. Charlemagne then laid siege to it, made a truce with the Moors; the Saracen chief was converted to Christianity and became the city's first governor.

The town of today is divided into two parts: the commercial

and residential district containing the shops, hotels, civic buildings, houses of the year-round residents and business people; and the second section known as "the Domaine," or Fief of Notre Dame. The busy "Main Street," ancient Rue de la Grotte, is a typical mountain-town thoroughfare, narrow, bustling, shouting; people and their vehicles jostling each other in good-natured confusion; shops with their varied wares crowding one another off the narrow sidewalks: Lourdes souvenirs, water bottles, perfumes, *patisseries*, notions. Pilgrims tramp up and down here all day long, with their knapsacks and lunchboxes.

At the top of the hill is the Square with the War Monument, the banks, the post office; the dry-goods stores, the bookshop, two or three cafés; and everywhere you look, hotels—scores of them.

At the bottom of the hill, Main Street runs into the Avenue Bernadette—equally crowded, equally noisy, and which leads directly to the Domaine. All day and every day, a continuous throng surges in this direction—people of many tongues, in many different costumes: a Scotch stretcher-bearer in a kilt, a Swiss pastor shepherding his picturesque flock with their wide lace headdresses; English curates, Italian *monsignori*, American and Irish bishops in colorful purple; city dwellers, peasants, soldiers and senators, mechanics and miners; the gentleman who gets out of his luxurious touring car, the wool salesman who comes in his truck.

The old and the new jostle at every turn: donkeys carrying huge bundles of laundry to the convent on the hill; young men tearing through on motor bikes; groups of humble village priests trudging along barefoot; an actress in a smart convertible, en route to Pau or Cauterets; big blue *charabancs* filled with tourists from Biarritz.

At the corner, hundreds of cars and buses rush by. All at once a girl with a big herd of sheep appears in the middle of the road. All halt, resignedly, and wait for her to go through. At Lourdes, a couple of cows can hold up traffic any time of the day. After all, it is still Bernadette's country town. This whole thing was started by a girl with a flock of sheep.

And here, now, directly in front, is the realm which her visions sanctified. Cross the perilous, tooting highway, enter at the big iron gate, and there you are at the Domaine: a long sweep of land, stretching for a quarter of a mile from the beginning of the town near the station, straight up to the Sanctuaries; bounded by the river Gave on the one side; on the other, the seething modern auto route of the Boulevard de la Grotte.

The Domaine was bought and set aside by the Church in the early days of the Shrine—to keep it apart and forever inviolate for the worship of God and The Lady. Within the high iron grille that surrounds it are the Sanctuaries, a hospital or "refuge" for the sick, the Medical Bureau, the printing press, quarters for hospital attendants and stretcher-bearers, and, most important of all, the Grotto itself. Higher up on the hill to the left are the ecclesiastical offices presided over by the Rector of the Sanctuaries, the Episcopal residence of the Bishop of Lourdes, and various other buildings connected with the complex administration of the shrine and the pilgrimages.

All day long, cars and buses tear up and down the boulevard —tradesmen and hawkers blare their traffic with the world outside. All day long the pilgrims come streaming into the Domaine, turning their backs upon that noisy world, giving themselves gladly, wholeheartedly to three days—or at least one day—of prayer and meditation.

Directly on entering this consecrated area, one feels more peaceful. The Esplanade opens its wide green lawns with their welcoming statues—Archangel Raphael, protector of travelers, Gabriel opening his book to the Ave Maria, Michael crushing Satan under his powerful foot—gazing down benevolently upon humble humankind and surrounding one with sunlit serenity. The marble figure of the young Bernadette nearby offers a homely human touch. And in the very center of the Esplanade and the Domaine is the statue of Notre Dame de Lourdes—

regal, benign, encircled day and night with pilgrims from every corner of the world sending their petitions and whispered supplications heavenward.

Standing there at the center, the newcomer faces the big Square which leads to the three Sanctuaries: the Church of the Rosary, the Crypt, and the Basilica—built one above the other, culminating in the Basilica at the top, with its pointed spire and its clock that strikes the Avé every hour. A great horseshoe Rampe sweeps out from the churches, making a promenade for pilgrims and a wonderful spot from which to see the processions and the town of Lourdes. On both sides of the Rampe underneath are various useful little bureaus and offices for the assistance of pilgrims.

Magnificent trees surround the whole place, and all about are rolling hills and the dreamy beauty of the gray-green countryside. Under the arcades of the Rampe, to the right, are the famous piscines, or baths, where the pilgrims come to be plunged into the waters of the Spring The Lady showed to Bernadette.

Pass the fountains where thousands of pilgrims come to drink and to carry away Lourdes water; walk a little farther under the trees beside the busy rushing river, and there you are at the Grotto: "that fiery hollow in the rock beneath the Basilica, a flaming cave burning in its side." An insignificant hole in the wall, it once was—a jagged rent in the mountain, unheeded, dark, forbidding, feared even by the populace; today the shrine most visited in all the world.

And here is the niche, the cleft in the rock where Bernadette first saw The Lady and heard her give the directions which resulted in all this vast structure and present activity. In that dark cavern where now a statue of the Virgin stands, one can well imagine The Lady shining forth from her niche, the child below on her knees, worshiping. Today thousands of people worship perpetually. The sides of the Grotto are worn smooth by all the hands and lips that have touched its sacred stones. Hundreds of flickering candles, tall pyramids of creamy white flowers, offer their perpetual praise. Along one side are heaps of crutches, plaster jackets, and steel braces, labeled "Thank You!" by the jubilant ones who discarded them.

The entire impressive edifice of the Basilica rests physically, as it does spiritually, on the Grotto. The one lofty and imposing (the mighty Church); the other simple and humble, close to nature, like Bernadette. All day long, people are praying here, absorbed, withdrawn. Procession after procession comes and goes —pilgrims from Brussels, from Bordeaux, from Strasbourg, Luxembourg, Madrid, Dublin. . . . Those who are praying do not look up—lost in recollection.

In the pulpit yonder, a priest from one of the pilgrimages is preaching, leading the people in this great lifting of the heart: peasant women on their knees, saying their rosaries; monks, Boy Scouts, taxi drivers, housewives; Breton pastors, Basque farmers, Dutch sailors, American college students; endless streams of people singing, kneeling, praying.

"*I want people to come here in procession. . . .*"

And all because a young girl had a vision, and was faithful to it to the end.

�⋙ *The great moments* of the day at Lourdes are the morning Masses, the Baths, the Procession of the Blessed Sacrament in the afternoon, the Torchlight Procession at night.

At dawn the hospitals begin to hum. Nurses and orderlies swiftly and skillfully wait upon their sick. Patients are washed, dressed, carried to Mass, carried back again. The morning trek to the Baths begins. The very sick are taken on stretchers, others are wheeled sitting up; the little carriages, each with its burden of agony, hopes and fears, rolled along by devoted stretcher-bearers or nurses. These are often praying aloud as they push their patients; the patients too are praying. One meets them swinging along the Esplanade in the morning sunshine.

Here are the sights that wring the heart: pathetic forms, worn but eager faces—some with closed eyes, motionless, numb. A young man with hollow cheeks and gray lips, his leg strapped to a wooden splint; mothers holding their children, some in heavy casts, some with huge lolling heads—pop-eyed, and Mongoloid; a girl with beautiful classic features peering out from a plaster cage imprisoning her from head to foot; a woman in a black veil, trying to conceal a face covered with flaming red sores; a priest, white and shrunken, in the last stages of tuberculosis; a little boy with black bandages covering his eyes; an old man hobbling along on two hideously twisted stumps. Literally, the lame, the halt, and the blind.

In front of the piscines, relatives and friends with their rosaries, praying audibly. Songs and prayers are heard also at the Chapel of Bernadette around the corner. As I pass those tragic little carriages, I pray too—that good may come to those poor souls. Surely a kind and good God could not but be touched by so much suffering.

All morning patients are being wheeled to and from the Baths and the Grotto. By eleven they are back in their hospitals for the midday meal and to rest until the events and ceremonies of the afternoon. Some visit with their families. Some are examined at the Medical Bureau. From two to four, the journey to the Baths begins again.

Soon after three, the stretcher-bearers start to clear the Square and rope off areas for the sick, for the Procession. Crowds gather with their camp-stools, milling along the Esplanade and up the Rampe, making sure of a good place.

At four, the bells begin to peal—the Procession begins to form. The priests in their varied robes assemble at the Grotto. "Everything starts from the Grotto," I am told over and again.

The Bishop appears with the monstrance, under the sacred canopy. Always it is a visiting Bishop or Archbishop who officiates—usually one accompanying a Pilgrimage. It is a great honor to carry the canopy. The first day I was at Lourdes it was carried by a Japanese, a Belgian, a famous Cure of former years, and a Negro with one of the most beautiful faces I have ever seen.

The loud-speakers open up. A great hymn rolls out, the huge crowd joining in unison, magnificently. The Procession begins its long impressive way down one side and up the other of the sunny Esplanade. First the Children of Mary, young girls in blue capes, white veils—girls of different pilgrimages, many nationalities. Then come the banners: Birmingham, Liége, Turin, Lisbon. Then forty or fifty priests in black cassocks— priests of all ages and features—some very fine faces among them. Other priests, in white surplices—the Chaplains of the Sanctuaries. Then come the Bishops in purple—ten or fifteen of them, and finally the officiating Archbishop in his white and gold robes under the golden canopy. Bringing up the rear, large numbers of men and women of the different Pilgrimages; Sisters, nurses, members of various religious organizations; last of all, the doctors. The head doctor—the President of the Medical Bureau—walks always at the very end of the line.

Hymns, prayers—fervent, unceasing. In the Square the sick lined up in two long rows—reaching from the Statue of Notre Dame all the way up to the entrance to the Rosary Church. Every few feet, in front of them, kneeling priests with arms outstretched praying earnestly, leading the responses. Nurses and orderlies on their knees, praying too—the same prayers, first in Latin, then Italian, then English, then Dutch, finally French:

"Lord, we adore Thee; Lord, we worship Thee; Lord, we love Thee. Lord, if Thou wilt Thou canst make us whole. Lord, Thy will be done! Lord, we believe; increase our faith!"

Ardor mounts as the Blessed Sacrament approaches. Prayers gather intensity, here at this spot where Christ is besought with the same cries as on the borders of Galilee:

"Lord, if Thou wilt, Thou canst heal me. Lord, he whom Thou lovest is sick . . . Lord, that I may see! Lord, that I may hear! Lord, that I may walk!"

The Bishop leaves the shelter of the canopy, carrying the monstrance. The Sacred Host is raised above each sick one. The great crowd falls to its knees. All arms are outstretched in one vast cry to Heaven. As far as one can see in any direction, people are on their knees, praying, in the form of a cross.

The sick raise their terrible faces, for the Blessing. Some pray that their own cure be forgotten, while imploring that their neighbor shall be healed. Souls long sealed within crushing agonies and suppressions open to the influx of divine and abundant Life. This is the moment when a sick one sometimes rises, and, pale but triumphant, follows the Procession with calm, victorious tread up the steps and into the Church.

Sometimes—but not today. The Bishop blesses the last sufferer, and mounts the steps of the Rosary Church to bestow the final benediction. Priests and chaplains follow him in. The crowd begins to disperse. The sun is going down. Nurses and orderlies take up the little carriages. The sick take up their burden of suffering again. People move off toward the Spring, to fill their bottles with Lourdes water; to the Way of the Cross on the hill, to do the Stations; to the statue of Notre Dame or of Bernadette. They talk in quiet groups.

There was no miracle today—except the only miracle The Lady asked for: Prayer and Penitence—mankind on its knees, in earnest common supplication.

5

Conditions for the Sick

Two million travelers and thirty thousand sick people pass through Lourdes every year; many of the sick in the last stages of some mortal disease. But in the hundred years since the Shrine's establishment, the city has never had an epidemic, there has never been a case of contagion, and the mortality rate has been not more than eight to ten persons per year. Certainly an amazing record.

True, the Lourdes sick do not travel with other passengers. Special pilgrimage trains protect both the patients and the general public, and are a guaranty for the public health. At the time when an anti-Lourdes movement was afoot in an effort to close the Shrine "for the sake of hygiene," Dr. Piraud of Poitiers wrote:

The movement of trains of sick across France affords no disadvantage to public health. As a member of the municipality of Poitiers and Vice-president of the Board of Health of this city, where hundreds of thousands of pilgrims have stopped and sojourned since the foundation of the National Pilgrimages, I declare that our city has remained absolutely free from all contagion and infection.

Lourdes hospitals are models of cleanliness—wards, kitchens, everything immaculate. Each pilgrimage brings its own nurses, but the two hospitals have also their permanent staff of Sisters. The Hospital of Our Lady of Lourdes, on the Esplanade, is staffed by the Sisters of Nevers, Bernadette's own Order; the

34

Hospital of the Seven Sorrows—just a few steps from my hotel —by the Sisters of St. Frai.

During the season, 1,200 to 1,300 invalids follow each other continuously in the wards—patients with all sorts of diseases— each pilgrimage staying only three to five days. The wards are remarkably neat and tidy, considering the poverty of many of the patients and the pathetic informality of their luggage— often just a cardboard box or string bag.

The dining halls are big, airy apartments, spotlessly kept; the kitchens the last word in modern equipment, with huge ovens and enormous round metal pots for cooking. Three enormous refrigerators keep the provisions fresh and appetizing. The chef has only one assistant. During the season, with the Sisters and nurses serving, a thousand are fed at each meal.

◆§ *Regarding conditions* at the baths, there has been at times heated discussion. Dr. Boissarie (in 1905) maintained that conditions at Lourdes were better than those at the typical hot springs—"where the pool is a large body of water in which the patients bathe all together, fifty or more at a time; where there is general contact, the water is not renewed, and the air soon becomes vitiated."

At Lourdes, he said, "the patients are bathed one at a time. Their immersions take only a minute. The sick person is protected by a curtain, the air circulating freely around him, and instead of a common pool he is dipped in a bath. Those seriously ill, those with heart disease and so forth, are not plunged in the baths, but are partially washed or 'lotioned.' Sores which might be contagious are bathed at the end of the session. With the large and experienced staff that directs the baths we are sure that every precaution is taken."

During 1953, 244,055 patients were immersed. There has never been an accident. Some 2,500 persons are given the baths each day.

The fact remains, as some writers have emphasized, that the water at the Lourdes baths is not changed after each patient. Some say it is not changed all day. It has been described as "dark and malodorous," "purplish," "inky," "a dreadful broth," etc. Where two thousand patients are bathed in four hours, one follows swiftly upon another. Persons suffering from syphilis, cancer, tuberculosis, and all manner of diseases are immersed in the same bath water.

The strange thing is that no infection ever results. When I was bathed, the water looked clear and clean. But the composition of Lourdes water has long been a matter of impassioned argument, from more than one angle.

⋙§ *The pools and the Spring* are of course a vital element in the life of Lourdes. Many of the greatest cures have occurred there. Before Bernadette discovered the Spring it was unknown. It appeared on February 25, 1858, during the sixth apparition of The Lady. The Lady said, "Go drink at the fountain, and wash there." Bernadette dutifully followed instructions and scooped out the sand in that spot—though everyone mocked and laughed at her. A small amount of water appeared —first a trickle, then a stream, finally a rushing torrent. People stopped laughing.

On the following Sunday, workmen came voluntarily and dug an excavation about 3 feet long and 1½ feet deep. The water that was conducted there by means of a small channel served as piscine in the early days, and here the first cures took place. (The Bouhohorts' baby, blind Bouriette, Blaisette Soupène, etc.) Later a small turbine engine was installed to provide a reservoir for the excess water and to meet the demands of the big pilgrimages.

The Spring is at the back of the Grotto to the left of the altar, behind a double grating fastened with a padlock. The water is conducted by pipes to the fountain in front of the

Grotto, to the taps where the pilgrims come to drink and to fill their bottles; and to the piscines, or baths. Each year, many thousands of bottles are sent to all parts of the world, by the chaplains' service.

The Spring furnishes 19 gallons a minute, 1,400 gallons an hour, and some 30,000 gallons every twenty-four hours. Many sick have been cured while being immersed or "lotioned" with Lourdes water; many others without drinking the water or taking the baths at all: at the Procession, at the Grotto, and so on. However, there is no doubt that the water has a powerful psychological influence.

Symbolically water is a sign of regeneration. In the Old Testament, Naaman the Syrian was cured in the Jordan; in the New Testament, John the Baptist plunged repentant sinners into it, and even Jesus went through this ceremony of purification. In ecclesiastical symbology, water stands for Christ, the angels, Gospel teaching, the science of the Saints—above all, as the symbol of the Holy Spirit. It does have a powerful suggestive value apropos of spiritual cleansing and restoration.

Chemically, however, the water of the Spring at Lourdes contains no curative or medicinal properties whatever.

In the early days some of the canny Lourdes citizens had rosy visions of exploiting the Spring and turning the town into a flourishing resort—like Aix-les-Bains or Vichy. They were bitterly disappointed when analysis revealed that the water contained nothing remarkable.

Professor Filhol of the Faculty of Sciences at Toulouse was engaged to make an analysis. He sent in the following report:

Carbonic acid	8 cc.
Oxygen	5 cc.
Nitrogen	17 cc.
Ammonia	Traces
Carbonate of lime	0 Grams 096
Carbonate of magnesium	0 Grams 012
Carbonate of iron	Traces

Carbonate of sodium	Traces
Chloride of sodium	o Grams oo8
Chloride of potassium	Traces
Silicate of soda and	o Grams o18
Traces of silicate of potassium	
Sulfate of potassium, of soda	Traces
Iodine	Traces
Total	o Grams 1 34

"The result of this analysis" (Professor Filhol noted) "is that the water from the Grotto of Lourdes has a composition that may be considered as a drinking water similar to most of those found in the mountains where the soil is rich in calcium. The water contains no active substance giving it marked therapeutic properties. It can be drunk without inconvenience." (Signed, Filhol, Toulouse, August 7, 1858.)

In a letter to the Mayor of Toulouse, Professor Filhol added: "The extraordinary effects which are claimed to have been obtained following the use of this water cannot, in the present state of science, be explained by the nature of the salts of which the analysis shows the existence." In 1934, a new analysis was made by Dr. Moog of the Faculty of Toulouse. The results were the same.

In 1938, Professor Lepape of the College of France undertook an exhaustive research to discover the possible existence of radium or radioactivity in the water. He writes to Dr. Vallet, with his report: "I send you herewith the report concerning the measurements of radioactivity which I have made on the water that you sent me. The search for radium did not disclose the presence of any radioactive element. From the point of view of radioactivity the water is entirely insignificant, containing only 0.7 millimicrocuries of radon at the point of emergence. Yours very truly, A. Lepape, Paris, November 16, 1938."

A bacteriological study of the water from the baths of the sick did, however, bring a remarkable discovery. As we have said, while only a small percentage of the sick who go to the baths

are cured, the uncured suffer no harm or any further infe
after their immersion.

The doctors at the Medical Bureau wished to check the ...y
of this, objectively, by facts. During the years 1934 to 1935, Dr.
Vallet, with several other physicians, arranged to conduct specific investigations. Two samples of water were taken from the
last bath where men's wounds are bathed, and these were sent
with all proper precautions, one to the laboratory of Dr. Bertrand of Anvers, the other to the Provincial Laboratory of Bacteriological Analyses of the Province of Gand, in Belgium—
neither office having any knowledge of the place of origin.

The resulting reports were identical. They stated:

"The water contains microbes of the most varied order—
colon bacillus, staphylococcus, pyocyaneus, etc. But none of
these microbes, after culture, showed itself pathogenic to the
guinea pig." Experiments made the same year at Tarbes, nearer
home, produced a similar report: colon bacillus, streptococcus,
staphylococcus, diplococcus, cocobacillus. That is to say, water
polluted in the extreme.

Six months after being inoculated with this water, all guinea
pigs were living and normal and in healthy condition. In short,
Lourdes water, even when polluted, remained perfectly harm-
less. Billions of bacilli were found, but they were inert.

At the same time, guinea pigs inoculated with water from
another source containing much the same bacilli, died.

Dr. Vallet arranged for similar experiments to be made with
guinea pigs inoculated with water from the river Seine. A
sample of water was taken from the river near the Concorde
Bridge at eleven o'clock in the morning, and was examined by
Dr. Deinse of the Pasteur Institute. It was found to contain the
same microbes as those reported in Lourdes water: streptococcus, colon bacillus, staphyloccus, etc. Three guinea pigs were
injected with this water. They developed fever of 104 degrees,
with rapid breakdown of tissue. Two out of three died.

Easy to understand, in the light of all this, how Lourdes water

came to be considered "miraculous." And here is a dramatic
footnote:

Many a Lourdes devotee—the stretcher-bearers and nurses
especially—at the end of the day, will scoop out a glass of water
from the baths and drink it down as an act of faith. Maybe this
will be too strong a "dose" for the average reader—but at
Lourdes it is an everyday fact.

The old Count de Beauchamp, President of the Hospitallers
and now eighty-seven, said: "I have drunk a whole hospital-full
of microbes, but I have never yet been sick!"

Naturally everyone wants to see the baths and to have a
bath himself, if possible. Walking along the Esplanade to the
right of the Sanctuaries, you come to the pointed-roofed bath-
houses.* They are divided into compartments—two for men,
three for women and children. Each compartment has a sort of
vestibule where the stretcher-bearers or nurses help the patients
to undress. Three of the walls are plain; at the far end on the
fourth side, is the shallow stone bath, with three steps leading
down into the water. Those who can walk use these steps;
others are lowered into the bath on their stretchers or in the
arms of their attendants. Immersion in the icy water lasts barely
a minute.

All morning and most of the afternoon, a steady stream of
people come to be bathed. Bath attendants are in these tiny
wet compartments for hours at a time, helping first one and
then another. Outside, the space in front is filled with the
stretchers and carriages of the sick, stretcher-bearers praying
with them and encouraging them as they wait their turn. Behind
them the tightly packed mass of friends and relatives, praying
passionately, each for his own, and for all the invalids: "the
assault on Heaven," as it is called at Lourdes.

* At present new baths are being built, and a number of improvements
created for the easement of the crowds around the Grotto.

Usually some pilgrimage priest leads the prayers, and with what fervor they pray, these poor country curés, flinging themselves on their knees with arms outstretched, invoking the Virgin with loud cries and imploring her to heal the patients who are being bathed.

"Mary, we love thee! Blessed Virgin, hear our prayers! Holy Virgin, save our sick! Jesus, save us or we perish!"

One after the other the ambulances roll in, bringing their pitiful cargo of human wreckage: the dropsied, the consumptive, the maimed, the paralyzed. Creatures who seem scarcely human any longer, so hideous and grotesque are their deformities.

A good place to view the scene is from the terrace up above— the top of the rocky cliff which falls sheer to the roofs of the bathhouse buildings underneath. I used to stand there for hours, watching the endless file of stretchers being carried in. Even from up there one can see those tense white faces of the sick, eager or twisted with pain, as they lie waiting, the crowd milling around them.

Loud above the shuffling feet come the cries of the priests— who stand now in a long row facing the people, with arms extended, always in the form of a cross. Now and again a burst of singing from the Grotto, where Masses are being said continuously—a great crescendo as the Gloria rings out.

And all around, the soft green countryside—the little white farmhouses, wide meadows, golden fields just ready for the harvest; the mountains, the sheep, the gray convent on the hill— everything Bernadette knew and loved.

The exquisite beauty of nature throws into sharper relief the agonies of those pain-racked bodies down below. One after another is passed along—lowered to rest briefly before that fateful door.

This is the moment. For this they have lived and planned, sacrificed and waited, for long weary months. And now—? This is where those others were cured. Will *I* be a chosen one? Will

I too drop the intolerable burden of pain and agony within
these damp walls, and come forth whole?

A lifetime of yearning and expectation is behind those closed
eyelids, those lips silently moving in prayer. One by one the
stretchers are lifted and swung gently over the threshold.

&§ *A person who is well* hesitates to take up space that might
be given to the needy sick. But such visitors are also permitted
to have a bath when there is time for them; and one is not considered a real Lourdes pilgrim until he has had a dip in the
piscine. So, in the afternoon when the crowds of sick had almost
finished, I took my place with the waiting women on the
benches near the bathhouse door.

"Partial or complete, madame?" asked a kindly, gray-haired
stretcher-bearer.

"Oh—complete." If I was going to do it, I had better do it
properly.

Two or three women ahead of me moved along toward the
door. One by one they were beckoned in. "And you, madame!"

I slipped through the portal into the tiny dressing room. Here,
in a space not more than five by seven, eight women—in various
stages—were undressing. At one end, behind the heavy curtain,
at three-minute intervals two sturdy attendants were helping
the bathers down the steps into the pool. The cries were not
reassuring.

We were told to take off all our clothes and to go into the
water *en chemise*—in nothing but our vests. Just before we
stepped in, one attendant swiftly slipped the vest over our
heads, while the other threw a wet towel around us—the same
towel that had covered the last person.

The women encouraged one another. "It's not so bad. Oh,
it's only a moment. You won't really mind it—I've done it three
times!"

The square, stone pool—a picture of Notre Dame de Lourdes

opposite—some prayers and invocations on the wall. The attendants praying without ceasing.

Down into the icy water. Gasps—cries—screams. "Now, now, madame, it's nothing. Just an instant. But really nothing, madame!"

"*Hail Mary, full of grace . . . Pray for us, poor sinners . . . now and at the hour of our death. Lord, if Thou wilt Thou canst heal me. Lord, that I may see . . . Lord, that I may walk . . . Mary, Mother of God, pray for us. Saint Bernadette, pray for us. Lord, hear our prayer!*"

My turn. The two pleasant-faced women grasp me firmly by the arms. One step down—two—*e-e-eh!* The water's freezing! In with the shoulders. Remember—this is where Joachime and the little Yvonne and Constance Piquet and Marie Lemarchand and all those others got their cure. This slippery wet little hole. Lord, help me to pray too. Help me to understand.

Up again. Quickly into one's clothes, damp, shivering. You aren't supposed to dry yourself after the bath. I know I must let Lourdes water dry on me. Six more timid, pink-fleshed women struggling into or out of their clothes. A stretcher-case being plunged in—a hunchback . . . Next, a woman with a dreadful, cancerous face. "*Lord, if Thou wilt. Hail Mary!*"

Out into the warm afternoon sunshine . . . the crowds, the kneeling pilgrims. More people going in—stretchers, little carriages—brancardiers skillfully moving their charges along. Through the crowds, past the kneeling priests, past the woman selling candles, out into blazing Square. . . . Glowing, a bit bewildered, moved in spite of oneself, wondering, hoping, praying for all those others—the really sick, waiting out there—the paralytics, the crippled, the idiots, the monsters, the blind. . . .

"*Lord, if Thou wilt—oh God, for Your sake, please do heal them all!*"

I have had a Lourdes bath.

6

Hospitality and Nursing Services

But how is all this organized? Who heads it? Who pays for it? What is the directing power behind it all? These questions naturally arise in the practical everyday mind. I asked them of the Rector of the Sanctuaries, soon after my own arrival.

We were sitting in his little office in the Administration Building—the unending procession of pilgrims winding past, up the hill, on their morning climb to the Way of the Cross. The Rector, a spare man with quiet dark eyes and a quizzical smile, regarded me benevolently across the plain deal table.

"Lourdes and its inner workings, eh? Very well—we'll begin at the beginning: The Bishop. He is supreme authority for all matters within the Domaine. Under him are the Rector and the corps of chaplains."

"And how many are they?"

"Fourteen, in permanent residence. In summer we call in twenty or thirty more, to hear confessions and give general assistance. These priests work very hard. Sometimes they are hearing confessions all night as well as all day. You see, hundreds of people want to confess at Lourdes who have not confessed for many years."

"I suppose each pilgrimage has its own priests, too?"

"Certainly. The number of pilgrims determines the number of priests who accompany it. Usually a pilgrimage runs from five hundred to a thousand persons; sometimes as high as sixty thousand, with the Rosary and the French National, for instance."

"And how does a person go about it when he wants to organize a pilgrimage? Suppose my friend Professor X, for example, wants to organize one, what does he do?"

The Rector shook his head. "Your friend Professor X can't organize a pilgrimage—nor your friend Madame Y, either, no matter how pious or devoted they may be. All pilgrimages must be organized under diocesan authority, and under the local priesthood.

"If a priest wants to organize a pilgrimage, first he gets authority from his bishop. Then he writes the Secretary-General at Lourdes to say how many pilgrims he wants to bring and at about what time. The Secretary-General arranges the schedule for all pilgrimages, and when you see the tremendous list—with three or four pilgrimages arriving every day—you realize what a terrific job it is.

"Look at that sheet of statistics here on the wall," he added. "In the year 1953, five hundred and fifteen pilgrimage trains came to Lourdes within the seasonal six months—not to mention planes and cars and other vehicles. They brought altogether two million pilgrims. That," said the Rector, laying the tips of his long fingers together, "is, in your language, 'a whale of a lot of people!' "

"Who," I asked, "makes the arrangements for all these people—the travel bookings, hotel accommodations and everything?"

"Again, the local pilgrimage priest and director. He is responsible for all arrangements. The Secretary-General simply gives that all-important thing: a date."

"What if a priest or group should arrive without the proper authority, or without fulfilling all the necessary requirements? I suppose that does happen sometimes?"

"They would not be admitted. You can understand how we would very soon be in chaos if these great numbers of people arrived helter-skelter, without complying with the regulations, or without the necessary staff to look after their sick members."

Each pilgrimage, he said, brings its own doctors, nurses, nurses' assistants and stretcher-bearers. The hospitals furnish free beds and shelter—as their name (Asile, or Refuge) implies. They provide food at a modest price, but no medical or nursing care. That is entirely up to the pilgrimage.

"What about the matter of expenses in general?"

Each pilgrim's expenses are borne by himself or his family— sometimes by a local Society of Notre Dame de Lourdes in the city or region that he comes from. The cost of a trip to Lourdes, for a sick person in France, ranges from thirty to fifty dollars, and for a well pilgrim about the same. Even the pilgrimage nurses and stretcher-bearers pay their own way, and consider it an honor and privilege to serve. All these are volunteer workers —most of them have to put in a fairly long apprenticeship before they are recognized as full-fledged yearly helpers.

"But as you know," concluded the Rector emphatically, "the backbone and central pillar of the volunteer work at Lourdes is the organization of the Hospitallers. That is an organization of which we are all very proud—a remarkable group of people."

Everybody here knows the husky, brown-faced men—popularly called brancardiers, or stretcher-bearers—who constitute a sort of combination nursing and policing service; and who serve the sick indefatigably from morning to night, asking nothing for themselves but the privilege of serving. The Rector told me something of their background.

Early in the Shrine history it became evident that some permanent organization was needed to give assistance of various kinds to pilgrims, and to maintain order. In 1884, the Association of the Hospitallers of Our Lady of Lourdes was established to meet these needs.

The Order had a picturesque beginning.

One day a poor woman, alone and helpless, arrived at the Lourdes station. An old pilgrim, Count Roussy de Sales, saw her getting down from the train with much difficulty. He went to help her into the little carriage that she had brought. She was looking for someone to wheel her to the Grotto. Roussy de Sales offered his services, and took her across town. The way was long and difficult in that hilly place; several times he stopped to rest.

On the Place Marcadal he saw, sitting in the Café Français, two young men whom he recognized and who, returning from a wedding in tail coats and top hats, looked at Roussy de Sales in amazement. "You really ought to lend me a hand!" he told them, smiling. They got up at once, and all three pushed the carriage to the Grotto.

Their task done, they began to discuss the need for organized assistance for the sick pilgrims, and thus the foundation of the Hospitallers was laid. In the early days it was in the hands of the French aristocracy, and these servants of the poor came from some of the noblest families in the land: the Count de Combettes de Luc, Count de l'Epinois, the Marquis de Luranes Castelet, the Viscount de Four de Pibrac, the Count de Villalba, and Baron de Saint Maclou. These formed the first Council, the heart of the great movement that followed.

The story goes that these early brothers prayed together for a long time at the Grotto; then, going to the Spring, they took a goblet, filled it with Spring water, and drank to the success of their project. That success went far beyond their hopes.

A year later, in 1885, the work was well advanced, and the Bishop of Tarbes received the first authorized members. The Order is based upon the old Knights Hospitallers of St. John for the sick at Jerusalem. The Hospitallers join the service with an act of consecration, and pledge themselves to give a certain amount of time and work every year. They are governed by a top ecclesiastic appointed by the Bishop of Lourdes, and administratively by a president, a secretary, and a certain number of councilors. They pay all their own expenses and give their services without any monetary compensation. There are now more than 2,000 in the permanent Association. They are assisted by the volunteer stretcher-bearers attached to every pilgrimage. (In 1954 these numbered 10,393.)

Three main virtues are enjoined: Charity, Piety, Discipline. Every Hospitaller is given a small handbook containing the rules he is to follow. He "must be ready to bear cold and heat, sun and rain, hunger and thirst, and long waits. He must not exceed a walking pace when in charge of invalid chairs. He must not smoke when in charge of sick persons. He must know how to carry the sick so that they suffer the least possible jolting." Last but most important: *"He must pray without ceasing."*

A brancardier is on duty from dawn until midnight, and sometimes later. His tasks are heavy, his meals uncertain, his rest slight and often broken by emergency calls. He may get his dinner at nine or ten o'clock—or not at all. He may be sent to the end of town or back to the station after a long and wearying day.

The President of the Order, Count de Beauchamp, records proudly: "In the course of thirty years' service, I have never once been refused by a brother brancardier, or even heard a murmur from him, when I asked him to perform still one more hard job at the end of the day." Some inner force seems to carry these men along and enable them to live at an almost superhuman pace while they are at Lourdes.

The work of the Hospitallers is organized in military fashion because of the large numbers of invalids to be helped and the size of the crowds to be controlled; and during their period of duty they take their meals together in a sort of officers' mess. They come from all walks of life—generals, judges, bankers, civil servants, sharing tasks and quarters with grocers, clerks, mechanics. They seem to work with extraordinary comradeship and harmony. At their office under the Rampe, a group is constantly in waiting to go wherever they may be needed.

Each morning, the president has posted on the door of the office the Order of The Day regulating the services—at the station, the hospitals, the Grotto, the outside and inside of the baths, the Esplanade and the Procession; so that everybody knows precisely what his duty is.

The brancardiers are the first people the sick see on arrival, and the last to see them off when they leave. Those on duty at the station help the invalids out of the cars with utmost care and gentleness, especially the stretcher cases who are lifted through the windows with great skill. Then they are placed in automobiles and carried to the hospitals. Sometimes the brancardiers are at the station for sixteen hours at a stretch. In the crowded season, as many as twenty-two pilgrimage trains a day are served.

In the hospitals the Chief of Service begins his work in the very early morning. First he goes through the wards and arranges to have Holy Communion brought to those who desire it. Then he sees to it that the sick are placed on stretchers or in carriages and are taken to the Grotto at the appointed time, the Rosary being recited by the whole caravan.

The Chief of Service at the Grotto, in the meantime, must have the space in front of the Grotto cleared and ready, and a set of stewards in waiting for those who are to receive Communion there. Thus, on arrival of the sick, everything is arranged for the hearing of Mass—after which the patients are grouped on the Esplanade and given their breakfast. This over, the move back and forth between the Grotto and the baths goes on till the return to the hospitals toward eleven o'clock. In the afternoon a similar service is in operation until time for the Procession.

This is the most strenuous hour of the day for the Hospitaller. He has to look to the safety of the sick in the midst of a crowd which sometimes numbers 40,000 to 50,000 pilgrims. When a cure takes place, the crowd may be carried away with excitement. The Chief of Service on the Esplanade has a large staff of assistants, posted so as to form barriers when necessary, and to prevent onrushes of the people. Well ahead of time, they have cleared the Square and the spaces on the Esplanade reserved for the sick, and these are then lined up in perfect order on each side, awaiting the great event of the day.

The Blessed Sacrament passes before each invalid whom the Chief of Service presents, and each receives a blessing. What jubilation when a patient is cured! And what a blessing when one can utter a word of help, give some bit of encouragement, or just tell a joke or a story to make the others forget their troubles for a few minutes and win a smile or a laugh from one of that suffering multitude.

All this service is wonderful enough just in a material way— of keeping order and making things a little easier for the sick. But over and above that, the spirit of self-dedication and constant prayer in which these brothers work, their powerful faith, their intense personal interest in every patient—in his physical welfare but especially in his spiritual estate, and in his getting all possible help and inspiration from these few days that have cost him so much pain and sacrifice to achieve: all this is deeply impressive and moving. Observing the gentleness, the tenderness with which these big men serve, day after day—many of them former invalids and Cures themselves—you begin to understand some of the factors that go into the making of that magic spirit of Lourdes.

Touching—and sometimes amusing—incidents color the life of a brancardier. Often the sick are very grateful for all this service and want to show it. Sometimes they offer a tip. One woman with more money than good sense offered a brancardier ten francs to get her in first at the baths. This one was rather curtly rebuffed.

Another time, a poor woman painfully took from her purse a ten-franc piece and said to the brancardier who was wheeling her: "Here, take it—for you!"

"But no, madame—keep it. I do not need anything."

"Oh," said the sick woman tearfully, "I understand. You won't take what I offer because it's too little. But I am too poor to give more."

"But no, madame—never!" And the brancardier took from her hands the little coin, respectfully, reverently, and put it into his wallet. The widow's mite—the alms of the poor! He could not refuse.

A favorite story of the brancardiers concerns two Oriental associates. Two Hindus presented themselves one day at the office of the Hospitallers and asked to speak to the secretary in charge. They had fine features and gentle manners, but their clothes were in tatters—their worn sandals tied up with string, their shirts clean but faded and full of holes. Evidently the poorest of the poor.

They explained in halting French that they had come from the middle of India to make a pilgrimage to Lourdes and that they wished to serve for those few days as brancardiers. The brancardier whose duty it was to inscribe volunteer helpers hesitated to enroll them, but was touched by their modest and imploring attitude and sent them to a certain Chief of Service, asking him to keep a special eye on these recruits who seemed a bit out of the ordinary.

The new brothers went to work and performed their duties with a zest and devotion, the Chief reported, "simply admirable"; and this went on for about a week. At the end of their time they came again to the office to return their equipment, and found there the same brancardier who had received them the week before.

He stared at them, amazed. There were at Lourdes just then only two Hindu brancardiers—these must certainly be his two friends. But what a transformation! He saw before him two distinguished-looking gentlemen faultlessly dressed in handsome suits, wearing gold watchfobs and magnificent scarf-pins, and with valuable rings on their fingers.

"But how is this?" stammered the brancardier. "I had thought you were—"

"We are two bankers from India," the men replied, smiling. "We wanted to make a real pilgrimage to Lourdes, especially

to give ourselves to serving the sick. We wanted to put ourselves in the same state as the poorest of them, in order to live
their life and really understand them. So we decided to dress as
miserable people, the better to carry out our plan."

The brancardiers marveled at the insight and sensitivity dis-
played by these visitors from afar, who had so thoroughly
grasped the Lourdes spirit, and given themselves so perfectly
and wholeheartedly to it.

The work of the Hospitallers extends beyond Lourdes itself
into many dioceses and faraway regions where local Associations
have been formed. These are now to be found in eighty-five
dioceses of France, also in Belgium, England, Switzerland, Holland, Italy, Spain, and Portugal. These local societies collect
the sick, raise funds for them, prepare them, both spiritually and
materially, for the pilgrimage, see that they get to Lourdes and
safely home again. During the year the local organizations hold
Lourdes conferences and reunions, monthly religious services
and retreats in common. Many help at home who cannot go to
Lourdes, but their help is just as important. Thus a vast network of Hospitality and knightly service is spread over France
and various foreign countries.

About the same number of nurses as brancardiers—that is,
around 2,000—belong to the permanent organization. The
women's membership has been a vital part of the Hospitality
from the very beginning. This too was originally under the direction of women from the great families of France and Italy
especially. Today its nurses and nurses' aids (known as "hand-
maids") who come with the pilgrimages each year, are recruited
from all classes: the wealthy and the nobility, but also salesgirls
and stenographers, dressmakers and filing clerks—all serving together in devoted comradeship just like the men. Many women
Cures of former years, come back each season as nurses, or to
help as scullery maids and with other menial jobs in the hospitals. Often 1,800 people a day are served in the women's section

at the baths, several hundred helpless and stretcher cases among them.

"I think," says the Comte de Beauchamp, "there is no service more meritorious and more humbly accomplished than that of these servants of the sick, both men and women, who for three consecutive hours of the morning and evening, behind curtains in an unpleasant atmosphere, aid the helpless, undo and afterwards remake the dressings of the most painful sores, and keep praying constantly."

The quiet order and efficiency of all this work is the more admirable when you remember that the assistant stretcher-bearers and nurses change every three or four days with each new pilgrimage; and that the men and women Hospitallers come not only from many different parts of France, but from many different nations.

7

The Medical Organization

D*own to the right,* on the Esplanade, stands the unpretentious gray building that houses the famous Bureau of Medical Verifications. That first day, I walked across the Square and toward its open door with mounting excitement. Inside those plain gray walls were the documents I had come six thousand miles to see. Here, for me, next to the Grotto itself, was the vital center.

Here in the court outside, patients with their families or physicians are waiting to be examined—stretchers, wheel chairs, little carriages lined up against the wall. Here visiting doctors come to register and get their official badges permitting them to visit the hospitals, talk to the sick, study the records—in short, to have the run of the place.

And here, during the next few minutes, I met the keen-eyed, cordial group of men who make up the staff of the Medical Bureau: half a dozen capable scientists, some seasoned veterans who return year after year, devotedly giving their time and skill; some strapping young interns just out of medical school, eager to learn all they can. The wife of one of them runs a little shop in Lourdes so that her husband can come in the summer and give his services at the Bureau.

These were to be my friends and generous helpers during the weeks to come—and a gold mine of valuable information.

They gave me a very kind welcome.

"Come in, come in, madame!" said the President, Dr. Leuret.

"Monseigneur has told us about you. Everything here is at your disposal. Madame has come all the way from America to do a book on Lourdes," he explained to the others, beaming. "The sort of book we like—careful, precise, well-documented."

He took me over to the office and opened a cabinet containing the precious dossiers. "Here you will find what you have crossed the ocean for," he said proudly. "And I believe you will find that you have not come in vain!"

This President of the Bureau is a remarkable person: Legion of Honor, Croix de Guerre, Councilor of France, Professor of Medicine; he is also head of a large clinic in Bordeaux—the worst section, which he has turned into a thriving parish house as well as hospital. A square, stocky man with sharp eyes and a heart as big as a cathedral, himself father of twelve children, he would pick up his little patients with infinite tenderness, talk to them, coax them as if they were his own, get them to tell him their pitiful little symptoms. Mothers gave their burdens into his charge with a sigh of absolute trust and confidence.

Sitting on a bench in the sunlight, after his morning office hours, he told me the story of his beloved Bureau.

"First and foremost: the medical work at Lourdes is run entirely by doctors and supported by doctors. Never forget that. Some are Catholics, some are Protestants; some are agnostics or unbelievers; others, followers of non-Christian faiths. There is only one criterion for membership in this work: the members believe that the study of Lourdes cures is something important which deserves their help."

He stopped to lend a hand to a stretcher-bearer who was rolling a little girl in a heavy steel brace out onto the boardwalk, then went on.

"Our beginnings were humble, though from the first the Bureau was served by men of the first rank. A certain Dr. St. Maclou who came to Lourdes with his wife on pilgrimage—that was in 1885—strongly felt the need for a permanent medical man on the spot, to examine the alleged cures. He offered himself for the post, and remained here till his death, a man of austere scientific standards and highest character.

"After him came Dr. Boissarie—the 'lion of Lourdes' he was called—one of the most brilliant young Paris interns of his time. He gave up several offers of big posts and chose Lourdes as his cherished life work. He died here, after thirty years of selfless service. Then there was Dr. Le Bec, a senior surgeon of St. Joseph's Hospital in Paris. You see the caliber of the men who have run the Medical Bureau. Dr. Marchand and Dr. Vallet followed Le Bec—both of them highly distinguished physicians. Lastly, myself—*pas grand'chose*, not much—but loyal and faithful to the great tradition."

"I don't wonder you're proud of it. But now tell me—what are the exact powers and functions of the Bureau? How does it work?"

"Of course—I knew you would ask that. Here"—he took a well-worn little book from his pocket—"I will read you the official statement."

" 'The Medical Bureau of Lourdes is a medical office officially charged to proceed . . . with the examination of the cases of cure on the day when they occur at Lourdes, and to note those cures which are patent, and which could not be the result of the forces of nature. It is also equipped for the study of healings which have taken place in any other part of the world, provided the name of Lourdes has been invoked.' "

"And is it open all the year round, or just during the summer?"

"Just during the summer, the pilgrimage season, from Easter to the middle of October."

He read further from his little manual: " 'Besides the President, the Bureau is composed of all the doctors who come each year to inscribe themselves in its register and to take part in its labors.' Any medical man is welcomed at the Bureau, whatever his religious opinions or lack of any. He may freely examine the evidence, criticize, and take part in the discussions. A simple identification card is all we require, showing that we have to deal with a reputable physician.

"And as I told you," continued Dr. Leuret, "these doctors are by no means all Catholics. During my time here, Jews, Moslems, Buddhists, Hindus, Protestants of all sects, have been among our colleagues; atheists and unbelievers, too. It's this study of the cures by men of such different beliefs and viewpoints that guarantees our competency and our good faith."

"How do you run as to nationalities?"

"Well, let us see—" He turned to his table of statistics. "In 1953, some fifteen hundred doctors signed the register and took part in the examinations at the Bureau. Two-thirds of them were French; the rest Belgians, Italians, Spaniards, English, Germans, Dutch. Very few Americans—distance, of course, has a lot to do with that. Though oddly enough we have quite a number from Oriental countries, and some from the Near East. Of course it varies each year. The countries near at hand, like Belgium and Italy, naturally send us the most."

"How about age? How do you rate with the younger men, for instance?"

"Very high when they see how carefully we scrutinize the cases. We get always two or three hundred doctors and interns among the younger crowd each year, who come to study the records and assist at the examinations of patients. It's a wonderful laboratory for them. The older men are professors of medical faculties, doctors of both city and country hospitals, surgeons, and specialists of many different kinds. Each is encouraged to give his views and opinions as freely as at any medical congress. We have lively—sometimes impassioned—discussions; but always in a friendly spirit.

"Here," he said, "is a grand opportunity to pool knowledge and to learn from one another; to compare the development of certain methods and therapeutic techniques as practiced in different parts of the world; to rub shoulders with confreres of many types of experience in many lands. Not to mention an opportunity to study practically every known disease—and for each one, usually several cases of his own specialty. It's the greatest polyclinic in the world!

"The alert modern physician appreciates all this, and, more and more, a visit to Lourdes is coming to be known as a valuable professional asset, as well as for some a memorable religious and spiritual experience."

He went on to fill in other details. By the end of that first morning I had a very good idea of the background and practical workings of the Medical Organization.

On the functional side, it's not so complicated, considering the mass of patients they have to deal with, the large numbers of sick who come to Lourdes each year.

According to official statistics, 33,276 came in 1954. Each pilgrimage is accompanied by one or more medical men, and no sick person is accepted without a medical certificate from his home physician, stating his disease, present condition, and progress of the disease at the time he left home. At the Bureau, when a supposed cure is being judged, everything is necessarily based on the accompanying medical certificates.

During the busiest season, several pilgrimages are held simultaneously each week—as for instance during the first week of my stay when 1,000 came from Newcastle, 1,200 from Brussels, and 1,000 from Turin, all at the same time. This means the presence of a number of medical men besides those visiting Lourdes out of personal curiosity or interest in the work there. All doctors are urged to register at the Bureau immediately on arrival.

When a supposed cure occurs, the doctor of the pilgrimage takes the patient to the Medical Bureau at once for examination—and eventually verification of the cure. The patient is thoroughly examined by the doctors who are present at the Bureau at that time and a careful report is drawn up on a special form. There follows an exhaustive and vigorous discussion of the case, around three principal questions: (1) Did the illness really exist? (2) Is there a cure? (3) Can the cure be explained naturally?

A *rapporteur* keeps precise record of all findings. And the patients give their testimony under oath. Note that this first record does not in any way constitute an argument in favor of a miracle. It is simply an initial document and opening of an inquiry. At this first session the patient is given a date and a place in the Bureau files; a study is made of the papers he brought with him on the pilgrimage; first accounts of witnesses are assembled; the patient is put through extensive physical and psychological tests, and the endeavor made to establish with all possible exactness his state before coming to Lourdes and his state at the moment of presenting himself at the Bureau.

At the end of this first session, either the record appears sufficiently significant and is retained for the following year, or it is inconclusive and is immediately discarded. If it is retained, the patient is put under observation; a physician of his own region is named as investigator. The latter will pursue this investigation—and his observation of the patient—for one year. He will gather new documents, will search out witnesses that may have been lacking, will talk with the patient's home physician, with his relatives and neighbors, and will be responsible for presenting the case again the following year, on completion of the inquiry.

The severity of this scrutiny by the Medical Bureau is shown by the fact that, in 1947, seventy-five cures were retained for investigation; only eleven came back the next year and of these only six were ultimately kept. In 1948, eighty-three records were set up at the first hearing; only fifteen came back, and nine were finally kept and sent on for study as possible Miracles. Sometimes cases are held over longer than a year for more complete inquiry, at the request of some physician. All of which explains why a cure is never announced under two years' time, and sometimes longer.

When a case has been retained, the patient under investigation is called to the Bureau again at the end of a year for a second examination, much more rigorous than the first. This time his case is gone over "with a fine-tooth comb." Much more information is now available on him. He is studied, discussed, and often sharply challenged by the group of doctors who are going to risk their professional reputations by signing or refusing to sign the statement certifying his apparent cure.

At the end of the second examination the following questions are formally put to the doctors participating:

1. Did the illness described by the medical record exist at the moment of the patient's pilgrimage to Lourdes?
2. Was the malady suddenly stopped in its course at a time when there was no tendency towards improvement? Which symptoms disappeared at this time?
3. Is there a cure? Can you prove it with certainty? Did the cure take place without medical treatment?
4. Is it necessary to delay a decision?
5. (Finally, the ultimate question): Is there any possible medical explanation of this cure? In the present state of science, can any natural or scientific explanation be given?

If not, and if after all this careful analysis and investigation the doctors of the Bureau are satisfied that the case appears to be a genuine supernatural cure, it is sent on for further study and judgment by the Medical Commission.

•ß *To make scientific competence and precision doubly sure*, a Medical Commission was set up which should study cases away from Lourdes, solely on the evidence of medical documents and from a purely technical standpoint. Its seat is in Paris and it has included among its members some of the foremost physicians and surgeons of that city. At first a national Commission, it has now been enlarged to take in doctors and experts of other countries—particularly those nearby (such as Belgium,

England and Italy) so that members may be able to attend the Commission meetings.

The list of names of the present Medical Commission shows the distinction and quality of the men who make up this body.

When the Medical Bureau of Lourdes is satisfied as to the genuineness of a cure, or if there is some question in their minds about it, they send the record of that cure—the documents, certificates, results of examinations, X-rays, bacteriological analyses, and everything to do with the case—on to the Medical Commission.

The Commission makes a thorough study of the case, calling in such specialists as may be needed for more extensive observation. The duty of the Commission is not to declare a miracle, but simply and solely to declare (or fail to declare): "We find no natural or scientific explanation of this cure." If they do so declare, the case is then sent on to the Bishop of the cured person's diocese, with the recommendation that a Canonical Commission be appointed to investigate it. It is the Church that decides whether or not it is a miraculous cure.

"As physicians," the President of the Commission told me, "we can only state our conviction as to whether the case is or is not outside natural and scientific law. The theologians have then to determine whether it shall be proclaimed a miracle." And the theologians, as we shall see, are even more strict and conservative than the doctors.

Far from trying to "contrive" a miracle, as critics of the Church sometimes suggest, the Canonical Commissions are so severe on every detail that when a case succeeds in passing their requirements, one may be sure it is indeed extraordinary and outside the laws of nature. Only fifty-one cases in a hundred years have passed this bar and been pronounced Miraculous Cures by the Church. The requirements of the Church are discussed in a separate chapter.

*   *   *

The Medical Commission of Lourdes

Dr. Grenet	*President. Specialist in Children's Diseases, Paris*
Dr. Auvigne	*Surgeon. Specialist Genitourinary Diseases, Nantes*
Dr. Biot	*Endocrinology. 30 Cours Albert Thomas, Lyon*
Dr. Ch. Lancrenon	*General Medicine. 3 Rue de la Trinité, Paris*
Dr. Langeron	*General Medicine. 63 Rue Vaubun, Lille*
Dr. Lanos	*Surgeon. St. Joseph's Hospital, Paris*
Dr. Lhermitte	*Neuropsychiatry. 9 Rue Marboeuf, Paris*
Dr. Mauriac	*General Medicine. 12 Rue Vauban, Bordeaux*
Dr. Merigot de Freigny	*Ophthalmology. St. Joseph's Hospital, Paris*
Dr. Michon	*Surgeon. Urinary Diseases. 40 Rue Barbet de Jouy, Paris*
Dr. Oberlin	*Surgeon of the Paris Hospitals. 121 Bvd. St. Germain, Paris*
Dr. Pasteau	*General Medicine. Parce, Sarthe*
Dr. Sendrail	*General Medicine. 26 Bvd. Carnot, Toulouse*
Dr. Huc	*Orthopedic Surgeon. 44 Rue Notre Dame des Champs, Paris*

The following international members have been added to the Commission:

Belgium

Dr. G. Van Schuren, *Professor of the University of Louvain*

Dr. Ch. De Gheldere, *Boussu, Tournai*

Germany

Dr. Ernest, *Chief Physician, Hildegardiskrankenhaus, Cologne*

Dr. Meixner, *Chief Physician, Schonmunzach, Schwarzwald*

Great Britain

Dr. Daniel O'Connell, *Charing Cross Hospital, London*

The Medical Commission of Lourdes (continued)

Dr. Dorothy Makepeace, 38 *Ashley Gardens, London*

Ireland

Dr. J. Stafford Johnson, *Richmond Hospital, Dublin*

Dr. F. J. Morrin, *Chief Surgeon, St. Vincent's Hospital, Dublin*

Spain

Dr. Juan G. Queralto, *Professor of Medicine, University of Barcelona*

Dr. Augustin Garcia Die, *Spanish President of the International Medical Association of Lourdes*

To go on with the medical organization: it is interesting to note the steady growth of interest by doctors. The first year the Medical Bureau was established, five doctors visited it; the second year fifteen; the third year twenty-seven. During the year 1953, 1,556 physicians have signed the Visitors' Book and taken part, many of them, in the examinations and activities at the Bureau. Here are some of the specialties and residences that one finds in the Visitors' Book:

Specialty	Residence
Otology	Argentina
Pathology	Edinburgh
Cancer	Paris
Ophthalmology	San Diego, Calif.
Psychiatry	Luxembourg
Stomatology	Casablanca
Cardiology	Wien
Orthopedic surgery	Glasgow
Neurology	Lausanne
General medicine	Amsterdam
Surgeon	Princeton, N.J.
Gynecology	Lille
Pediatrician	Turin
Dermatology	Lisbon
Cancerology	Newcastle
Radiology	Grenoble

Specialty	Residence
General medicine	Calcutta
Genitourinary *spec.*	Rouen
Pharmacology	Louvain
Eye and ear	Dublin
Tropical diseases	Tunis
Diseases of the brain	Bordeaux
Tuberculosis	Toronto
Bacteriologist	Liverpool
General medicine	Brussels
Obstetrics	Aberdeen
Urology	Rome
Skin diseases	Oslo
Cardiology	Geneva
Surgeon	Hongkong
Tropical diseases	Madagascar

What is the attitude of these doctors, when confronted with the facts? How do they react? What do they say?

Some are curious and unbiased; some are honestly stumped, frankly admitting they have no explanation. Some are definitely hostile and declare, with Zola: "Even if I saw a miracle, I wouldn't believe it!" Some are exasperated by the embarrassing problems put before them. Others are incredulous but sincerely interested in searching for the truth, and sometimes are lucky enough to find it—in the presence of an extraordinary cure. But more and more men of worth come to listen and to see for themselves, to study and weigh the evidence presented to them. They soon gain respect for the Lourdes cures when they observe the scientific procedure and strict practices at the Medical Bureau. Many become firm friends and helpers with the work.

One of the younger doctors, who has been coming every year, confided to me: "I don't mind telling you, I had my doubts about this place. But when I first came, Dr. Leuret told me, 'Here, you are a doctor first, a Catholic second. Never forget it!' I certainly never expected to find such merciless rigor in going over the cases. The doctors seem to lean more toward proving that no miracle has occurred than toward trying to find one!" This professional skepticism makes them very solid with the younger generation.

⊷§ *With all their interest and goodwill*, however, the visiting doctors are birds of passage. They cannot be counted on for the methodical checking and supervision of cures during the "probationary" year, or for other duties connected with involved and lengthy research. The Bureau is thus dependent on its own means—often very insufficient—to continue its diverse inquiries in the home area of the patients, not only in France but in foreign lands.

Recognizing these limitations, some of the doctors habitually assisting at the Bureau decided to create an International Medical Association to supplement the work of the Bureau and to become, so to say, laboratory workers for it in the field. The extraordinary development of the Association since its creation in 1927 is the best proof of its usefulness and its practical service.

AMIL, as it is affectionately called at Lourdes, is an international organization of doctors banded together to support the work of the Medical Bureau and to help in every way with the medical investigations and the scientific study of cures. It consists of 5,000 doctors from some thirty countries, each of whom pays 200 francs a year as dues; some give much more. This meets the annual budget of the Bureau—one million francs per annum. The Church gives them not one penny; "The Work of Lourdes," the general fund for Lourdes institutions, not one penny either.

"When I was invited here," says Dr. Leuret, "I was told we were to be entirely self-directing, self-supporting. 'You are to be technically autonomous, financially autonomous also.' While sometimes difficult, this has its advantages, too. For me this is a fact of major significance: *The medical work at Lourdes is run by doctors and supported by doctors.* Thus it can never be said that our work is under ecclesiastical domination or for propaganda purposes."

AMIL has two main objects: (1) to support the work of the Medical Bureau; (2) to help organize the pilgrimages and the study of alleged cures, so that the medical side—doctors' certificates, laboratory reports, and so on—shall be scientifically correct and well put together.

Each country, province, and region has an AMIL member in charge. When special research is needed on a case or when some particular type of specialist is wanted, AMIL supplies the technical information and the doctor required. Before the existence of AMIL, records at the Bureau and for the sick going on pilgrimage were sometimes very sketchy. The Association makes the Lourdes medical work scientifically much more exact and has added enormously to the prestige of the Medical Organization.

Growing interest in psychosomatic medicine has also undoubtedly played its part in increasing respect for and interest in the study of Lourdes cures. Last summer the National Psychiatric Association of France—400 doctors meeting in convention at Pau—came over in a body and spent an entire afternoon listening attentively to the accounts of cures and activities by the doctors of the Medical Bureau. Twenty, even fifteen years ago, such a thing would have been unheard of.

Let us not be overoptimistic. A large number of doctors still exist to whom the very name of Lourdes is anathema. But the number is steadily decreasing. In another twenty-five years it may be negligible.

8

An American Doctor
Analyses a Lourdes Cure

Every day, patients are examined at the Bureau from nine to twelve in the morning, and from two to four in the afternoon. All doctors who happen to be in Lourdes, either on pilgrimage or on visits of personal interest or curiosity, are invited to take part in the examinations and discussions. I was kindly permitted to be present at a number of these.

The Bureau occupies two entire floors of its present building —ten good-sized rooms, airy and well-equipped. Various Pilgrimages and Associations have contributed a good part of the equipment.

Through wide double doors the patient enters first a waiting room with many benches, where a nurse receives him, registers his name and address, and the name and address of his home physician. This puts the Bureau into immediate contact with the doctor who has been in charge of the person up to this time.

All day long, people are waiting here to see the doctor on duty —mothers with their children; Pilgrimage doctors with some specially interesting case or patient needing attention; paraplegics, diabetics, heart cases, tumors, polio victims. Every sort of malady and agony is studied within these plain gray walls.

A door to the left leads to the official examination room—a

large workmanlike place, with benches for forty or fifty doctors, an examination table for the patient, a desk for the presiding doctor and *rapporteur*. Over the desk (somewhat ironically) a plaque with Zola's observation: "There is no more heroic task than to establish even the smallest of truths." Zola, the arch-enemy of Lourdes!

Behind these formal outer apartments are the X-ray rooms, the office of the President of the Bureau—a comfortable study where the doctors gather for conferences and discussion of the cases—and the library, containing many valuable medical works and early Lourdes records. Farther on is a series of rooms equipped for special examinations—gynecological, urological, ear-nose-and-throat, and so on. Downstairs is a room for eye examinations and rooms for developing X-ray films.

X-rays are a vitally important factor in the study and appraisal of alleged cures. A fine Phillips X-ray apparatus given by the Dutch Catholics has enabled the Bureau to make some two thousand fluoroscopic examinations and about as many X-ray pictures within the past five years. The French colony of San Francisco presented splendid electrocardiographic equipment, in charge of none other than Bernadette's grand-nephew, Dr. J. M. Soubirous, who is a heart specialist and a thoroughly up-to-date physician.

When a cure occurs, the Pilgrimage doctor, or sometimes a brancardier, takes the patient as soon as possible to the Medical Bureau. A preliminary examination is made—then usually a much more detailed one on the following day, when there has been time to assemble all the physicians available.

Even the most coolly detached and skeptical must feel a little of the thrill and excitement that pervades the room when the newly cured patient walks in, followed by a beaming nurse or relative and a group of doctors and professors of Faculties from half a dozen countries—all on the *qui vive* to see for themselves this extraordinary phenomenon: a "miraculous" Lourdes cure!

Often the President will invite one of the visiting physicians to preside over the examination. An American physician, Dr. Smiley Blanton, directed the examination of one of the most famous cures—Charles McDonald. Thirty-two doctors gathered at the Bureau to study this remarkable case. Dr. Blanton afterward read an account of it before a joint session of the American Psychoanalytic and Psychiatric Associations. Here is a summary of the case taken from that account and from Mr. McDonald's own story.

Charles McDonald was born in Dublin on August 12, 1905. He had a healthy childhood. His brothers and sisters were also healthy. At sixteen he left school to work in his father's carpenter business. He was keen on sports and a capable athlete. He married at nineteen and has now three children, girls, all in good health.

His illness began in 1924. He became tired and irritable and had to give up work for several weeks. He resumed work in November but kept losing weight. Then he began to have night sweats and his cough became so aggravated that he consulted Dr. Young of Sandymount, Dublin. Tubercle bacilli were found in his sputum and an X-ray showed active tuberculosis of the lungs.

McDonald was sent to a sanatorium for five weeks, then entered a Dublin hospital (in April, 1925). There he had two hemorrhages from the lungs. He lost thirty pounds in six months.

On July 3, 1925, disobeying medical orders, he set out for Johannesburg, South Africa, where he remained for six months. Here his cough ceased and he regained weight and strength. He took up work in one of the gold mines, working always on the surface, however. For five years his health remained good.

Early in 1931, after a strenuous football match, he felt pain in hips and neck. Soon after, pain began in his left side and in the lower part of his back, especially when he rode his motorcycle. Things got so bad that he could not apply the brakes of his car without feeling a stinging pain in the lower back. In

October, 1931, his doctor, after taking a spinal X-ray, said that he had tuberculosis of the twelfth thoracic vertebra.

McDonald was put into a steel corset from the shoulders to the hips, opening so that he could take a sun bath. After three months he was no better. The doctor suggested a bone-graft operation. McDonald refused and decided to return to Dublin. On the voyage he abandoned his brace, finding it too hot and tiring. Back at home he tried to work, but pains on the left side and in the back were so severe that he had to stop. For three months he rested, under no medical care meanwhile.

In June, 1932, he was examined by Dr. Lane of Dublin who diagnosed tuberculous disease of the vertebra and sent him to Dr. Lynch to determine whether the condition of the lungs would permit an operation. Dr. Lynch said no—the lungs were too bad. Once more the young man was put into a steel brace.

In September, 1932, a large abscess developed in the right lumbar region, and another, later, in the left shoulder. The shoulder abscess was aspirated but that in the lumbar area had to be opened, as the pus was too thick. Both these abscesses discharged freely during the spring of 1933.

In June, 1935, McDonald became very ill. He collapsed during a violent fit of vomiting. A week later his body was badly swollen. He consulted still another doctor, O'Connell of Dublin, who diagnosed his trouble as acute nephritis (inflammation of the kidneys). He was taken to Meath Hospital where he remained for thirteen weeks—again under the care of Dr. Lane, also of Dr. Boxwell. Examination of the urine showed albumin, blood cells, and granular and hyalin casts. Any movement caused severe pain especially in his back, and he had to be given frequent sedatives.

In November, 1936, Dr. Boxwell said the patient would have to be sent to a hospital for incurables. The cheerful name of this institution was Hospital for the Dying. McDonald refused, and went home. He called in Dr. O'Connell again. The doctor visited him weekly for three months. The family was now being supported by a small tobacco shop which Mrs. McDonald ran in one part of the house.

The doctor told Mrs. McDonald that he could do little for her husband and that he considered him a hopeless case. Finally, in June, 1936, he said to his patient: "McDonald, I'm sorry—I can do nothing more for you."

It was then that McDonald thought of Lourdes. He had a strong presentiment that he would be cured there. He kept telling his friends that if he went to Lourdes he would certainly come back on his feet. He insisted that his wife should pack for him the suit and clothes in which he would return as a well person.

He joined the Catholic Young Men's Pilgrimage of Ireland, which took place September 4–10, 1936. The journey had to be made on a stretcher, sitting being too painful. "I had been an invalid for over four years," says McDonald, "and for fifteen months before going to Lourdes was confined to bed. Twice I was given the Last Rites and pronounced by more than one doctor to be beyond medical aid. I was unable to sit up for more than four minutes to have the wounds dressed. Pain had nearly driven me mad at times. When the ambulance came to take me to the train, I was placed in a carrying sheet and with infinite care transferred from bed to stretcher and thence to the ambulance."

For admission to the Pilgrimage, he had a certificate from Dr. O'Connell stating that he had Pott's Disease of the twelfth dorsal vertebra, nephritis, and tuberculous arthritis of the left shoulder. Some fifteen X-rays at Meath Hospital established the diagnosis. Dr. Hannigan was in charge of the pilgrimage which included a dozen medical men.

McDonald left Dublin for Lourdes on the night of the third of September, 1936. His wounds were dressed on the fourth of September by Nurse Falvey on the Pilgrimage train. She testified that there was considerable pus draining from the sinuses in his back and shoulder.

He arrived in Lourdes on Saturday, September 5, and his wounds were dressed that day by Dr. Hannigan. At this dressing the doctor noted that McDonald had two large sinuses (draining abscesses) in the lumbar region, a large sinus just below the outer end of the collar bone, and two more in the left shoulder.

On the morning of September 6, he was taken to the baths and carefully lowered by six brancardiers into the pool, lying on a special webbing. His bandages were taken off, and when he came out they were put on again. In this way Lourdes water touched his wounds directly and cleansed them. He was considerably chilled by this bath and felt no benefit from it.

On September 7, he was bathed again. He felt confused and cold but after he was dressed and removed from the piscine to the Grotto where a service was being held, he began, as he said, to feel "the first glow of health."

"It should be remembered," says Dr. Blanton, "that for fifteen months the patient had been in bed, so helpless that he had to use a bedpan, unable to move his hips or shoulders without severe pain. But now, lying on a stretcher in front of the Grotto, he experimented by moving his arm slightly. There was no pain. He loosened the brace strap on his shoulder and raised his shoulders from the pillow—without pain. He thought that perhaps he felt no pain because the shock of the bath had taken his mind off his condition. He waited an hour, and moved his hips again. Once more there was no pain."

"My expectations had become a certainty!" said McDonald jubilantly. "The Blessed Virgin had healed me!" He said that there at the Grotto he "felt more fit than I had ever felt in my life. I knew I could get up and walk." The brancardiers and nurses restrained him.

All that day he was outdoors in front of the Grotto. Back at the hospital in the evening, he told the doctor he was going to get up in the morning. He was forbidden to do so.

Next morning (September 8) when the doctor and nurse were out of the room, McDonald got up and walked to the foot of the bed—the first time he had been on his feet for fifteen months. He said, "My knees would have given way and I would have sunk to the floor had I not held on to the bed." He dressed himself with help from no one and walked without pain.

That day he was taken to the Grotto, not, as usual, on a stretcher but in an invalid chair. "I remained in the chair until after the Blessing of the Sick, in the afternoon. Then I left the chair . . . and walked up the steps into the Rosary Church where I was able to make a complete genuflection and to kneel in one of the benches. On rising some minutes later I repeated my genuflection and walked out of the church down onto the Square, where I resumed my chair for the official photograph of the pilgrims."

This the man who for more than a year had not been able to make the slightest move without agonizing pain, or raise his head and sit up for more than four minutes at a time.

"That night," says McDonald, "I told the doctor he could roll up my stretcher and place it in the guard's van of the train, as I was traveling home as an ordinary passenger. On Wednesday morning I dressed without assistance and when brought to the baths for the third time, walked in, undressed and dressed myself unaided. This I had not done for more than three years.

"I left Lourdes on Wednesday night. Our homeward journey was full of rejoicing. On arriving at Dublin Station I had the supreme pleasure of dispensing with the ambulance which had been so vitally necessary one short week before. I ordered a taxi, thus fulfilling my promise of returning on my feet."

At the time when McDonald left Lourdes it was still not a complete recovery for, according to Dr. Vallet's statement, his wounds were not yet entirely healed and were draining pus. Under these conditions he was not taken to the Medical Bureau for examination. It was on the return trip, before the train arrived in Paris, that his wounds healed. Dr. Hannigan stated as follows:

I certify, as doctor in charge of the sick in the Irish Pilgrimage, that I examined Mr. Charles McDonald. He presented then: three fistulas of the left shoulder, two fistulas in the lumbar region all of which discharged pus. During the trip going and coming from Lourdes I personally cleaned his wounds. While on the way out, discharge was abundant and the patient had to remain lying on his stretcher.

After the second bath there was a marked improvement and I authorized him to try to walk, which he did with facility. During the return voyage his wounds were dressed in Paris by the nurses. There was only a slight fluid from one of the lumbar fistulas. All the rest had healed up.

Dr. Hannigan wrote again on August 29, 1937:

I have seen Mr. McDonald twice since his return from Lourdes. I can declare definitely that there are now no traces of his former illness. Mr. McDonald is a well-balanced, active, healthy man, who can get through his day's work without trouble or undue fatigue. [He had now gone into the insurance business.] All the former sinuses are firmly healed. Personally, I am very glad to be able to testify to this cure, as when I first saw him I regarded this case as hopeless. (Signed, Ch. Hannigan.)

From Dr. Young, 49 Tritonville Road, Sandymount, Dublin, came another certificate:

I certify that in 1934 I examined Mr. McDonald and found him suffering from active tuberculosis of the left shoulder and a lumbar abscess. I have recently examined Mr. McDonald and found no active signs of his disease and as far as I can see he is completely cured.

From Dr. C. J. O'Connell, 35 Fairview, Strand, Dublin:

I certify that on September 1, 1937, I examined Mr. Charles McDonald and found the abscesses, two in the lumbar region and three in connection with the shoulder, completely healed. The urine contains neither blood nor albumin. At my first visit in 1934 this patient was suffering from acute nephritis and active tuberculosis of the dorsal vertebrae. He was sent to Meath Hospital under the treatment of Dr. Lane and remained for thirteen weeks, leaving at his own request. Seen by me the day following at his own home, the urine contained albumin and pus. I wrote out the certificate for the Pilgrimage and considered this man's case incurable.

The diagnosis given by Dr. O'Connell on the pilgrimage certificate read: "Pott's Disease, caries, nephritis, and tuberculous shoulder."

The report of an X-ray given on September 9, 1937 by Dr. R. A. Ruyert of St. Kevin's Hospital, Dublin, is as follows:

The left shoulder joint clearly shows old trouble in the joint between the humerus and scapula which had made definite progress. This trouble exists no longer, the cure having taken place by ankylosis. The left kidney shows foci of disease now completely cicatrized. An examination by injection of uroselectan shows as regards the kidneys that the left kidney is hypertrophied, the pelvis dilated, and its outline changed. The function of this kidney is, however, perfect. The right kidney is slightly dilated but otherwise normal. Both lungs show several tuberculous lesions now healed. There is some thickening of the pleura at left apex. It is difficult to say if the disease is completely cured, but it is certainly inactive. (Signed, Dr. Ruyert.)

As soon as McDonald returned to Dublin he began to walk about half a mile a day. Two weeks later he was able to walk several miles. In December (1936) he began to ride a bicycle. On September 16, 1937 he returned to Lourdes, where Dr. Blanton and other physicians examined him on September 17.

Thirty-two doctors were present at the Medical Bureau during McDonald's examination. In their concluding remarks they made the following statement:

Charles McDonald has been afflicted with (1) tuberculosis of the left shoulder with three fistulas; (2) tuberculosis of the dorsal spine with two fistulas; (3) chronic nephritis characterized by the presence of pus, blood, albumin. These three conditions were in full evolution at the moment of the pilgrimage to Lourdes, the five fistulas giving off pus.

They were abruptly halted in their evolution on September 7. An immediate functional healing after a bath in the piscine was followed in less than four days by a definite cicatrization of the five fistulas, of return of normal urinary secretion rid of its infectious germs; cessation of pain, return of partial movements of the left arm and lumbar region.

This healing, obtained without the use of medicaments or of any therapeutic agent whatever is confirmed by one year of excellent health and work. . . . No medical explanation, in the present state of science, can be given; considering the extraordinary rapidity of the healing of these tuberculous affections, judged incurable by the specialists called in to treat him, and whose beginning was noted by general infection, later by bony localizations. This healing is written down as on the margin of the laws of biology.

The signatures of the thirty-two doctors end this statement.

In his report to his American confreres Dr. Blanton concludes:

To summarize, we have a man who seems certainly to have had tuberculosis of the lungs. He also had an infection of the twelfth thoracic vertebra which had destroyed it, and an infection of the shoulder which had practically destroyed the bony structure of the joint. In bed fifteen months, he had to have his wounds dressed twice daily. After the second bath in the piscine he was able to move without pain; he was able to walk that day; within three weeks he was able to walk several miles a day; his sinuses were practically healed in a period of two weeks.

What is the explanation of this healing?—for that it is a healing I am myself convinced. The records seem adequate to support this conclusion and they were made by well-trained and reputable physicians. Furthermore this is not an isolated case but one of approximately ten or twelve that occur at Lourdes yearly, in which the records seem well and honestly made.

We must lay aside as untenable the accusation that these cases are in any way "fixed" or the histories "doctored." There does appear to be at this shrine . . . a sudden quickening of the healing processes, a removal of symptoms, and a feeling of well-being. The percentages of such cures . . . are certainly too great to be laid to coincidence, nor do the details of the cures conform to the laws of recovery as we know them. Even coincidental cures in our hospitals do not, in the space of two or three days, get up and walk without pain after fifteen months of life in bed with continual pain. . . .

The basis of the cures seems to lie in some aspect which has to do with the psychology of the situation. . . . It is my feeling that in this case and in similar cases at Lourdes there is a quickening of the healing process, due to the emotion aroused by the transference to an all-powerful, all-loving Virgin Mother. . . .

I feel that we are justified by what we saw at Lourdes in stating our tentative belief that processes leading in the direction of death were not only halted but reversed, and the libido liberated in this way was put to the use of the individual in the restoration of health. I believe that something does occur which is, as Dr. Vallet has remarked, on the margin of the laws of nature.*

* Charles McDonald is in excellent health today—a robust man of forty-nine. He comes to Lourdes frequently, and was there with his daughter shortly before my own visit.

9

Lourdes Atmosphere: Psychological Influences

Dr. *Blanton thinks* that psychological factors have a great deal to do with the cures. This may seem true to some—at least in the matter of creating an atmosphere, opening the way.

The little room at the Bureau where I work on the records looks out on the river Gave on the one side, the pavement along the Esplanade on the other. On both sides pilgrims are walking up and down all day long; families, Sisters, priests, young people, old people. And all these people are praying.

Families come saying their prayers aloud, together; offering their united supplications for some suffering loved one. Sisters lead their groups of little girls or boys, reciting the Rosary. Now and then a distraught father or mother with a compassionate confessor wheel their child toward the Grotto, uttering low, desperate pleas for help. Sometimes a lively procession of students swings along, energetically beseeching; sometimes just some tranquil old priest murmuring his Collect for the day.

At the Statue of Notre Dame, people are on their knees all around; at the statue of Bernadette also; at the Grotto, in front of the piscine, up along the Way of the Cross, on every path and colline. Even the clock chimes *Ave, Ave—Ave Maria!*

All day long, this praying army passionately offers its prayers toward heaven. One would have to be made of stone not to be affected by it. The rhythms get into your blood. You find yourself humming and saying the things *they* say and hum. And if this affects the able-bodied, how much more must it affect the sick—relaxed, receptive, many of them semiconscious, with no positive activities or plans of their own to engage their attention.

Another powerful element in the Lourdes atmosphere, already referred to, is the devotion of its workers: the spirit of dedication and self-giving that permeates the whole place. It is the spirit of the early Christian community, where all give their services and share alike in the daily tasks.

Hundreds—even thousands—of people work hard all winter, save bit by bit, do without, so that they can come to Lourdes for some days or weeks in the summer and work hard there from morning till night. Brancardiers, nurses, nurses' aids give their vacation time this way, year after year; public-school boys, daughters of famous families, teachers, lawyers, scores of clerks and business people.

The girl in the souvenir shop at my hotel works in the shop mornings (comes from England every year) so that she can help at the baths in the afternoon, dressing and undressing roomfuls of wet, frightened women. The girl at the Cook's Travel Agency, who works from nine to six at her job, goes every night to help at the Grotto until midnight. "Every night when I go to the Grotto . . ." she would say, her face alight.

One brancardier said: "These few days at Lourdes each August fix me up for the whole year. I *live* for twelve months on what I get here in just this one week!"

Two thousand brancardiers are here for the Rosary Pilgrimage alone. Many brancardiers and nurses are Cures of former years. The Cures coming back, strong and well, caring for them, nursing them, give tremendous inspiration and hope to the sick.

The service of these voluntary workers is lavish and untiring. They run up and down long flights of stairs, they carry bedpans; sit beside idiot children whose guttural cries never cease. They change fetid dressings, bathe malodorous wounds. It is not their profession—they are not paid for this. They do it not only cheerfully but joyfully, happily. Why? They pull those invalid carriages to and from the Grotto and the hospital twenty times a day. Everybody with a smile—joking, laughing, encouraging. And praying constantly—at the baths, while carrying the patients, dressing and undressing them, while washing and feeding them; at the station, at the Procession—everywhere.

Psychologists today are measuring mental and emotional wave lengths. If they could measure the wave length of such an atmosphere, surely it would be found to have a powerful effect on the human organism.

⊷§ Sometimes prayers are answered in a roundabout way.

I asked one of the English doctors who had been coming to Lourdes for several years whether she had ever seen a miracle.

"Not literally—not right under my nose. But in a way I saw one."

"Tell me!"

"A woman came to Lourdes one year with a mongoloid child. You know what a lot of those there are. This one would draw anybody's pity: such a horrible-looking little monster—great pop eyes, enormous head, slobbery mouth—*you* know, you've seen enough of them around here. And the mother such a dainty little thing—so young and pretty, so utterly wretched. I stood near her at the Grotto several times, and, one day at the Procession, I heard her desperate prayers."

"Were they answered? Was the child cured?"

"The child died. But next year the mother came again to Lourdes, and on a pilgrimage of thanksgiving. For she had another child, a beautiful baby, perfect in every way."

"Wonderful!"

"Yes. But the interesting thing is that she kept praying: 'Oh God, give me a well child, a perfect child!' And that is just what God did. So often people don't watch what they're saying," the doctor added. "They're surprised when they get, quite literally, what they pray for!"

One of the Italian doctors told another interesting story. A young Genoese girl, desperately sick with some strange disease of the spleen, came to Lourdes—but was going home without her cure; if anything, worse than when she arrived.

On the last day of the pilgrimage, a Belgian doctor coming through the ward stopped to have a special look at this girl, Maria. He became very much interested in her case.

"Where are you from, Maria—Genoa? You know," he said suddenly, "there's a doctor very close to you there, who has made a special study of tropical diseases and particularly diseases of the spleen. I sat next to him at a medical meeting last year. His name is Dr. Liebermann. When you go back, go to see him. I'll bet he can help you!"

The doctor in Genoa not only helped her, he cured her. When she was completely well—and had become his office assistant—Dr. Liebermann teased her about it.

"Well now, here's a fine thing! You go all the way to Lourdes and the Blessed Virgin does nothing for you. And you come back home to Genoa and a Jewish doctor makes you well! How do you account for that? It looks very much as though the Blessed Virgin let you down!"

"Don't you say such a thing!" cried Maria indignantly. "It was the Blessed Virgin who brought the Belgian doctor into the ward to tell me about you. That was Her way of curing me. The Blessed Virgin knows what She's about!"

Much of my time was taken up, necessarily, in work on the medical records. Thus I met many of the visiting doctors and heads of pilgrimages. Always something doing, around the Bu-

reau. The first day I was there, a young priest from India sat
reading at the table beside me, his face alight with pride in
"Facts of Lourdes." Another day, a Chinese doctor from Hong-
kong was poring over the files. Often young French interns on
holiday with their wives will spend several days of their precious
vacation time laboriously copying out data on some of the most
interesting cases. They like to discuss these, even with a layman
and a foreigner, and regard my thick notes with respect.

Getting these stories of cures is not a simple process. After
you have been given permission from the authorities to use the
files, and have selected your chosen case for the day, a big black
folder, or dossier, is set in front of you, filled with a great mass
of papers, pamphlets, and photostats. A dossier may contain as
many as a hundred papers—including doctors' certificates, laboratory reports; testimony of witnesses to the illness and witnesses
to the cure; depositions of relatives, neighbors and nurses, of
brancardiers and bath attendants (where the baths are involved); hospital charts, surgeons' notations; pilgrimage officers'
statements, statements by the patient's employers; detailed reports of the Medical Bureau examinations and conclusions; also
the report and conclusions of the Medical Commission; and
various other documents, such as personal letters from friends
and associates—often the most interesting and significant of all.

If the cure is one of those recognized by the Church as Miraculous, there is an entire second set of notes and findings handed
in by the Canonical Commission—after the Medical Commission has finished with theirs.

Most of the papers are written by hand—the spindly French
hand, a good deal harder for Anglo-Saxons than their own. To
wade through this mass of material, translating every paper
from the French as you go, and with proper punctiliousness as
to medical and ecclesiastical terms, means long hours of careful
work.

Records all morning, the Procession and the sick all

afternoon. If I'm not at the baths or the Grotto, I'm at the hospitals visiting patients, or up on the rampe looking on. The days are filled to overflowing—*and* the nights, with the pilgrims running up and down the halls of the hotel, singing and talking till all hours.

And then the constant arriving and departing of thousands of people—by trains, planes, cars and autobuses. Lourdes is a strenuous place. You get very little sleep. Your nerves and emotions are under constant assault: a succession of tragic sights and sounds, each time you set foot in the street.

Sometimes you feel the need of getting away from it all for a while. Then there is the lovely Bearn countryside—where in ten minutes you can lose yourself in green woods and heavenly quiet. Or, you can sit on the terrace of the Café Royal and watch the world go by.

The Royal is at the crossroads of all Lourdes traffic—directly in front of the Boulevard and the entrance to the Domaine. Everybody "falls in" there for a bit of a rest and refreshment at the end of a hard day. More cosmopolitan than the Paris boulevards, it is *the* place to study the extraordinary mixture of Lourdes types and nationalities: Spanish women with fans and black lace mantillas, chatting with their Director as they drink their chocolate; Belgian and Dutch farmers enjoying big mugs of beer; country priests sipping lemonade and casting sidelong glances at foreign priests drinking liqueurs; a group of English university students ordering Dubonnet and looking deliciously sophisticated; little French girls and boys gorging ices and *patisseries*, while their parents mop hot faces and drink Cinzano.

The brancardiers unharness. The Directors of the pilgrimages lean back in their chairs and relax over coffee and little cakes. Some of the old priests enjoy a joke and a good cigar with the younger men, and perhaps a thimble of cognac in their coffee. You might think all this not quite "correct" in a pilgrimage town. But then you remember that these men have been up since daybreak, working incessantly—both priests and brancardiers. By five o'clock they are tired out and it is only right that they should rest a bit and enjoy themselves before taking up their burdens again.

This is a place too for friendly interchange among the different pilgrimages, and for mutual confidences and stirring tales of Lourdes. Some of the most thrilling stories of cures, some of the most deeply touching accounts of faith reborn and lives remade, have been told me over these cups of coffee at the Royal.

Just a few steps farther on, along the Avenue Bernadette, is the Hospital of the Sept Douleurs. Even here at the café, stretchers and invalid carriages go by all day long; but for a few moments one can forget them, and under these gay awnings relax and recover one's forces.

Autocars swing by, bearing crowds of singing pilgrims to and from the station—the Basques and Italians waving a last good-by to the Dutch and English in the café, with whom they have shared their five pilgrimage days. Traffic is terrific, as the different groups and organizations pour out of the Domaine after the Procession. People overflow from the sidewalk onto the pavement—a solid mass, through which autos and motorbikes weave amid incredible shouting and hooting.

Tour leaders wave their arms and call frantic orders, which nobody can hear. Newsboys run up and down hawking the latest Paris papers. At the corner the candid-camera man is doing a rush business among stout Flemish and British matrons and demure Breton girls in lace caps and gaily decorated aprons. The rug vendor and the watch peddler slip in and out between the tables, importuning in their eternal singsong; the sellers of postcards and the sellers of vanilla double their shrill cries. An Arab chief in full regalia causes a sensation striding along with his picturesque retinue—flowing white robes, gold-thonged headdress, shiny black beard.

Suddenly, through all this hubbub and commotion, a swirl of figures over at the gateway—the mighty roll of the Magnificat. All spring to their feet, rush to the pavement, cross themselves,

View of Lourdes (*Photo Viron*)

Blessing of the Sick at the Procession (*Photo Viron*)

Pilgrims at prayer (*Photo Viron*)

The Grotto (*Photo Elcé*)

Brancardiers at work
(*Photo Viron*)

Below: Doctors and
patient at Medical
Bureau (*Photo Lacaze*)

The Comte de Paris, Bishop
Théas, and the Comte
de Beauchamp (*Photo Viron*)

then laugh and ask questions excitedly. Something is happening. A cure perhaps—a miracle? Then you see them.

Following the long line of stretchers and carriages returning to the hospital comes a jubilant little procession: a group of brancardiers forming a guard of honor for a radiant young girl who walks up the street as if on air. She had been carried down to the Grotto that afternoon on a stretcher, after four years in bed with a tuberculous spine. She is returning on her own two feet, singing and praising God.

Everybody joins in the singing. The Dutch and Spanish women hug each other. The little boys throw their caps in the air and cheer. The waiters smile and bring a double order for everyone. They know the splendid aftermath for *them* in the expansive, heart-warming hour after a miracle.

Was it a miracle, really? Time will tell. But that girl's eyes—!

I recognized one of the "unbelieving" French doctors, standing at the curb quite near me. "Well, what did you think of it? Quite exciting, wasn't it?" I said casually.

"It was—" He suddenly turned and fled into a shop, handkerchief held up to his face. I didn't realize until afterward that he was weeping. Never again did he have anything derisive to say about miracles.

At dinner everybody is talking about it. The Dutch are staying at our hotel. The girl is a member of their pilgrimage. They are all tremendously pleased and proud.

One of their nurses is telling the wonderful story, with personal elaborations:

"So I told our pilgrimage doctor, I said, 'Well sir, you have a miracle!' 'Well, well, we shall see. We don't know about it yet.' 'But it's true!' I insisted. 'I saw it with my own eyes! While I was bathing your patient, whom we had plunged stiff as a board into the bath, I saw her arms and legs *bend*, and she whom we had had to carry—four of us—to put her in the bath, I saw her sit down on the edge of the bath and help us while we put her clothes back on again.'"

"She left her cast and brace at the Grotto," another verified joyfully. "Never any need for *those* again, she said!"

"And how do the other patients feel about it?" I asked; "the ones who didn't get their cure? Are they envious, or disappointed, or anything?"

"Madame, they are enraptured! They are in the seventh heaven. They had all been praying for this girl day and night— she was the worst of our cases. All they can think of is that their prayers were successful, and Suzie will go home *whole* and on her own feet!"

Everyone was electrified—beaming; all round the big dining room, faces alight, eyes shining, broad smiles from the ambulant patients delighted at their comrade's good fortune. This was not just the usual exuberant summer crowd, full of *joie de vivre* and healthy physical energy. The joy in these faces, the spirit in that room, were something different, something to cherish and remember.

"Well do I recollect," mused an old brancardier, "the first miracle I ever saw. I may live to be a hundred, but I'll never forget *that*—or the thanksgiving Mass that followed in our village church after we went home. People made up quarrels who hadn't spoken to each other for years. Estranged children came back home to their parents. It's—well, a miracle does something to you; brings people back to God."

And does all this come about, as certain scientists tell us, through mere "mass delusion" and "some unusual psychological phenomenon," "a sort of 'explosion' in man's brain cells"? They must be very different cells from those we know in ordinary everyday operation.

◄§ *After dinner* we gather in the hall downstairs with our wraps and candle shades. No one wants to miss the greatest of all Lourdes spectacles—the Torchlight Procession. Even the concierge, seasoned veteran of many summers, softens at the mention of it.

"But yes, madame, I still go sometimes. It is *va-iry* beautiful!"

People are streaming out of the hotels up and down the street. Nurses and brancardiers off duty catch up their candles and fall into line with the rest. Bishops and bank clerks, truck-drivers and duchesses; pilgrimage leaders vainly trying to keep track of their straying flocks: all hurry along to the meeting place. At eight o'clock in the evening every pilgrim's feet are turned in one direction, toward the Domaine.

It is night when we reach the Square, but the whole place is brilliantly illuminated. The churches are lit up, and the statue of Notre Dame de Lourdes and the huge cross on the Pic du Jer. The old castle on the hill shines against the sky. High up on the left the Basilica, outlined in fire.

The crowd, too, soon becomes a serpent of fire, weaving in and out along the steps and parapets; and from this undulating throng, great joyous bursts of singing. Each pilgrim carries a candle protected by a paper shade, and sings with his group.

They sing in different tongues but always the same song: the "Canticle of Bernadette," that tells the story of the little shepherd girl and her visions, each stanza ending with *Ave, Ave, Ave Maria!*

This is the theme-song of Lourdes. It is sung on the pilgrimage trains and at different times during the day at the chapels; and it is *the* song of the Torchlight Procession. It is heard every night at Lourdes, for two hours and longer. It is not "good" music; parts of it are very poor poetry; but it has a haunting quality. One hears it, dropping off to sleep, and again when the chimes ring out first thing in the morning. That simple refrain, slipping up through the mind, can recreate the whole Lourdes scene for me in two minutes.

The groups gather at the Grotto, wind along the rampes in an enormous horseshoe, then to the Esplanade—down one side and up the other. Each person holds his candle. Each group carries its pilgrimage sign, also illuminated: Newcastle . . . Limoges . . . Brussels . . . Oran. . . . The tiny flames form larger and larger blocks, till they become a huge wheel of fire.

Seen from across the river, the procession is a scene of eerie beauty. Out of the enveloping darkness shine a myriad lights. The candles burning at the Grotto form a great wall of light, the church ablaze above it.

My favorite place is high up at the rail in front of the Basilica, where I can watch the whole vast panorama and see every part and each pilgrimage as it comes along. French families often stand near me—little boys and girls singing lustily with their fathers and mothers, uncles and grandparents. An astounding sight, that crowd as it comes by—matrons and midinettes, stalwart young men, grizzled veteran pilgrims; a bride in her veil, an old woman in her tattered shawl, each face illumined by the paper-shrouded candle, each pilgrim singing with all his might.

Down the path they wind, pealing forth their hymns and *Aves* under the stars—the hospital doors open; the sick looking out from their rows upon rows of beds and singing too. On any night it is an amazing and wonderful scene. At the time of the great pilgrimages—such as the French National, or the Rosary in October—when as many as sixty thousand people march and sing, it is overwhelming.

Have you ever heard sixty thousand people singing one great hymn together? Have you ever seen sixty thousand faces lighted up not only by candles but with radiant love and devotion? It's something you won't forget—in this bomb-ridden, disillusioned twentieth century.

The marching continues for two hours. At the end, the marchers come together in the Square in one huge block in front of the Rosary Church. Hundreds of pilgrims are massed along the rampes and beside the river too. The Bishop on the steps of the church holds up his hand, and the singing stops. He raises his hand again—and the people burst forth into the majestic chanting of the Credo.

Visitors to Lourdes often say that the singing of the Credo is the most impressive moment of all. An instant before, each pilgrim was singing in his own tongue, the result a confused though not unpleasing jumble. Now, suddenly, everyone is declaring his belief in God in Latin—universal language of the Church.

This ends the day's ceremonies. You may be Catholic, you may be Protestant, you may be an out-and-out atheist and unbeliever. Whoever you are and wherever you come from, you will never forget the Torchlight Procession at Lourdes.*

* Lest the figures regarding the Torchlight crowds be considered exaggerated, I may add that in 1946 the space along the Esplanade and the rampes was scientifically measured and found to have a capacity to hold 100,000 persons.

10

The Church and Lourdes

Twin peaks stand guard over Lourdes—on top of one a great Cross, shining day and night; on the other an observatory where groups of scientists pursue their studies. There they stand, exactly opposite each other: Science and Religion, the two great servants of man—and of truth.

For a long time people have wondered whether the gulf between the two would ever be bridged—whether they would ever get together. At Lourdes—by a miracle?—they do. Down there in the valley, the Bureau and the Grotto live side by side, working in thorough harmony; under the aegis of an International Association of 5,000 doctors and of the most conservative ecclesiastical body in the world.

We have seen the change in attitude of the Church after the findings of the Episcopal Commission which vindicated Bernadette, and the official establishment of the Shrine under the direction of the Bishop of Tarbes in 1862. From that time on, Lourdes has won the steadily increasing interest and affection of the Church through the years. Witness the large numbers of churches and organizations dedicated to Our Lady of Lourdes—in cities and countries all over the world, the interest of various pontiffs in the Shrine; the great number of bishops and clergy who prepare and conduct the pilgrimages; the magnificent work of the Hospitallers and their continuous activity in the dioceses.

From having been at first an obscure stepchild, regarded with some hesitation and embarrassment, Lourdes has come to be a beloved daughter; next to Rome, the brightest jewel in the Catholic crown.

From early days the Popes have followed the development of the Shrine and the pilgrimages with an attentive eye. Pope Pius IX, in Bernadette's lifetime, was greatly devoted to Notre Dame de Lourdes. He often visited a small replica of the Grotto which had been built in the Vatican gardens. Under Leo XIII the Sacred Congregation of Rites (July 16, 1890) approved the office of the Feast of the Apparitions of the Immaculate Virgin at the Grotto of Lourdes. In 1900, the Bishop of Tarbes asked permission to erect in the Vatican gardens an exact reproduction of the Grotto. The Holy Father approved, and watched the construction with lively interest.

The present Pope, Pius XII, has been a devoted friend of Lourdes for many years—especially since 1935 when, as Cardinal Pacelli, he was sent by Pius XI as Papal Legate to preside over the three days and nights of prayer which closed at Lourdes the great Jubilee of the Redemption.

On that solemn occasion, when fears of war and prayers for peace reached their climax on the part of the whole Catholic world, the present Pope paid his moving tribute there before the Shrine:

Oh Lourdes—Holy City! In you is united the enchantment of Nazareth, the sacred charm of Bethlehem, the healing power of Bethesda. How many miracles of the Redeemer have you not seen, renewing themselves here! What marvels of grace have been accomplished within your walls. For more than one Thomas you have become the Upper Room where his eyes have been unsealed. For more than one Saul, the road to Damascus, where he has become Paul.

But it was the wise and much-loved Pius X (recently canonized) who perhaps exercised the most powerful and lasting influence on Lourdes destinies. His portrait stands in the center of the baluster of the Church of the Crypt "as a witness [he wrote] for all time to come of my great devotion to Notre Dame of the Blessed Rosary and a proof of my particular affection for the Sanctuary of Lourdes."

It was he who extended to the Universal Church the Office of the Mass of the Apparition of Notre Dame de Lourdes. He delegated the Cardinal of Bordeaux to preside in his name at the ceremonies of the fiftieth anniversary of the Lourdes Shrine. He enlarged and improved the Grotto in the Vatican gardens, so that henceforth the slender spire of the Lourdes Basilica would shine near the Dome of St. Peter's. On August 13, 1913, he signed the decree introducing the cause of Bernadette Soubirous for canonization.

It was this great and far-seeing Pope who inaugurated the system of Canonical judgments regarding Lourdes cures; his wise mind that first conceived the idea of "an international board of scholars and physicians who should give to the Medical Bureau guarantees that cannot be contested."

In April, 1904, two hundred and fifty Catholic physicians went to Rome to pay homage to the Holy Father, taking with them fifteen persons who had been miraculously cured at Lourdes. The Bishop of Tarbes headed this pilgrimage,* accompanied by representatives of the various sections of Lourdes activities. The physicians were for the most part habitués of the Medical Bureau. Thus the Pope could get an idea of both the institutions and the work of Lourdes.

He was deeply impressed; also he realized the need for discretion and dignity in the conduct and direction of such a place. "The word miracle," he said, "should not be uttered lightly." Safeguards must be thrown round it—precautions must be taken.

In October, Dr. Lapponi, the Pope's physician, advised the President of the Medical Bureau that "in his (the Pope's) judgment it would be well for the Reverend Curia to institute a

* The name of Lourdes was added to the Tarbes bishopric by Pius X in 1912. It then became the Diocese of Tarbes and Lourdes.

regular process on the most remarkable cases, especially as to the identity of the persons, on the authentications of the physicians, and the depositions of witnesses who saw the patients before their cure."

Shortly after, the Bishop of Tarbes (in a letter dated Nov. 15, 1906) begged "the Bishops of the Dioceses where people are living, called in popular language *miraculés* of Lourdes, to be good enough to establish, upon canonical inquiry, the reality and the supernatural character of the cures"; adding, "it belongs to ecclesiastical authority to declare whether certain cures should be classed as among miraculous acts . . . it is the Bishops who have the power to recognize and to approve new miracles, after having consulted the canonical commissions . . ."

Following these instructions, and the desire formally expressed by the Pope, the Bishops appointed commissions and set them to work investigating alleged cures. In consequence of these investigations twenty-eight cures were declared miraculous by Episcopal ordinance on the eve of the Golden Jubilee of Lourdes (1908). These were cures pronounced by canonical judgments of various Cardinals and Bishops, following upon the inquiries and reports of canonical commissions and the procedure as directed.

This same procedure is in force today.

When the doctors have finished their work and rendered their decision on an alleged cure, if the decision is in the affirmative the case is sent on to the ecclesiastical authorities for consideration by a Canonical Commission. The Canonical Commission is named in each diocese by the Bishop of the Diocese and each case is determined upon separately.

The Commission usually consists of five persons, two of whom must be physicians. The Church requires that two experts or specialists in the disease under discussion shall be included, that "the experts must enjoy a certain renown in medicine or surgery; furthermore, specialists chosen must be distinguished for the diagnosis and the cure of the maladies which are concerned in the proposed miracle. The report of the experts, briefly written, and clearly supported by arguments, will reply to the following questions:

1. If it is a question of a cure, may the one named as beneficiary be considered as truly cured?
2. Can the event proposed as a miracle be explained by the laws of nature, or can it not?

Benedict XIV enumerates the seven characteristics which must exist whenever there arises a question of a miracle—and these are to be applied by every Canonical Commission studying an alleged supernatural cure at Lourdes:

1. That the malady was a grave one, and impossible or at least difficult to cure.
2. That the cured malady was not in a state of decline to such an extent that it could have declined soon afterward.
3. That no medication had been used, or if there had been, that its inefficacy was certain.
4. That the cure was sudden—instantaneous.
5. That the cure was perfect.
6. That there had not been beforehand a crisis produced by some cause and at its natural hour; in this case one cannot say that the cure was miraculous but natural, wholly or in part.
7. Finally, that after the cure there has been no relapse of the illness.

Dr. Leuret notes that "one can conceive true miracles which do not present one or another of these characteristics. . . . The Church does not deny the possibility of miracles 'less complete,' but she refuses to authenticate them, so strongly does she exact precise characteristics, easy to verify and which exclude all possibility of error."

Certain doctors are astonished at the severe requirements of the Church in accepting as miraculous an extraordinary cure. Dr. Leuret speaks of having been a member of a tribunal charged with investigating an alleged miraculous cure, and having heard one of the doctor-witnesses exclaim: "How is it that I, who am not a very firm believer, see a miracle in this cure, while you—ecclesiastical judges—are more difficult to convince than I?"

The rigorous attitude of the Medical Bureau itself is in line with that of the Church. Monseigneur Théas emphasized it in his address to the General Assembly of AMIL physicians in 1949:

"Your only role is to be true. You have neither to be severe nor indulgent, but only to be exact and to furnish to the Church medical observations which are indisputable—leaving her to judge in each case whether there has or has not been a miracle."

As stated earlier, only fifty-one cases have been declared Miraculous Cures by the Church, during the ninety-seven years of the Shrine. It may be well to mention again that cures of nervous maladies are not considered—nor are cures of hypersensitive patients "whose emotions would be susceptible of provoking 'nervous discharges' which could modify for example their mobility."

In spite of all these precautions, not only lay people but some of the clergy have occasionally been overzealous with premature announcements of "miraculous cures" at Lourdes. In 1924, the Bishop of Tarbes and Lourdes issued a stern warning in this regard:

The haste of certain pilgrims to proclaim "miraculous" certain happenings which have not yet been the object of sufficient scientific study or of official confirmation, is incontestably of a nature to furnish weapons to the enemies of the supernatural and of the Catholic Church. . . .

Inspired no doubt by most honorable intentions, too much haste in naming such happenings as supernatural, far from producing conviction with unbelievers, favors on the contrary attacks of impiety and of bad faith.

It is of utmost importance then, in order to prevent opinion from falling in error, that no act of a cure at Lourdes shall give rise to a religious ceremony or be set forth in the accounts of

pilgrimages, before having been rigorously checked and authenti-
cated by the inquiries and official publication of the verbatim proceedings of the Bureau of Medical Verifications of Lourdes.

In disregarding this rule—imperatively dictated by Christian
prudence—newspapers and other Catholic publications will expose
themselves to an official denial which, to their very great regret, the
President of the Medical Bureau and even the Bishop of Tarbes
and Lourdes will be obliged to bring upon them. (Signed, Francis
Xavier, Bishop of Tarbes and Lourdes.)

⊷§ *It may come* as a surprise to many that the Catholic
Church, while maintaining the possibility of present-day miracles, does not require its followers to believe in them, and some
do not. Bernadette showed no interest in them. The Lady never
mentioned them, or gave any indication of the great healings
that were to take place at the Shrine. What The Lady wanted
was Prayer and Penitence. This is what the Church wants too.

Among Catholic doctors one finds sometimes the strongest
conviction, sometimes the most stubborn skepticism. I talked
with a number of Catholic doctors who were greatly interested
in Lourdes cures but who are still uncertain as to the forces
that may produce them. (These of course are definitely in the
minority, and by some might not be considered "good Catholics.")

"There are vast areas of knowledge as yet almost completely
unexplored," said one Catholic physician. "All we can say now
is that such healings are at present *inexplicable*."

I must add that no one appears to be trying to convince or
change the skeptics, or to change the views of doctors of other
faiths either. The declared freedom offered to all hands in the
work is a genuine freedom—and very fine.

I have never seen any proselytizing at Lourdes, except that
of example. During the months that I was there no one inquired
about my faith or suggested that I change it. What impressed

me was the sincere and simple faith, the true religion being *lived* all about me. One thought for the thousandth time how much more eloquent preaching is the silent kind—*being* your religion—how profoundly and permanently that impresses.

The Church does practice one open—and very interesting— piece of propaganda, each summer during the pilgrimage season. Up on the hill behind the Sanctuaries, it presents each year a Missionary Exposition—bringing before its masses of Catholic pilgrims (and other interested visitors) the story of Catholic missionary work in faraway lands. A different area is presented each summer. The year I was there, Africa was the continent under discussion; the year before, India and Ceylon.

Photographs, surveys, arts and crafts, exhibits of all sorts of work done by the native Catholics of the various countries are on view; priests and Sisters, with native helpers, give hourly talks and explanations. Every day, several thousand people see these exhibits and hear these talks. They form a colorful supplement to the regular routine of the pilgrims, and bring in quite substantial returns for the missionary cause, if only through the very modestly priced tickets of admission. They bring these thousands of peasant folk into dramatic and vivid touch with people of other lands and with the work of the Church throughout the world.

⋅§ *This national and international unifying work* is one of the most interesting aspects of Lourdes, quite aside from the healing and spiritual side. The bringing together of scores of pilgrimages from different provinces and territories of France is in itself a fine, patriotic work. Coming here brings a person in touch not only with people of the different parts of the country itself—its many regions and departments—but with French citizens from many parts of the world: Madagascar, Syria, Morocco, French Guiana, Algeria, Indo-China, and so on.

I have often thought of the amazing way in which the sup-

posedly un-unitable French come together in such complete
unity here. Lourdes has united Frenchmen of all types and
classes, all shades of religious and political opinion, and during
times of greatest intellectual division and irreligion. Here, from
the beginning—and even in the strait-laced and snobbish nineteenth century—French people of all social castes, all grades of
education, have come together spontaneously, wholeheartedly,
in common worship and in common work of love and compassion. Any Hospitallers' mess is a shining example of this, all
political discussion being strictly ruled out. Thus, among such
passionate individualists, in a nation we are accustomed to think
of as a conglomeration of conflicting and irreconcilable views
and groups, we find at this one spot an extraordinary sense of
unity and the smoothest and most contented teamwork im-
aginable. And this extends back into the local units when the
people all go home.

Lourdes is a great national center. It is a great international
center. Not only for the doctors and pilgrims but for the
priests and bishops of many countries who meet here too: a
perpetual ecumenical conference, enlarging their individual out-
look, permitting them to share experiences, discuss problems of
their various lands and dioceses; and through them carrying
this wider viewpoint back for the better education and en-
largement of thousands of parishioners in their homelands.

As hosts, the Lourdes clergy are famous. It takes real genius
to make all these various visitors feel at home and so welcome,
so much wanted and appreciated, as they all do feel at Lourdes.

One of the nicest things about the place is its democracy
and unpretentiousness, notwithstanding all its splendid ceremonies. The humblest little priest from the back of beyond is
invited to say Mass. It is always the visiting Bishops—from
Liverpool or Turin or Seattle—who lead the processions, not
the resident clergy.

"Just imagine, they asked me—me, a little missioner buried
in a tiny village in Japan—to say Mass at the Grotto. And I
did!" a young Maryknoll Father told me, joyfully.

The Lourdes Bishop says Mass only once a week—at eight o'clock on Saturday mornings, throughout the summer. When he became ill recently, he had himself carried down to lie with the other sick in front of the Grotto. "Now I am one of you!" he said with great content. "I who have lectured and preached to you so often. Now you will teach and instruct me!"

And here a word about this remarkable person, His Excellency the Most Reverend Pietro Maria Théas, The Bishop of Lourdes. He lives in a modest "Chalet Episcopale" on the hill above the Sanctuaries. His waiting room is open to anyone— and is usually full: Sisters, priests, brancardiers, nurses, townspeople. The first day I was there, two Turks, a French sailor, an Egyptian scholar, and three young men from a seminary in West Africa were waiting to see him.

The Bishop is friendly, charming, *simpático*. His unfailing graciousness and kindliness is from the heart. Day after day I watched the tenderness, sensitiveness, with which he greets the sick. Seeing these multitudes as he does—month after month, year after year, it would be understandable if he became, not blasé, but sometimes perhaps just a bit perfunctory in his greeting and feeling for them.

With Monseigneur Théas—never! Each group, each occasion, each new pilgrimage and ceremony, is a new opportunity for him to show his never-ending compassion and concern for their welfare. The healing of their souls and bodies is ever in his mind.

Everything that a great ecclesiastic can be to his Church— a tender father to his "children," both sick and well; a generous and devoted friend to his colleagues; a genial and self-effacing host to his visiting confreres; a magnificent orator and presiding officer at the never-ending succession of celebrations and ceremonies—all this and much more Monseigneur Théas is to the people who surround him in the office he so ably and humbly fills. There is no office quite like it anywhere else in the world.

Part Two

MIDDLE YEARS AND SOME FAMOUS CASES

11

Five Characteristics of Miraculous Healing

*A*nyone *who studies* the records and reports on the cures at Lourdes must be impressed with the extreme prudence and care of the doctors of the Medical Bureau and the Medical Commission in judging alleged cures. Far from being in haste to declare a supernatural cure, they seem to turn up every possible argument against it.

No hysterical or neurotic cases are considered for study, either by the Church or by the Bureau. *No case is studied unless some organic change has occurred,* with medical and laboratory documents to prove it. When this has happened—as for example when a tumor has disappeared or bony structure altered—the alleged cure is examined. If the case appears to be a genuine cure, it "goes into the works" of the intricate and meticulously severe scrutiny and time-process required before a Lourdes cure is officially announced.

The doctors of the Medical Bureau list five special characteristics which mark "miraculous" cures * and which differentiate them from natural cures that the physician ordinarily finds among his patients and that medical science can explain:

---

* I am greatly indebted to Dr. Vallet and Dr. Guinier for permission to incorporate substantial portions of their observations in this account; and to Flammarion & Co., publishers of *La Vérité sur Lourdes* by Dr. Vallet.

1. *Absence of a curative agent* (such as drugs or injections, special treatments, etc.)

2. *Instantaneousness.*

3. *Suppression of convalescence.*

4. *Irregularity of the method of healing.*

5. *Function restored without action of the organ—still incapable of accomplishing it.*

Any one of these five could mark a case as outside the borders of the cures ordinarily known to medical scientists—and therefore to be sharply challenged by them.

In regard to Point 1, and any material aid that might help to bring about a sudden cure: the hospitals at Lourdes (or as they are properly called, "refuges" or hostels) give no medical treatment of any kind. And the majority of the sick are chronic invalids who have exhausted all drugs and therapies, during long years in various hospitals and clinics; who have been given up to die by famous surgeons and doctors powerless to save them; and who have come to ask at the Shrine at Lourdes that which has been proved—not once or twice but over and over again—medically impossible.

Thus no one can say, when a cure takes place, that some wonder drug or injection of cortisone or penicillin has been the cause of the sudden bounding back to life. The water of the Grotto is the only material agent used, and that, as we have seen, has no medicinal properties whatever.

2. *Instantaneousness:* this, for the doctors of the Medical Bureau, is the main characteristic by which they identify a miraculous cure. Obviously, instantaneousness is a severe shock to the medical man. It goes against all the basic laws and procedure impressed upon him throughout his medical training.

Dr. Guinier, who worked for four years at the Medical Bureau making an intensive study of Lourdes cases, describes the bafflement they cause the average physician:

The laws of biology that we have studied have taught us that all the work of organic recuperation requires, to be perfect, *time* and *slowness*; and here all at once these laws are completely set aside. That which ought to have required a month of attentive care, even granting it might be successful, occurs instantly—perfectly, and permanently—without any apparent intervention of any kind. Microbes are annihilated . . . carcinomas vanish, tubercle bacilli exist no more; gangrenous bones are re-formed, severed nerves joined together, wounds cicatrized. Sometimes this happens in a few seconds, sometimes a few hours, but so rapidly that we can say that the factor *time* has disappeared, consequently the cure has operated beyond the laws of biology.*

Imagine the state of mind of a doctor suddenly confronted with such things. Here is a young physician just starting out. He has spent four years—maybe eight or ten—learning the rigorous precepts of the science of medicine, studying what he believes to be unalterable biological principles. He has spent hour after hour and year after year drilling all these things into his mind. Scientific law is his alpha and omega. He has been told that any superhuman power higher than science or man's own mind is a myth.

All of a sudden everything he has been taught is overturned. He sees before his own eyes things which his professors and all the learned books and authorities have taught him could never happen. Yet there they are, happening—becoming facts of human experience.

No wonder Lourdes is hard to take; when, for example, the average medical man is brought face to face with a case like that of Elizabeth Delot, instantly cured of cancer.

Mlle. Delot was a teacher in a girls' school at Boulogne. In

---

* According to biology, the healing of the arteries requires forty or fifty days; that of a nerve entirely severed, three or four months, at least, to heal over and recover its lost function; for a broken bone to knit, thirty to sixty days—according to the thickness of the bone and extent of the fracture. The healings at Lourdes require neither time nor slowness for cicatrization and the production of no matter what tissue—bone, muscle, kidney, lung, or whatever.

her late forties she became seriously ill—so ill that she had to give up her work and go into a hospital. X-rays and clinical tests brought the terrible news that she had cancer of the stomach. Besides, bismuth tests showed that there was a block between the stomach and the beginning of the intestine. This meant death by starvation, unless surgery could effect the passage of food.

When the surgeon who performed the operation, Dr. Houzel of Boulogne, saw the condition, he told Miss Delot's attending physician, Dr. Wallois, that the size of the tumor was such that it could not be removed. All he could do was to make an opening from the stomach into the intestine which would permit the food to pass into the lower digestive tract.

This was done, and at first there seemed to be a slight improvement; but after three months the trouble became worse. The original cancer of the stomach had spread to the liver, and the operated opening itself was invaded by cancerous cells. In July the blockage was complete. Eating became impossible for the patient—even liquids were thrown up. Physicians agreed there was nothing ahead but the misery of constant hunger and thirst until death. Mlle. Delot was lost.

In this desperate state she joined the Lourdes Pilgrimage from Arras, arriving at Lourdes on the morning of July 30. She was so exhausted after the journey that they put her into the water at the piscine with extraordinary precautions. Her first sensation was of pain so intense that she cried with all her strength for death to deliver her. She felt "a terrible burning and stabbing" in the stomach and intestine—as if, she said afterward, "they were holding her under a fiendish hammer."

But when the nurses helped her out of the water, the agony gave way to an unaccustomed sense of well-being. A strange feeling of calm and health took possession of her, also an unexpected vigor. She dressed herself without assistance. At the same time she felt a strong sensation of hunger—unknown to her in a long while. Back at the Hostel, she ate some soup and some vegetable purée, without feeling any discomfort. That night she ate some meat, and felt nothing but a renewal of strength. The next day a repetition of the same diet confirmed the cure. The intestine emptied itself normally.

Examining her at the Medical Bureau, the doctors noted the suppleness of the stomach and the part that had been operated on. They observed that the liver was resuming its usual outline. After her return to Boulogne, her home physician reported that "Mlle. Delot eats just like everyone else—meat, vegetables, everything," and that "she experiences no fatigue, and all her organs are in excellent state." New X-rays taken three weeks after her cure showed a complete reversal of the former condition. Eight months later Dr. Houzel wrote to the Bureau that Mlle. Delot, "operated on by me for a malignant tumor of the stomach, today shows all the signs of perfect health. She now leads a very active life, and has resumed her work at the school on a full-time basis."

The following year she returned to Lourdes and was again examined at the Bureau. After minute investigation, eighteen doctors gave the following unanimous report:

At the time of her first arrival at Lourdes, Mlle. Delot was suffering from (1) a malignant tumor of the pylorus with extension to the operated mouth of the gastrointestinal passage; (2) a spread of the disease to the liver. There has been a proven cure, proven by the disappearance of the tumor, the reestablishment of general health (increase in weight of 18 pounds), the perfect functioning of the pylorus, liver and intestine, and the proof of time. This sudden healing cannot be attributed to natural processes. It goes beyond the portals of our knowledge.

Since her cure Mlle. Delot has remained in excellent health. "It has never ceased to be excellent," she writes, "from the moment when I came out of the piscine full of life, where a few minutes earlier they had plunged me dying. From that day I have entirely forgotten what it is to suffer with one's stomach. I digest anything."

Here was a cure that certainly could not be laid to errors of diagnosis, or autosuggestion, or any of the classic explanations of the medical skeptics.

&ऽ *Another celebrated case* was that of Marie-Louise Arnaud, who was instantly cured of disseminated sclerosis while lying on her stretcher in front of the Grotto. This disease, generally called incurable, is caused by patches of inflammation occurring in different portions of the brain or spinal cord. It often begins with weakness in the limbs; later come muscular incoordination and wavering eyesight. The patches spread, and the disease is usually fatal.

With Mlle. Arnaud the first symptoms appeared with pains in the legs, frequent falls for no apparent reason, violent headaches, and inability to use her hands properly. She could not sew or knit, her writing became almost indecipherable, reading more and more difficult.

Two physicians, Dr. Boudet and Dr. Rimbaud of Montpellier (her home town), examined her and returned the same diagnosis: disseminated sclerosis. She rapidly lost weight, could walk only when held up by someone, had frequent attacks of vertigo, and her vision was much involved. No treatment seemed to help, and death appeared certain.

A devout Catholic, and knowing that from the human point of view her case was hopeless, she decided to join the French National Pilgrimage to Lourdes. Dr. Boudet wrote her certificate. She made the journey on a stretcher, attended by a nurse at every moment. After reaching Lourdes, she was so ill that on the second day she was taken only to the Procession in the afternoon. Being carried there on a stretcher increased her giddiness. She seemed to be very near the end.

August 23 was the anniversary of her brother's death. She begged to be taken to the Grotto that morning, wishing to offer up her Communion for him. When the priest mounted the pulpit, he asked that the sick should try to forget their own sufferings for a few minutes, and to pray for the dead. Mlle. Arnaud was much struck by this coincidence, and began to pray earnestly. After she had received the Communion she wept quietly, thinking of the brother she had loved so much, and, as she records, "quite oblivious of myself and my illness."

Turning her head on her pillow to hide her tears, "I was astonished (she said) to feel quite distinctly the shape of my right slipper resting on my left foot—for sensation had been so completely dulled by my illness. I opened my eyes. Before me, everything was steady (where before everything seemed to oscillate and wobble about). I could see clearly.

"All this happened in a lightning flash, while the Sacred Host was still on my tongue. With my fingers I could say my Rosary; I sat up without falling over to the right, as usually happened. Sensation had returned to my legs and my limbs now seemed to obey my will. . . .

"At twelve o'clock I was back in the hospital. One of the ladies asked me: 'Well, how are you?' 'Cured, I believe,' I replied. The stretcher was set down and I got up and walked. . . . At two o'clock I was taken to the Medical Bureau. That same night I slept the whole time, calmly and peaceably. I had not had such a night for twenty months." Next evening she started on the return journey to Montpellier. She spent most of the night in the train on her feet, helping with the sick.

At the Medical Bureau the doctors could find nothing wrong with her except an absence of the abdominal reflexes and some exaggerations of those of the knee and ankle. Her eyes were perfectly normal. However, with its usual caution, the Bureau did not declare a cure until it had proved itself with time.

The following year Mlle. Arnaud came again to Lourdes, bringing with her another certificate from Dr. Boudet in which he said: "I have seen Mlle. Arnaud on several occasions since her return from Lourdes. At the present time there is neither vertigo nor loss of consciousness; no headache or pain in the back; no contraction or tremors; no nystagmus [oscillation of the eyeballs]. Writing is easy and normal; no trouble with the sphincters; Babinski's reflex is normal. The ankle and knee remain brisk—the sole remaining sign of the former illness."

Another letter received from Dr. Boudet several years later stated that in spite of a good deal of trouble in her family, Mlle. Arnaud had been able since her cure eight years ago to lead an active life. There had been no return of any of the previous symptoms. Her handwriting just before and just after her cure makes an interesting footnote to her doctor's observations. (See illustrations for photostat.)

These are only two of the long list of cases described in Lourdes medical records, illustrating the instantaneous character of miraculous cures.

3. *Absence of Convalescence* is another characteristic which goes hand in hand with instantaneousness.

The natural cure of an infectious disease usually proceeds slowly and progressively over a certain period, during which the organism gradually gets rid of the unwanted germs and poisons and the various organs gradually get back to normal. Convalescence lasts sometimes for days, sometimes for weeks or months. It requires special treatment, special care, sometimes a more temperate climate, and various other inducements to coax the body back to normal activity.

But those who are cured at Lourdes do not know that in-between period of gradual strengthening and return to health. The instantaneousness appears to suppress the disease at its source. No matter what the affliction, the degree of acuteness or chronic condition, it is *immediately* that all the organic functions—digestion, breathing, circulation and so on—are restored to normal vigor. The function of digestion and assimilation is first to get back in order—to the astonishment of the invalid, amazed at his sudden imperious hunger.

This hunger is a tremendous need of the whole organism for these individuals who have been reduced to the point of death. There is so much to be regained, so many empty spaces to fill, flaccidity to make firm again, injured tissue to repair. Patients have been known to put on two pounds a day at first, and as much as seventy pounds during the year following their cure. "I am hungry!" is the leit-motif of the miraculous cure, says Dr. Vallet, and one of the first symptoms by which it makes itself known.

This was strikingly evident in the case of little Henri Mieuzet, a boy of seven who came to Lourdes dying of a serious digestive ailment.

Henri was a quiet little boy, highly intelligent, but always delicate. From the time he was a year old, he began to suffer from the illness that nearly killed him: enteritis, or inflammation of the intestines, as diagnosed by three doctors—Chevalier, Basser, and finally by Dr. Vannier, who made out Henri's pilgrimage certificate.

The child's sister had died of the same disease. In his case, occasional attacks soon developed into chronic illness. Living in the country, it was sometimes hard for him to follow the prescribed treatments. In spite of the doctors' efforts, the child's health steadily declined. By the time he was seven, he was in a very critical state.

He had now been in bed for two years, refusing almost all food but milk, and in acute pain most of the time. While his brothers ran and shouted outside, he lay helpless and in agony.

Dr. Basser's notations over this two-year period are weekly repetitions of the symptoms: "Severe abdominal pain, night sweats, blood in the stools—of which six or seven a day, extreme anemia, and loss of weight," all pointing to classic tubercular symptoms as well as the immediate digestive miseries.

"At the present moment," (i.e., when leaving for Lourdes) wrote Dr. Vannier, "this child has almost the look of a dying person. He has become very thin, and eats less and less—lately only liquids. He has not left his bed for long months. He weighs only 28 pounds, whereas eighteen months ago he weighed 42 . . . In his present state, and in view of the apparent uselessness of all the remedies and diets tried up to this time, the child seems beyond therapeutic help."

The doctors considered it folly for him to travel, and said it was unlikely he would come back alive.

Henri's parents nevertheless took him to Lourdes—like so many others, as a last desperate hope. During his time there, his condition, far from improving, seemed to grow worse. The trip itself was very hard on him (300 miles in a third-class carriage), and on the night after their arrival his mother thought he was dying. Wheeling him about on his stretcher to the various ceremonies, plunging him into the icy water at the piscine, might certainly have killed a child in his condition.

On Tuesday, the day set for the return journey, the mother cried her heart out as she looked at the wasted little body and admitted despairingly: "He is no better! It has all been for nothing. I know now that he will die!"

He seemed unconscious after they got him into the train. He lay back on his pillows, white and spent.

One of the nurses on the train later wrote the following account to the Medical Bureau:

The train departed. After taking a last look at the Virgin as we passed above the Grotto, nurses and patients began to recite the Rosary. They could not finish it without real emotion, for it was during our Rosary at the Grotto that the little Saget girl—a Pott's Disease victim—had been cured.

When the recitation was finished, little Henri, motionless on his mattress up to that moment, suddenly sat up and said, "I want to go see the little girl who was cured. I want to see her right now!"

He stepped down on the floor. His mother, stupefied, began to laugh and cry all together. "I want to see the little girl who was cured," insisted Henri. "Now, right away—at once!"

And here he is, standing up, walking, followed by one of the nurses ready to hold him up if need be. "Very well, come," she said soothingly. And he walked the length of the corridor—this child who had not stirred from his mattress for eighteen months.

When he reached the compartment of the little girl he threw his arms around her, and the two children hugged each other joyfully. By this time everybody in the car was in the corridor, laughing and crying with the mother. And giving thanks to the Blessed Virgin who had wrought this double miracle.

After things had quieted down, Henri went back to his own compartment and, for the first time in several years, *he said that he was hungry.* His mother gave him first a little milk, but that was not sufficient. They gave him then a banana, and a bowl of hot chocolate, which went down very well. Two hours later, for supper, he ate two slices of bread and some pâté—a diet certainly not indicated for intestinal disease! Next morning when he woke up he ate three sweet rolls and a cup of black coffee. And then he was hungry and ate again before he reached his destination.

Henri Mieuzet was cured instantly, with no period of convalescence afterward, nor any interim condition. From the day of his return home he shared the family meals, which were substantial. His digestive functions were entirely normal. It was, said the doctors, "a complete restoration of the entire digestive tract."

Dr. Vannier saw him immediately after his return and at monthly intervals afterward. His notations on these occasions coincide almost identically with the report of Dr. Vallet who visited the boy seven months after his cure:

"The present state of the child is very satisfactory. Splendid appetite. Easy digestion. Stools regular and normal. He eats like anybody else, has no more pain, spends his days running about and playing with his brothers. Since his cure he has gained eight pounds and has grown almost an inch taller. This child is admirably cured.

"It is a cure," Dr. Vannier adds, "profoundly disconcerting to the physician."

"What especially marks this case," says the Medical Bureau report, "is the suddenness with which the symptoms disappeared, and the rapidity of the recovery. The child passed immediately from a state of most serious illness to a state of health full of promise—which has since been amply realized."

Henri Mieuzet has never ceased to have good health from the moment of his cure. He became a student at the Grand Seminary of Rennes, a vigorous young man, of fine abilities.

⋅§ Another dramatic example of instantaneous cure with no convalescent period following—after a long and desperate illness—was the case of Ernestine Guilloteau.

This girl, aged twenty-four, arrived at Lourdes with a certificate saying that for three years she had suffered from tuberculous peritonitis. The diagnosis was confirmed by five physicians: Charrier, Valla-Brochart of Thouars (her home), Renon, Collon, and Corbin of Niort—a town nearby. The doctors were unanimous in refusing to operate, saying that the unfortunate girl was simply "a compote of decompositions," that all treatment or medication was useless.

She suffered horribly, took no food at all, and was kept going with parenteral injections. Dr. Valla-Brochart's certificate stated that "for two years she has had only a little milk, tea or coffee —often thrown up for the most part." A living skeleton, she weighed 48 pounds on her arrival at Lourdes. She was unconscious most of the time, and death was declared imminent. The Sisters at the hospital showed her mother the cell where she could put the body. But Ernestine was not to need it.

During the passing of the Blessed Sacrament at the Grotto, the morning after her arrival, this living skeleton suddenly raised itself. She got up from her stretcher, walking unaided, and followed the Procession into the Rosary Church. The crowd looked on, dumfounded. Then a resounding Magnificat broke forth.

Ernestine was taken to the Medical Bureau, where fifteen doctors examined her. They found no trace of lesions; the abdomen had become supple, and there was no pain whatever. She was ravenously hungry, and was able to eat and digest any food. Before her cure she had been unable to move without excruciating pain. Now she walked and moved about with perfect ease. She had been in bed for two years, but the muscles and fat were restored with a rapidity that was abnormal.

She returned to Lourdes a year later on a pilgrimage of thanksgiving, having gained 66 pounds. From the moment of her cure she continued to lead a healthy and happy life.

A professor of the University of Paris with whom I discussed this case told me he was acquainted with Ernestine Guilloteau. He and his family are frequent visitors at a guesthouse that she runs at a summer resort in the Vendée. He says she is in wonderful health—"a very attractive and remarkable woman." The name of the guesthouse is Villa Massabieille.

4. *Irregularity of Method* is another marked characteristic of a miraculous cure. With natural cures, a doctor can gauge the effectiveness of such and such a treatment with two persons suffering from the same malady. At Lourdes, no such determination is possible. No one can foretell who will be the fortunate chosen one of this mysterious healing force. We frequently see two patients suffering from the same disease, and having arrived at precisely the same stage in the course of it. One is healed, the other not. Why, nobody knows.

For one person, the first indication of a cure is strong hunger and a sense of well-being; for another, a tearing pain through the whole body. One gets his cure on the very first day of his visit to Lourdes, another not till his second or third visit, when his illness has apparently grown very much worse.

These, the doctors say, are some of the mysteries peculiar to miraculous cures, and marking them as definitely outside scientific law which operates always uniformly, universally, and forever the same under the same conditions.

5. Point five is perhaps the most amazing of all: where a person with a diseased organ—eye, lung, brain, or heart—finds the function natural to that organ working perfectly, though the organ itself remains unchanged, and biologically incapable of performing that function.

We saw one brilliant example of this in the case of Madame Biré, who was blind for many months—the nerves of her eyes were completely atrophied. Yet after that miraculous moment at the Grotto, Madame Biré saw well enough to read the finest print, months before the optic nerves had regained their normal aspect. (And this last a medical impossibility too, said the doctors, for atrophied nerves do not recover.) She was able to see, they said, when organically she had no right to see. She saw with "dead" eyes.

Almost identical was the case of Gerard Baillie * where, again, the examining doctor said: "The child has a chorioretinitis with double optic atrophy. He should not see." But he *did* see.

The case of Guy Leydet was even more spectacular.† Here, a child in a state of complete idiocy for two and a half years suddenly began to think and move and act, with a brain at least partially destroyed, following acute meningo-encephalitis. He was thinking with a brain that "could not think," just as Gerard Baillie was seeing with eyes that "could not see."

How can such things possibly happen? They can't, says medical science. But at Lourdes they do.

These are not pious inventions of religious devotees, seeking to add luster to their cherished faith. These are actual occurrences, observed by physicians of top standing and set down by them in official medical records over their signatures. They are among the most impressive illustrations of some of the characteristics of supernatural or "miraculous" cures.

* See page 220 for full account of this case.
† See page 236 for full account of this case.

12

The Author Interviews a
Miraculous Cure

I myself saw and talked with one well-known Cure whose case illustrates several of these "miraculous" characteristics.

The cures of men had particularly interested me—I suppose because so many people say, "oh yes, the cures at Lourdes—just neurasthenics and a lot of hysterical women!" They forget that some of the greatest cures have been those of Charles McDonald, John Traynor, Abbé Lochet, Abbé Dessailly, and other male pilgrims.

One of the most famous of the male cures, Fernand Legrand, I interviewed in his own home.

Legrand lives in Gisors, a small town not far from Paris. In my travels to visit the Cures, I soon got into the habit of using the little branch omnibus trains that dawdle along the French countryside, stopping every ten or fifteen minutes at some tiny station, spending half a day to go seventy miles, but finally arriving; as I did that day, at the pleasant little town of Gisors.

It was market day. Steep little streets, plodding beasts and vehicles, crowding good-humored people. . . . I made my way through the teeming market place and across the square. I was bound for the shop of the local cobbler who is known as one of the "grand Cures" of Lourdes; twenty-seven years old at the time of his cure, now fifty.

It is a modest little place halfway up the hill, Legrand and his wife smiling a welcome from the doorway: a very small shop, with a narrow house at the back where the family lives. But every year, Fernand Legrand saves the necessary 18,000 francs ($50) to go to Lourdes and give his services as stretcher-bearer with his diocesan pilgrimage. He has an extraordinarily fine face: the face of an Emerson, the hands of a shoemaker.

"*Bonjour, madame!* We were waiting for you. Did you have a good journey? Was it cold in the train? Come inside and get warm, and we will talk of Lourdes and the great things that God has done there!"

We sat by the fire in the cheerful little sitting room, and there, with the dog beating a drowsy tom-tom with his tail on the floor beside us and customers coming in every few minutes to claim a pair of boots or slippers, Fernand Legrand told me his story. Here it is, with a few additions from the Lourdes Medical record.

A healthy childhood—no unusual incidents or illnesses. He lived at that time at Vernon, another little town in the same *département,* not far from Gisors. When a husky young fellow of twenty-six, calamity came upon him. He was injured by a shot in a hunting accident. The lower part of his left leg had to be amputated.

"I recovered well from the operation, and soon got used to the artificial leg. But a year later severe pains began in that leg, then numbness which gradually spread up both legs and to the spine, finally to the right arm until I was completely paralyzed." He had spells of high fever; he lost weight rapidly and was in constant pain.

He was hospitalized at the hospital in Clermont. After two years, he was sent back to the hospital in Vernon, labeled *Incurable.* On March 20, 1933, he came under the care of Dr. Decrette of Vernon, who diagnosed his case as polyneuritis, involving particularly the spinal nerves and the cord itself.

All the classic treatments were put to work to combat the disease, but Legrand only grew worse. The arm and both legs were immobilized—a plaster cast for the right leg, splints for the stump of the left leg and right arm. His legs were greatly swollen and became gangrenous. He ate nothing, became thin as a skeleton (except for the legs), and suffered "the tortures of the damned."

The girl to whom he was engaged urged him to go to Lourdes, and he decided to join the Evreux Pilgrimage. Dr. Decrette, writing the certificate for his admission, answered the pilgrimage questionnaire as follows:

1. What is your prognosis—good, serious, or very serious?
   Answer: *Very serious.*
2. Is the disease incurable?
   Answer: *Incurable.*
3. What end do you anticipate for the present disease?
   Answer: *Progressive development of the paralysis, until death.*

Legrand, held rigid in a horizontal position, could make no movement of any kind. Each effort, each disturbance of the bedclothes even, gave him excruciating pain. It took six men to get him from the automobile into the compartment in the train for Lourdes. The journey was a horror.

He arrived at Lourdes on the morning of the tenth of September and was taken to the Sept Douleurs Hospital. That day and night passed as usual, with morphine injections to calm him. In the meantime, Dr. Decrette had arrived to look after his patient. At the Medical Bureau he described the case to the doctors present, with so much earnestness and concern, that the President of the Bureau appointed Dr. Clement of Hyères to go with Dr. Decrette to the hospital and examine Legrand. The two set out at ten-thirty next morning.

Legrand had already been to the Grotto and the baths with the other sick. As Dr. Clement later recounted, "The patient had just returned from the piscine when we got there. When we reached his bed, Decrette asked me to examine him—'but go gently,' he said. 'He suffers very much when anyone touches him. His legs are so swollen he can't budge.' I took a look at the patient, who was all smiles, and said: 'Well, anyhow, he can smile!' 'Yes, you're right,' said Dr. Decrette, adding to Legrand: 'How is this? I've never seen you with an expression like that on your face. How do you feel?' 'I feel very well,' said Legrand."

Meanwhile, Dr. Clement had taken the right leg out of its cast, and the bandages which enveloped it. "Look here," he said to Dr. Decrette, "you told me he had a swollen leg. This one doesn't seem to be swollen, and it is dry."

"Impossible!" said Decrette. Then, as he looked, he gave a quick exclamation. "But—since when?"

"Since just now," said the patient. "Since during my bath in the piscine. All at once I felt a great warmth through all my body, my legs could bend, and I no longer had any pain."

At these words, Dr. Decrette was so moved he could not speak, and it was several minutes before he got himself in hand. He had seen this man in such a horrible condition, every day, for so long. "Tell us what happened," he managed to say finally.

And Legrand told them . . . this same story he told me now, here in his own home, twenty years later.

"I was carried to the Grotto, and then to the piscine on my stretcher, with the other sick. When they dipped me in the water, I felt as though all my arms and legs were being broken to pieces. But then—that strange and heavenly warmth, all through my body. The pain for a moment was agonizing; then I sat up and began helping the brancardiers to dress me. I could move my arms, and bend my legs. Can you imagine that—I could *move!*"

They took him back to the hospital. He was very hungry. They gave him several pieces of bread and a big bowl of *café au lait*. He ate it all and demanded more—*three times*, though he hadn't eaten more than "the size of a nut" in two years!

"When my doctor saw me like that, he began to weep. It was too much for him. They had brought me there in a dying condition. The only thing left for the doctors was to help me die with the least possible suffering. And now they saw me like this!"

The two doctors examined him. They verified that all the swelling of the lower limbs and of the arm had disappeared; that movement was possible, though still limited, that pain no longer existed. The patient could sit up in bed, and—always the special sign of a miraculous cure—he demanded something to eat and ate heartily.

Next day he was examined at the Medical Bureau. Fourteen doctors were present, among them two from the Royal Academy of Medicine of Italy and several from the Paris hospitals. The patient undressed himself like any normal person, and replied good-humoredly to questions during the two hours of interrogation, at the end of which the doctors set down the following conclusions:

1. Fernand Legrand has indeed been afflicted for twenty-six months with polyneuritis (ascending) and myelitis, characterized by symptoms of fever, pain, edema, arthropathy.
2. The above morbid symptoms totally disappeared on September 11, 1934, at ten o'clock in the morning at the moment of his immersion in the piscine of Lourdes.
3. The patient still has muscular atrophies, and some stiffness of the joints and tendons in which we see rapid improvement from hour to hour. These symptoms are consecutive to the illness, but not constituent of the illness. They should disappear in a relatively short time.

The cure was steadily maintained during the next twelve months. Legrand worked during that time as a practical nurse in the hospital of Vernon, without a single day off on account of indisposition. He returned to Lourdes the following year and came to the Bureau for his second examination. This time eleven doctors confirmed his cure. They found that all stiffness had disappeared, that reflexes of both arms and legs were normal, the heart was normal, and the patient had gained eighteen pounds.

"In conclusion (they stated): there has been a definite cure of the illness. No specific medical treatment had been given for more than six months—except certain drugs to keep the heart going, and numerous injections of morphine. In view of the instantaneousness of the cure, it cannot be attributed to natural causes."

The next year when Legrand went back, he went as a stretcher-bearer in the service of other sick people.

"Doesn't your artificial leg make it difficult for you?" I asked him.

He laughed. "Difficult? Madame, you should see me! Since my cure I can run like a rabbit—wooden leg and all. None of them with real legs can get ahead of me!"

He went to Lourdes on his honeymoon trip and has served there every year since his cure, except during the war.

A stretcher-bearer I frequently saw at Lourdes told me that he was one of those who had helped carry Fernand Legrand off the train on his arrival that day, twenty years ago, as a *grand malade*.

"The most terrible case I ever had to carry. That, madame, was truly a miracle!"

✑§ *Two other stalwart Cures* frequently seen at Lourdes are Robert Guyot and Lucien Belhache. Guyot, a worker in the mines of Dourges, suffered for months from an abscessed left kidney. Under the care of three physicians—Drs. Leroy, Dereux, and Sennelart—he was operated on, but instead of improving grew steadily worse.

Severe pain developed in the left leg and he could no longer bend it or stand upon it. The wound failed to heal, his state of weakness increased alarmingly. Transfusion after transfusion was given him, and he received the Last Rites. His condition was so serious, his wife brought linens to the Hospital for the Sisters to use in preparing him for the grave.

He rallied from this crisis, however, and was carried to Lourdes, convinced that no medical aid could save him. He was cured after his third bath in the piscine. That night his wound was completely healed, he could stand erect and walk without difficulty. At the Medical Bureau he was found normal in every way, and has not missed a day's work since his cure.

The cure of Lucien Belhache is interesting because it occurred in a family of complete unbelievers. Lucien's father and mother had been married "outside religion," and none of the five children had ever been inside a church or even baptized. They lived as carefree pagans, in their home city of Toulouse.

Then, when he was twenty-two, Lucien became ill. While working at his aviation plant he suffered a violent fall which sent him rolling along the ground several yards. During the weeks that followed he had severe pain in his spine, and soon a stiffness that prevented his standing erect.

Dr. Verdier, the family physician, diagnosed his trouble as Pott's Disease, or tuberculosis of the spine, brought on through the crushing of the fifth lumbar vertebra. The diagnosis was confirmed by X-rays and the detailed report of a second physician, Dr. Constantin. The doctors wished to put the young man immediately into a spinal jacket. But Lucien's father had read somewhere that at a place called Lourdes several cases of this disease had been cured. He insisted that this "special treatment" should first be tried.

In order to join a pilgrimage, Lucien received religious instruction, and was baptized before the pilgrimage left Toulouse. He was not in a cast when he left home, but so weak and bent over that others had to support him in walking.

After his first bath he felt considerable improvement, but his real cure came at the Procession, when the Blessed Sacrament was raised before him in blessing. At that moment he had "an indefinable sense of well-being"—he knew he was cured. No more stiffness or pain of any kind. He could stand erect and walk freely!

He was examined at the Medical Bureau the following day. The report states: "There remains no stiffness whatever and the suppleness of the spinal column is complete. All movements free and easy; the walk normal. The illness—attested by doctors' certificates and X-rays—certainly existed. In the present state of science, the cure, in several hours, of caries with disintegration of a vertebral body, has no natural explanation. It awaits confirmation after the required year's testing."

The following year Lucien returned to Lourdes, himself to serve the sick and carry them back and forth between the baths and the Grotto. He was again examined and the doctors present verified that the young Pott's Disease victim of a year ago now enjoyed perfect health. He was working in his father's business of piano repairing, with long motorbike trips around the country; and as a Scout of the Toulouse troop he went on hikes of ten miles or more with a pack on his back. His cure was definitely confirmed.

In consequence of this cure, the entire Belhache family were baptized and became devoted practicing Christians. Both Lucien and his wife come every year to Lourdes to help with the care of the Toulouse sick, he as brancardier, she as nurse. He now has an important post in the radio department of Air-France. Lucien, now a husky man of fifty-two, was among those who had the honor to "carry the canopy" during the great Rosary Pilgrimage of 1953: the same Pilgrimage where he was healed, thirty years before.

❧ *Skeptics are sometimes* to be found among the clergy as well as the laity. An interesting example was the Abbé Fiamma of Paris, who suffered from a severe case of varicose veins with ulcerations, and who had little faith in Lourdes cures.

He told his doctor: "My Archbishop wants me to go to Lourdes, but I go without any confidence that I shall be cured."

He arrived on the last day of the pilgrimage and did not bother going to the baths. Then a brancardier friend told him bluntly that he was a fool not to do at least as the others did. Even then the Abbé did not take a complete bath, but immersed his legs only. He felt intense pain—"like thrusting a red-hot iron under the skin."

He was cured—suddenly and permanently.

So was the Abbé Dessailly, afflicted with tuberculosis of the larynx and of both lungs, according to Dr. Pradal of Pau, who stated in his certificate to the Medical Bureau:

"The patient was suffering from tuberculous laryngitis and complete loss of voice. Swallowing was very difficult. He lost 11 pounds in one month. Fever was constantly present, with temperature varying from 100 to 103 degrees. His general condition seemed to indicate a speedy fatal issue."

The diagnosis was corroborated by both X-rays and clinical examination. The sputum contained tubercle bacilli. The X-rays showed that the upper two-thirds of both lungs were affected.

He was kept in bed, as much as possible in the open air, and urged to eat more; but he seemed to be slipping steadily downhill.

Finally he decided to go to Lourdes. Directly after his first bath he showed marked improvement. He recovered his voice; he could dress himself; and was seized with a great desire for food. He gained 40 pounds in the next two months, 68 pounds within six months, and was hale and hearty when he came to Lourdes the following year.

Since his cure he has never coughed, has had no medical treatment whatever. He returned to work at his Seminary and has been able to perform all his duties with perfect freedom.

13

The Cure of a British Soldier
Gunshot Wounds — Paralysis — Epilepsy

Perhaps the most celebrated of all men-cures is John Traynor.

Traynor was a soldier of World War I, seriously wounded in a bayonet charge at Gallipoli. One bullet entered the inner side of his right arm, traveled up to the level of the collarbone, severing the large nerves of the axilla which supply the skin of the arm with sensation and actuate the muscles. The result of this injury was loss of sensation, paralysis, and muscular atrophy. Doctors urged him to have the right arm amputated, "as it would always be useless." He refused.

Several physicians operated on him—Sir Frederick Treves and Major Ross while he was still overseas, Dr. McMurray and Major Montserrat in hospitals in England after his return home —in a series of attempts to suture the severed nerves. All were unsuccessful.

Traynor was discharged from military service and awarded a pension of 100 per cent, the Ministry of Pensions recording that "the right arm is useless and will probably remain so."

He was sent from hospital to hospital—five in all—in well-meaning but futile efforts to relieve his condition. During his last hospitalization his skull was trephined in the hope of helping his epileptic attacks which now averaged three a day. Besides the atrophied arm, both legs were partially paralyzed, there was loss of control of the bladder and rectum. On the skull at the site of the last operation was an opening which revealed the pulsations of the brain; whenever he coughed there was a protrusion of the membrane. In this condition Traynor was discharged from Springfields Hospital and returned to his own home in Liverpool. Here is his own account of his condition at this time:

When I was a little better I was discharged in an ambulance and carried to my own bed . . . I could not walk or stand, and was in a very bad way. I had not moved my right arm for eight years. I was on special home treatment under Dr. Turner, medical referee of the Ministry of Pensions, and Dr. McConnell and Dr. Aiken. My wife received "attendance allowance" for helping and looking after me. I was on a special milk diet ordered by Dr. Turner. After several months in bed the British Red Cross lent me a chair so that I could get out in the fresh air; my wife or my daughter always carried me from my bed to the chair, or from the chair to my bed. I was supplied with an air cushion on account of bed sores at the bottom of my spine. The Ministry of Pensions supplied me with a light special propelling chair.

After some time he was told that on July 24, 1923, he could be admitted to the Hospital for Incurables at Mossley Hill. But Traynor, a devoted Catholic, decided instead that he would go to Lourdes to ask for his cure. Again, in his own words:

In the month of July, 1923, I was at home, helpless as usual, when a neighbor woman came to the house and spoke of an announcement that had been made in our parish. A Liverpool diocesan pilgrimage was being organized for Lourdes. It would cost thirteen pounds to go. A down payment of one pound would engage a place.

My wife was out in the yard and I called her in. I told her to go upstairs and get a certain box in which we kept a gold sovereign which my brother had given me and which we were treasuring for some special emergency. I told her I was going to give it to Mrs. Cunningham, our neighbor, as a first payment on a ticket to Lourdes. My wife was very disturbed but finally did as I told her and the neighbor went off and made the booking.

Soon one of the priests in charge of the pilgrimage came to see me. "You cannot make the trip," he said. "You will die on the way

—please give it up." I said I had made my first payment and that I was going to Lourdes.

Then came the matter of a medical certificate. We called in several doctors—every one of them said that such a journey would be suicide. The priest came again and begged me to give up the idea. I would not—and finally succeeded in going without a medical certificate. To raise the twelve pounds, the balance due on my ticket, we sold some of our belongings, and my wife even pawned some of her bits of jewelry.

The day of departure came. At the station, in the press of people and confusion of getting all the sick aboard, Traynor missed the first train—the one he was supposed to board. Again the priest tried to persuade him to give it up and go home. Traynor was stubborn. There was another train.

"I said they could put me in the coal tender or anywhere they liked—*but I was going to Lourdes!* By being stubborn about it I won my point."

The journey was a nightmare. Three times they tried to take him off the train, as he seemed to be dying. Each time there was no hospital at the town where they stopped, and the only thing was to keep on.

The Pilgrimage reached Lourdes on July 22—Traynor by then in a terrible condition. He was taken to the Asile Hospital and kept under sedatives. On July 24 he was examined by three physicians—Dr. Azurdia of London, Dr. James Marley of Wallasey, and Dr. Dennis Finn of Liverpool, who issued the following certificate:

This is to certify that on July 24, 1923, we examined Mr. John Traynor, of 121 Grafton Street, Liverpool, and found his condition to be as follows:

1. Epileptic. We ourselves saw several attacks during his journey to Lourdes.
2. The radial, median, and ulnar nerves of the right arm are paralyzed, the hand is *en griffe* (clawlike), there is wrist drop and muscular atrophy.
3. The shoulder and pectoral muscles are atrophied.
4. The trephine opening in the right parietal region is about 2 cm. 5.

(That is, slightly under an inch in diameter.) The pulsations of the brain are visible. A metal plate covers the trephine orifice.

5. There is absence of voluntary movements of the legs, with loss of sensibility.

6. Incontinence of urine and feces.

The Pilgrimage was to remain six days at Lourdes. During that time Traynor was desperately ill. He had several hemorrhages as well as epileptic fits. Nevertheless he succeeded in being immersed in the baths nine times. On the morning of the second day, as he was being wheeled to the baths, he was seized with a severe epileptic fit. . . .

"I felt something burst in my chest, and blood flowed freely from my mouth. The doctors in attendance were much alarmed and when I came round—very quickly—they refused to let me go to the baths, saying I would surely collapse. I insisted on being taken, putting the brake on my wheel chair with my usable (left) hand, and refusing to change my mind. The doctors at last gave in, and I was wheeled to the baths and immersed in the water. When taken out of the water my condition was much the same as before, except that some change unknown to me had taken place which marked the end of my epileptic fits. I never had another."

Nothing remarkable occurred between this and his ninth and last immersion. The pain, paralysis, and sleeplessness continued. Once more Traynor tells the story:

We were to leave on the morning of July 27. The afternoon of July 25 came. I seemed to be as bad as ever. A young Frenchman, Felix Douly, came into the ward selling rosaries and medals, and I spent the last few shillings I had on little religious souvenirs for my wife and children. Then it was time to get ready for the baths.

There were many to be bathed and we all wanted to be finished before the afternoon Procession . . . which began at four o'clock. My turn came. When I was in the bath, my paralyzed legs became violently agitated, so much so that I almost emptied the bath. The brancardiers and attendants were terribly alarmed, thinking no doubt that I was in a fit, though I knew it was not so. . . .

I struggled to get to my feet, feeling that I could easily do so, and wondered why everything and everybody seemed to be working against me. [People were holding him down.] When I was taken out of the bath I cried from sheer weakness and exhaustion.

The brancardiers threw my clothes on hurriedly, put me back on the stretcher, and rushed me to the square in front of the Rosary Church to await the Procession. Practically all the other sick were already lined up. I was the third last on the outside, to the right as you face the church.

The Procession came winding its way back, as usual, to the church, and at the end walked the Archbishop of Rheims, carrying the Blessed Sacrament. He blessed the two ahead of me, came to me, made the sign of the cross with the monstrance and moved on to the next. He had just passed by when I realized that a great change had taken place in me. My right arm, which had been dead since 1915, was violently agitated. I burst its bandages and freed the arm.

I had no sudden pain that I can recall and certainly had no vision. I simply realized that something momentous had happened.

I attempted to rise from my stretcher, but the brancardiers were watching me. I suppose I had a bad name for my obstinacy. They held me down and . . . immediately after the final Benediction rushed me back to the Asile. I told them I could walk, and proved it by taking seven steps. I was very tired and in pain. They put me back in bed and gave me a morphia injection.

Drs. Azurdia, Marley and Finn certify that they examined Traynor after his return to the Asile after the Procession. This was to see if he could really walk, as he claimed.

"We find," they certified, "that he has recovered the voluntary use of his legs; the reflexes exist. There is intense venous congestion of both feet, which are very painful. The patient can walk with difficulty."

Traynor was put in a small ward on the ground floor, with brancardiers to watch him and keep him from doing anything foolish. The effect of the morphine began to wear off during the night, but he still had no full realization that he was cured. He was awake most of the night. No lights were on.

"At five-thirty," says Traynor, "I heard the bell of the Basilica begin to ring out the *Ave* . . . I jumped out of bed and knelt on the floor to finish the Rosary I had been saying before I fell into a short sleep. Then, I dashed for the door, pushed aside the two brancardiers, and ran barefoot out of the Asile. I may say here that I had not walked since 1915 and my weight was down to 8 stone [about 112 pounds].

"Dr. Marley was outside the door. When he saw me run out of the ward he fell back in amazement. Out in the open now, I ran towards the Grotto, which is about two or three hundred yards from the Asile. The brancardiers ran after me but they could not catch up with me. When they reached the Grotto, there I was on my knees, still in my night clothes, praying to Our Lady and thanking her.

"After I had prayed for about twenty minutes, I got up— surprised and not pleased to find a crowd of people gathered round, watching me. They drew aside to let me pass as I walked back toward the Asile. By now the hotels of Lourdes were emptying and an excited crowd had gathered in front of the Asile. I could not understand what they were doing there as I went in to dress. I put my clothes on in a hurry, but kept away from the bed for fear those doctors and brancardiers would tackle me again and treat me as a sick man.

"I went to the washroom to wash and shave. Other men were there before me. I bade them all good morning but none of them answered me—they just looked at me in a scared way. I wondered why.

"It was still pretty early in the morning when a priest, Father Gray, who knew nothing about my cure, entered the ward where I was and asked if anybody there could serve Mass. I answered that I would be glad to, and went off and served his Mass in the chapel of the Asile. It did not seem strange to me that I could do this, after being unable to stand or walk for eight years.

"I went in to breakfast in the dining room of the Asile. The other men drew back, as if they were afraid of me. I could not grasp the situation nor could I understand why people were staring at me so hard." Every time he tried to leave the hospital that day the crowds made a rush for him. He tried taking a carriage, but was obliged to abandon it and retreat back into the Asile. Excitement ran high in Lourdes that day. The priest who had urged Traynor not to come to Lourdes broke down and cried—openly and unashamed.

The Pilgrimage left for home on the nine o'clock train next morning, July 27. Early that day the three doctors again examined Traynor. Their statement recorded that he could walk perfectly; that he had recovered the use and function of his right arm; that he had regained sensation in his legs; and finally, that the opening in his skull had diminished considerably.

As far as Traynor knew, the metal plate in his skull just disappeared. When he took off the last of his bandages on returning from the Grotto on the morning of July 26, he found every one of his sores healed.

He left Lourdes amid scenes of tremendous enthusiasm. The train went up through France with Traynor "still in a daze," but traveling in his seat like any normal person. News of his cure had of course been telegraphed back home. At the station in Liverpool there was a stampede. The police were compelled to draw their batons in order to force a passage for Traynor and his wife to a taxi. Finally, "We drove home," he said, "and I cannot describe the joy of my wife and children."

He was not presented that year to the doctors of the Medical Bureau. The following year, he came to the Bureau bearing a certificate from Dr. McConnell of Liverpool who had been his physician for sixteen months, the time that had elapsed since he left Springfields Hospital. The certificate, dated June 24, 1924, states:

"John Traynor, aged forty-one, living at 121 Grafton Street, suffering from gunshot wounds in the head and chest, and from epilepsy, has been under my care since his discharge from the hospital. There have been no epileptic crises since July, 1923. Signed, Dr. McConnell."

On July 7, 1926, Traynor was examined at the Bureau by the President, Dr. Vallet, by the three physicians who were present when he was cured—Drs. Finn, Azurdia, and Marley—and several others, including Dr. Harrington of Preston and Dr. Moorkens of Antwerp. After the examination the doctors signed the following statement:

The right hand is slightly *en griffe* and shows a little wasting of the interossei muscles. The right forearm is less than the left by 1½ cm. in circumference (about one-third of an inch). No atrophy of the pectoral or shoulder muscles now exists. All the movements of the wrist are perfect. The trephine opening has been obliterated; with the finger a slight depression only is found in the bone. There have been no epileptic crises since the cure, in 1923.

The official report issued by the Medical Bureau at Lourdes on October 2, 1926, declared that "this extraordinary cure is beyond and above natural causes."

The most striking part of the cure was probably the instantaneous healing of the right arm. The nerves of that arm had been severed for eight years. Four surgical operations had revealed that they were truly severed, and had failed to reunite them. More than a mere suture would be necessary before the arm could feel and move again; the shrunken nerves would need to go through a long process of regeneration. A feat that expert surgery had four times failed to accomplish, and a process that required months of gradual restoration, were achieved instantaneously during that fateful moment when the Blessed Sacrament was raised over John Traynor at Lourdes.

Traynor arrived in Lourdes a veritable wreck—as Dr. Vallet said, "a pathological museum"; paralyzed in the right arm and in both legs. He went back from Lourdes pushing his own wheel chair, arms and legs normal and with a complete cessation of the epileptic fits and other painful troubles with which he had been afflicted.

"I am in the coal and haulage business now," he states in his conclusion. "I have four lorries [trucks], and about a dozen men working for me. I work with them. I lift sacks of coal weighing around 200 pounds with the best of them and I can do any other work that an able-bodied man can do. I go to Lourdes every year and serve as brancardier there."

14

The Uncured: What of Them?

But what," people ask, "is the actual percentage of cures? Isn't it terribly small—infinitesimal almost—compared with the vast number of sick who come seeking health? What are the vital statistics?"

To answer that question intelligently, we must first take account of the fact that there are several different kinds of Lourdes cures.

1. There is the official Miraculous Cure which is recognized by the Church and a Canonical Commission as well as by the Medical Bureau and the International Medical Commission.

2. There is the cure which is recognized by the Medical Bureau and the Medical Commission as being "inexplicable under scientific and natural laws" but which is not recognized by the Church as a miracle.

3. There are cures—some 1,200 of them—recognized by the Medical Bureau (after repeated examinations at the Bureau) but which have never gone before a Medical or Canonical Commission for lack of sufficient documentation: certificates, clinical reports, X-ray analyses, and so forth.

4. There are large numbers of cures which have for one reason or another received no official recognition but whose beneficiaries are enjoying the bliss of being whole and well after years of agony. These people care not at all whether their cures are recognized as miracles; they come to Lourdes and give thanks every year, just the same.

Every Pilgrimage has in its local records its own substantial number of verified cures never publicly proclaimed. And scores of people who are cured make no official report of their cure to the Bureau, simply because they dislike publicity.

As indicated under class 3, a large number of actual cures go without official recognition because of insufficient data. Sometimes the evidence from relatives or home physicians is too indefinite and unsatisfactory to declare a cure; sometimes doctors have not kept sufficiently precise records. Other doctors refuse pointblank to furnish X-rays, diagnoses, or biological reports showing the condition of the patient before the journey to Lourdes and the change which occurred there. "If it's Lourdes, we're not interested," they say.

Under these circumstances it is extremely difficult to obtain accurate data and statistics regarding cures. The President of the Medical Bureau told me, in August, 1953: "We have at the Bureau some 1,200 records and files of 'inexplicable' cures for which we have systematic and orderly accounts—many of them with accompanying X-ray and clinical reports, and all with doctors' diagnoses and certificates. We have notations and material concerning some 4,000 cases that are very probably complete and genuine cures. We have insufficient data to record them as cures but the individuals and their families are unquestionably enjoying the blessings and benefits of a genuine cure."

It is probably safe to say that during the hundred years of the Lourdes shrine, at least ten thousand people have been cured there. This may seem a small proportion, in view of the millions who come; but ten such cures—or even one, as Dr. Smiley Blanton said—would have been dumfounding.

The proportion of women in relation to men is easier to gauge, and runs about three to one. But as three times more women then men come to Lourdes, the proportion of cures runs about parallel. One of the interesting facts is the relatively large number of children who are cured; some at Lourdes itself, others at home or in some local sanctuary where a Novena has been held or the name of Notre Dame de Lourdes invoked.

One of the baffling things about Lourdes cures is their extreme variability and unpredictability. Some people are cured at the baths, others at the Procession; some with intense pain, others with no pain at all—only a sense of sudden ineffable well-being.

Some cures happen at once—in the first bath; some not till the eighth or ninth; some when the patient, having given up hope, is about to leave; others after the patient has returned home and renounced the whole experience. Cures have occurred when the patient did not even come to Lourdes but was lotioned at home with Lourdes water. Sometimes a person is not cured at his first pilgrimage but achieves his cure suddenly at the second—or even the third. Persistence often seems to be an important factor.

Strangely enough, religious faith or deservingness on the part of the patient seems to have little to do with it. Tiny children, who believe and know nothing, may be cured, while saintlike persons are left to endure their agonies to the end.

Devotion to the Catholic faith or to the Blessed Virgin apparently is not an essential factor. Some of the most extraordinary cures have happened to people of no religious faith whatever—such as Gargam, Auclair, and Madeleine Guinot. Mlle. Guinot, an advanced tubercular case, was an unbeliever both by education and personal conviction, who came to Lourdes with a sort of bored acquiescence (and her tongue in her cheek), to satisfy her friends. After her cure she became an earnest, practicing Christian.

And there is also the case of Germaine Birsten, a Protestant, in the last stages of Pott's Disease, who was cured at the Procession. A New England Congregational minister's wife, another tuberculosis victim, had the same good fortune; and numbers of others.

Catholics believe that Our Lady of Lourdes performs some of

these cures to bring nonbelievers into the Faith. "She knows She *has* me!" said a young priest who, notwithstanding several pilgrimages, had not received his cure.

The Cures are almost invariably simple people—the poor and the humble; people who do not interpose a strong intellect between themselves and the Higher Power. "The Blessed Virgin does not interest herself much in the rich," they say at Lourdes.

But why this apparent favoritism on the part of a compassionate Mother or Divine Creator? Why is George chosen and not Marcel? Why sinful coal heaver but not saintly nun who returns unrelieved of her hellish pain? This is the inscrutable mystery.

A determining factor, in certain cases, may be some inner psychological or moral conflict. Modern psychiatry points to mental and emotional blocks in some people which retard their cure even under ordinary psychotherapy. Some, for example, have firmly accepted the belief that they are incurable; others that their sufferings have come as a just punishment for sin. Conscious moral guilt, too, can stand in the way of a perfect healing.

Modern clergymen and psychiatrists stress the significance of a guilt fixation and urge the patient to get rid of it by frank and full confession and changed habits. How powerfully it works may be seen in case after case among the health seekers and sufferers who come to Lourdes. "I'm too wicked . . . I don't deserve it . . . I've sinned too much and too long . . . no, it can never be for *me!*"

Conversely, the attitude of expectancy and childlike readiness to accept and to believe appears to open the way, following the injunction laid down long ago: *"Except ye become as little children . . ."* Those who do often enter into the kingdom of health and healing too.

"But it doesn't always happen!" No, and cures by drugs and

physical means do not always happen either. We are dealing with that incredibly intricate and mysterious thing, the human organism with its long and complicated evolution—physical, mental, emotional, spiritual; its strains and reactions; interwoven attractions and repulsions, aversions and rejections; of eons to be probed before we can reach even a rudimentary understanding of this great mystery. Meanwhile we can give thanks for the wonderful things that come to pass occasionally now in the midst of our ignorance.

Even when no physical cure takes place, it has been noted time and again that the most important thing that happens at Lourdes is the cure of souls. Those who have to go back, and live on with their physical miseries, seem to get such a spiritual transformation and inspiration that they can go on cheerfully and gratefully.

People come to Lourdes weary and worn out with pain, hardly able to make the journey because of the suffering it involves, bitterly resenting their sickness and wondering why God has thus afflicted them—a burden to themselves and to those who bring them here. And then they arrive at Lourdes Station and are so warmly welcomed, so gently transported and looked after. They arrive at the Hostel and are surrounded with all that lavish care, and love, and devotion—the humblest of them, the despairing and the lost. They arrive at the Shrine, and there at the Grotto in company with hundreds of other sick—many worse off than they—the transforming touch begins to work. They stop thinking about themselves. They begin to think about their neighbor—the one in the next bed or in the next little carriage. They begin to pray for him, earnestly, repeatedly, when the "big" prayers of the day are said. They begin to long, above everything else, for his cure.

In sum, *they forget themselves.* They become absorbed in love of God and love for fellow man: the two great solvents for all human ills, as Jesus taught. And so their real healing takes place—imperceptibly almost, but none the less actually and dynamically.

Time after time I have been told at Lourdes—by Dr. Leuret, by nurses, brancardiers, even the man who sweeps the paths: "The sick? Oh, madame, they've forgotten about their own cure. They've forgotten why they came here. All they care about is that that man in the next row shall get well . . . 'Don't bother about me—that fellow over there needs you more . . .' 'Never mind, nurse, I can wait.' 'Look after this poor lady in the next carriage—she really needs attention.' "

Naturally the pain comes back again, but not so terribly. It hasn't the same bitter hold on them. Their minds are not centered on it any longer. The mind is elsewhere—absorbed in something new. They have all these other people to think about —the friends they've made, the nurses, the Sisters, and all those who have served them and cared for them so devotedly; the sufferers everywhere in the world who need their prayers.

And when the time comes to go home, though they haven't been physically cured, though it means another long difficult journey with all sorts of sacrifices and miseries, their one cry is: "If only I can come back next year! If only I can come again to Lourdes!"

It would be absurd to suggest that there are *no* disillusioned or disappointed ones. Unquestionably certain people do leave bitterly disappointed and resentful, still longing passionately for the cure they did not obtain. But—and I believe all Lourdes workers will bear me out—these are a handful compared with the vast majority who go away happy and (despite failure to obtain a physical cure) profoundly grateful for the spiritual and psychological lift which is their lasting reward.

"Of the uncured none despair," says an old pilgrim. "All go away filled with hope and a new feeling of strength. The trip to Lourdes is never made in vain."

This was borne out by a man who worked at the desk of the Hospitality. His own crutches stood against the wall behind him. His strong, tanned face was that of a healthy and happy person. Seeing him there interviewing the sick day after day, an American visitor asked him, "What about this great question of the uncured? Doesn't it spell unmitigated tragedy?"

"No," he answered, "I don't think so. In fact I *know* it doesn't. I often interview patients before they leave. I have never seen a case downcast—not even the worst. The words you usually hear are, 'God's will be done.'"

He gave several examples. As they talked the visitor again noticed the crutches leaning against the wall. What was this man's own story? What was he doing here, serving without pay during the hottest part of the summer—cooped up in this tiny office, besieged by an unending line of people? He ventured to ask the man about himself. Later he got the whole history.*

His name was Lemarchand. He was a native of Brest. He had been crippled from birth, and longed to go to Lourdes where he hoped he might be cured. But he and his sister were alone in the world; they could not afford to make the trip. Finally, a special opportunity came and they were able to join a pilgrimage.

"On our arrival we went directly to the Grotto. My first impression was very deep, and made up both of hope and sadness —sadness at the sight of the sufferers we passed, hope for my cure. . . . Two days later it was time to leave. The farewell was heart-rending. Not that I was disappointed, but it seemed as if I was leaving my home and best friends."

How often one hears that. People have an extraordinary feeling about this place. Always they speak of it as "home," and of their sadness at leaving, even at the end of a few days.

"I could not have believed that I could become so attached to a place in three summer days," said an English visitor. "There was everything hostile to my peace—crowds, heat, dust,

* This story was first published in an article by J. B. McAllister in *Commonweal* magazine. Reprinted by kind permission of the editors.

weariness; yet I felt such a home for the soul as I had never before experienced."

Lemarchand felt it too, along with so many others. He promised to come back the following year—and did, for eight days.

"I still prayed for my cure," he said, "but on the second day, while I was sitting among the sick during Benediction, I began to feel ashamed of myself. On my right, a blind man sat rigid in his chair; on my left lay a consumptive. I looked around at all the sufferers and then up to the green mountains and higher to the sky. I could see; and I could move about; I had the free use of my ears and tongue and arms. I had not known sickness or disease—and I was praying for my cure! I started praying for the blind man and the consumptive. Since that moment I have felt that I should think of others and not of myself."

The following year he and his sister came to Lourdes again. The year after that, his sister, a nurse, worked in the baths. He felt useless. Then he decided to offer himself for clerical work. His knowledge of English proved valuable, and his services were readily accepted.

"I felt like a new man. I, even I, was doing something to help the sick!" He returned each summer and worked during his vacation.

"Perhaps it sounds foolish," said Lemarchand, "to speak of the happiness I have found at Lourdes, I who went there to be cured and am still a cripple. But I have found contentment, and my soul has been cured. And, for more persons than anyone knows, Lourdes has done the same thing."

A famous American pilgrim was Fred Snite—"the man in the iron lung." Snite had contracted infantile paralysis in 1935 and was obliged to lie flat in his respirator or "iron lung" from that time on. He was unable to breathe if out of it for more than a few minutes at a time.

Naturally his going to Lourdes created tremendous interest.

Newspapermen and photographers followed him, every step of the trip.

What a moment this would have been for a miracle! But that is not the way things happen at Lourdes. Cures are usually given to the obscure, quietly—in secrecy, almost. "The Blessed Virgin is not seeking the newsreels!" say the Lourdais. "She operates without fanfare or publicity."

This millionaire patient came with a humble heart and a submissive spirit. One would have thought maybe She might have made an exception. . . . He was not asking for a miracle —only that the best might be done.

Snite's doctors begged him not to bathe in the piscines. To leave the iron lung and go into the cold water was suicide, they said. But Snite insisted. In his diary that day, he wrote:

Early this afternoon I had another new experience—a bath in the famous Lourdes waters. . . . In that I had to leave the respirator during the bath, I was quite nervous and excited. Everything went smoothly however, and I was so glad I had decided to do it. The water was very cold, but I did not mind it. There was some kind of happiness in connection with it which I am unable to analyze. . . . All I can say is that I was glad for the opportunity.

He told friends that, as he bathed, a wonderful feeling of peace came over him, a feeling he had never before experienced. Later he had a second bath, and again everything went smoothly. The water hardly seemed cold.

After attending the procession of the Blessed Sacrament he wrote: "Seeing some of the other sick people makes me feel very fortunate."

Snite wrote in his diary: "And so tomorrow is Saturday, the ninth of our stay and Sunday the last day. I have not in any way given up or lost hope. I am praying very, very fervently, and if nothing happens, as I have often said before, God certainly knows what is best for Him, for me, and for the world in general."

The entry for June 4 closes with two short sentences: "Our pilgrimage is at an end. God's will be done."

Snite returned to America, still in his iron lung. Everyone thought he would be terribly depressed and disappointed. Had the journey then been entirely futile?

The answer from Snite or from any of his close friends would be an emphatic "No." He referred to Lourdes afterward with deep appreciation and affection—he named one of his daughters Bernadette. Everyone marveled that he could be so cheerful. This final extract from his Lourdes diary may explain his feeling:

"Life here at Lourdes is so wonderful—such a series of unending thrills, that I find it difficult to record my reactions. Everyone is happy. . . . Here there is no talk of war, of politics, of bodies; here life is a prayer. It's no wonder we are happy.

"We are in a place apart from the world—a place halfway to heaven!" * †

* This account of Mr. Snite's pilgrimage was taken from the book *After Bernadette* by Don Sharkey, with kind permission of The Bruce Publishing Co.

† Fred Snite died in his sleep in November, 1954, sixteen years after his Lourdes pilgrimage.

15

Cures away from Lourdes

It's hard enough for the medical man to admit the fact of miraculous cures at Lourdes. But when he is confronted with cures that have taken place hundreds or thousands of miles away, just by calling upon the name of Notre Dame de Lourdes, or by using Lourdes water—that, he says, is really *too* much to ask us to believe!

And yet it happens—not once or twice, but many times. And the Medical Bureau states that "it is also equipped for the study of healings which have taken place in other parts of the world (i.e., outside of the Domaine itself), provided the name of Lourdes has been invoked."

Such cures have occurred in many different corners of the earth—in America, Oceania, Canada, Ceylon. They have occurred after Novenas * to Notre Dame de Lourdes; at Lourdes shrines or replicas of the Grotto; in Lourdes chapels; or at home after the application of Lourdes water. Accounts of such cures fill a substantial portion of the Bureau records, and fascinated me from the beginning.

One of the most spectacular of these cures in the early days was that of Pierre de Rudder, whose case caused a storm of discussion and argument all over Europe. Here was a case that could not by the wildest flight of imagination be attributed to autosuggestion or hysteria, for it had to do, not with nerves

---

* A Novena, as all Catholics know, is a nine-day period of prayers and devotions, directed toward some special end.

or emotions or even altered tissues, but with broken bones that were instantaneously joined together—the leg bones of an adult man.

De Rudder was a Belgian peasant who lived in Jabbeke, near Bruges. His leg had been broken by a falling tree. The break was so bad that, after the fragments of bone were removed, the two bones that remained intact could be seen in the wound over an inch apart. The lower part of the limb, no longer attached to the top, "swung in all directions like a rag."

Eight years later, the shattered bones still refused to knit, and an abscess had formed round them, causing a horrible running sore. Surgeons, one after another, pronounced the case incurable, and Professor Thiart of Brussels, consulted as a last resort, advised amputation of the leg. De Rudder refused. For more than eight years he suffered fearful torture, having to dress the wound several times a day, and dragging himself along on crutches.

Finally he decided to make a pilgrimage to the statue of Notre Dame de Lourdes that had been erected at Oostacker, a town near Ghent. Three men lifted him into the train. Arriving at Ghent, he got into the Oostacker omnibus, and his leg, though well wrapped, discharged so much blood and pus that the driver loudly complained about the damage to the seat of his vehicle.

At the Oostacker Grotto, Pierre prayed long and earnestly. First he asked forgiveness for all his sins. Then he begged Notre Dame de Lourdes the grace of being able to work and take care of his children, and no longer to live on charity.

As he prayed, all of a sudden he felt a profound movement through his whole body. Hardly realizing what he was doing, he started to walk—without crutches—all around the Grotto. He did this three times. After that he walked to the carriage which was to take him to the station. On arriving at home, he got off the train in normal fashion.

When he examined his leg, he found that the wound had

closed. In a few brief minutes at the Grotto the bones had become solidly knit together. His legs were as firm and sound as anybody's. There was no gap left, and his bones had united. He did not even limp, for both his legs were the same length.

The news spread swiftly. Soon the whole of Belgium was in an uproar over this astounding cure. Pierre's doctor, an agnostic, at first refused to believe it—but went to see for himself. He found his patient hard at work digging in the garden. The physician, Dr. Van Hoestenberghe, later wrote to the head of the Medical Bureau:

Pierre is undoubtedly cured. I have seen him many times during the last eight years, and my medical knowledge tells me that such a cure is absolutely inexplicable. Again, he has been cured completely, suddenly, and instantaneously, without any period of convalescence. Not only have the bones been suddenly united, but a portion of bone would seem to have been actually created to take the place of those fragments I myself have seen come out of the wound. But if a miracle, then there is something beyond natural law—a God exists, and surely He must have given some revelation of Himself.

The doctor returned to the faith of his childhood. And so did scores of others in that part of Belgium. The cure had a tremendous effect in the religious life and practice of the entire district. It caused a sensation throughout Europe.

Twenty-eight doctors undertook a study of the case. They made minute inquiries, superintended by both Catholics and unbelievers. They questioned the physicians who had attended de Rudder, the neighbors in Jabbeke who had witnessed the state of the wound on the day of his departure, and the people who had been present at the Grotto. They put de Rudder himself through the strictest possible examination. In the end, they were forced to admit the authenticity of the unprecedented fact: the instantaneous growth of a piece of bone over an inch long, filling up the gap where it was wanting, the whole process following upon a simple prayer. On the leg where it had been broken there remained merely a bluish spot.

Twenty years went by without any weakening of the leg. De Rudder died of pneumonia at the age of seventy-five. An autopsy revealed nothing new regarding the case, except that "the leg was restored as the most skillful of surgeons might have done it, had an operation been possible. And it was done by getting rid of a suppurating wound immediately, and by the instantaneous creation of a bone."

De Rudder's leg bones are preserved at the University of Louvain, but copper models of them were given to Lourdes and may be seen there at the Medical Bureau office.

Dr. Leuret, writing of this case in 1951, says:

There was an instant formation of bony callus, filling the void between the bony extremities. Whence came the bony substance, and notably the calcium salts necessary for the solidity which was immediate? Dr. Le Bec has shown very definitely that, in view of all the conditions, at least fifty days would have been necessary for the formation in question by normal processes. But in the cure performed at the Shrine of Notre Dame de Lourdes, it took barely sixty seconds.

❦ *Lourdes shrines have been* the scene of cures not only in Europe, and not only to members of the Catholic faith. Some of the most interesting accounts come from the countries of the East.

In 1880, the Georgian Fathers, banished from France, established a convent at Constantinople. There they dedicated an altar to Notre Dame de Lourdes, adorned with a statue like the one at the Lourdes Grotto; and they kept on hand a supply of water sent them from the Spring.

At once miracles began to happen—so many that Cardinal Vanutelli, Apostolic delegate of the Holy See in Turkey, appointed a Commission to examine them. Palsy, epilepsy, and cancer were reported to have vanished instantaneously. A Jew of Orta, and a child who was born clubfooted, as well as many blind people, were suddenly healed. A woman of Pera got rid of a piece of needle for many months lost in her finger, four

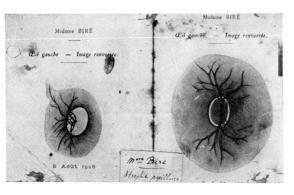

Group of doctors at the Bureau; President Leuret is in first row, center (*Photo Lacaze*)

Photographs of drawings by Dr. Lainey of Madame Biré's eye

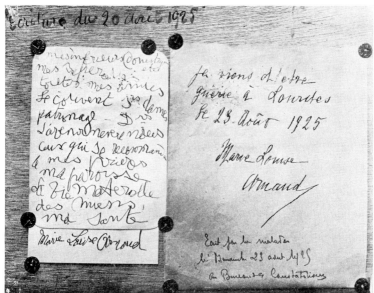

Mademoiselle Arnaud's handwriting—three days before her cure and a few hours after

Left: John Traynor: cured of gunshot wounds, paralysis, and epilepsy

Center: Madame Pillot: brain tumor

Right: Lucien Belhache: Pott's Disease

Far left: Jeanne Fretel: cured of tuberculous peritonitis. Center left: Colonel Pellegrin: abscess of the liver. Left and above: Mademoiselle Clauzel: rheumatic spondylitis—shown before and after her cure

Francis Pascal: cured of blindness, paralysis of arms and legs—shown before and after his cure

Yves Joucan: Pott's Disease—shown before and after his cure

Henri Mieuzet: chronic enteritis

Guy Leydet: idiocy, quadriplegic paralysis—after cure (*Photo Grange*)

years before a like event in the case of Celestine Dubois, at Lourdes. Greeks, Armenians, Moslems, and Jews were cured as well as Catholics. Among the crowds about the convent could be seen people of all types—soldiers, pashas, women of every class, dervishes, eunuchs, and Turkish officers.

"And why not?" says a Catholic writer. "Are not all men Her children, and did not Christ come to redeem them all?"

Catholics say it is no wonder that Mary's mercies should be granted to these Eastern peoples, for the Oriental liturgies— Armenian, Maronite, Coptic, and Syrian—glow with praise of Mary. It must have been strange to see these processions, made up of all sorts of people and creeds invoking her whom the Moslems call Meriem-Ana, or Bikir Meriem, praying for and being granted these amazing cures.

After the invocation in the chapel at the Virgin's altar, (says one of the records) the pilgrims would go into the sacristy. There they were sprinkled with holy water and had the Gospel read to them. They were then blessed, by placing the Holy Gospels on their heads and kissing the cross engraved in the flat part of the book. Afterwards cures were wrought by the drinking of Lourdes water.

Sometimes the Moslem women would unfold handkerchiefs or shirts meant to be worn, in accordance with Turkish custom, by those for whose recovery they were praying. Before beginning their invocations they placed them on the first steps of the altar, and came to fetch them away afterward. They burned from four to five thousand candles in the chapel, and distributed quantities of water and medals gratuitously. From Mesopotamia and Turkestan came requests for it, and—stranger still—from Mecca and Medina, the two holy cities of Islam.

Many years have gone by since that record was written. The little convent of the Georgian Fathers has grown into a huge abbey, but the church and the altar to Notre Dame de Lourdes remain as they were then. Thousands of thanksgiving tablets cover the walls. People of all creeds continue to pour in, declaring that "Our Lady of Lourdes still dispenses her favors." *

* This account is taken from J. K. Huysmans' *The Crowds of Lourdes*, with kind permission of the publishers Burns, Oates & Washburne, Ltd.

✑ *Here and now*, in our own time, remarkable cures have occurred in cities far away from the Domaine, during special prayers or a Novena made to Our Lady of Lourdes.

One of the most interesting personalities seen at Lourdes every year is Madame Pillot, who lives in the big industrial city of Nancy in northeastern France. To see her today, in her nurse's garb moving vigorously among the sick, one would never guess that she herself was once a desperately sick patient.

At the age of forty-two, Madame Pillot had a tumor of the brain, certified by three physicians—Drs. Malaterre, Lamy, and Guillemin. Both clinical and X-ray reports supported the diagnosis.

The illness began in 1930 and by 1932 had reached an acute stage. Dr. Guillemin writes:

In the winter of 1932–33, the patient had appalling headaches, delirium, periods of aberration, with fixed ideas. She ran up and down the street during the day, and also at night, in nothing but her slip. Often her husband had to search the streets for her. She would wander off, talking to herself deliriously. At other times she would pile onto the bed anything that happened to be at hand— chairs, chests, different objects. Sometimes she had a fixed idea concerning water and wished to throw herself into the canal. Her husband was obliged to restrain her during such moods. I myself have been present on some of these occasions. Morphine alone would calm her.

These crises would be repeated sometimes twice in one night. The shutters had to be locked in her house, for she had tried several times to throw herself out of the window. She could not be left alone for a single minute.

Between these crises, there were flashes of lucidity even more painful for the patient, accompanied as they were by terrible headaches and the realization of the doom that was upon her.

Despite all sorts of treatment and efforts to help her, the condition became steadily worse, and it appeared, as her physician said, "that the approaching end would inevitably take place in an asylum."

But Madame Pillot was cured—after all human efforts had failed, and all the skill of the physicians had proved futile. The Sisters and nurses in the sanatorium where she had been taken began a Novena for her to Notre Dame de Lourdes, praying earnestly for an end to her sufferings. She was cured on the first day of the Novena. Suddenly all pain ceased and, Dr. Guillemin records, "It is a fact that from that day Madame Pillot suffers no more." He adds:

"Her condition has improved remarkably. She has taken up her usual tasks again, and I have seen her do a day's work that few people in sturdy health could accomplish.

She was examined at the Medical Bureau in August, 1933, and again in 1934. In the meantime the Bureau kept in touch with her and received several reports from her home physician who testified to her excellent health. No more headaches, no more crises, or troubles of any sort; good appetite; and never a drug or sedative of any kind, from the moment of her cure. Prior to that, for a long time she had been having massive doses of morphine. "In short," says the Bureau report, "a negative examination, all along the line."

Madame Pillot comes to Lourdes every year as a nurse with the Nancy pilgrimage, always asking for the hardest cases. Last year again she was there, a most attractive woman, in splendid health and spirits. She did magnificent Resistance work during World War II, and was awarded the Military Medal.

◀§ *Other extraordinary cures* have occurred through Novenas and invoking the name of Our Lady of Lourdes. Catherine Lapeyre was cured of cancer of the tongue in her own little attic in Toulouse on the last day of a Novena made for her by the Sisters of the Redemption. She had shown no improvement after a visit to Lourdes the previous year. She longed to make a second pilgrimage but hadn't the money for the journey.

"There is no reason why you cannot have your cure right here at home," said the Sisters. And this is exactly what happened.

An English boy, Joseph Duncan-Bothman, was cured of a suppurating ear and complete deafness at his home in Dover, after a Novena to Our Lady of Lourdes. The boy's father, a member of the Senate of Cambridge University and a former Anglican rector, gave an account of the cure to the doctors of the Medical Bureau.

"For ten years my son suffered from otorrhea (a discharge from the outer ear passage), involving almost complete destruction of the middle ear cavity of the left ear, and total deafness. He was treated by many well-known specialists in England and abroad. Finally a celebrated Harley Street physician declared that the inflammation might reach the brain at any moment and cause death. An immediate operation was necessary to save the boy's life. Even if the operation should be successful, the doctor said, permanent deafness was certain."

The father, a Catholic convert especially devoted to Our Lady of Lourdes, wished "to take the case to a Higher Power." He obtained the promise of prayers from several religious Communities, to coincide with Novenas he and his son made each night and morning. He applied Lourdes water—"a supply of which I kept always on hand; and we performed daily devotions at a miniature Grotto which I had erected in my garden. We made a vow that if our prayer were heard we would make a pilgrimage to Lourdes and offer our services to the Hospitality there. I had the firmest conviction that Our Lady of Lourdes would grant our prayer."

The Novena ended. On the following Sunday the boy served Mass at the convent of the Augustinians, near Dover. At the Elevation of the Host he felt an acute pain in his left ear, almost unbearable. After Mass he told his father that he could hear as he had not been able to do for years. The running sore had dried up completely.

Next day he was examined by Dr. Murphy of Dover, who certified that his hearing was normal and that the ear condition was perfect in every respect. Shortly after, the boy, with his father and mother, set out on their pilgrimage of thanksgiving to Lourdes.

Dr. Murphy had cautioned them. "Yes, this cure is wonderful. I congratulate you. But don't set your hopes too high. There might be a relapse."

The relapse never came.

⊷§ *Psychotherapists say that* a cure can be blocked through the conscious or unconscious opposition of a relative. Often with Lourdes cures the persistent faith of a devoted relative can be the effective means of bringing a cure to pass.

As, for example, in the case of Madame Gardelle. One of the greatest Lourdes cures ever known came to this little brown nut of a farmer woman, tucked away in a tiny country town in the middle of France: Crevant, near the city of Clermont-Ferrand. People who have lived in France know these sturdy peasant women—valiant, hard-working, good as men at their jobs—not unlike our New England pioneer type.

One day Madame Gardelle woke up with a very bad toothache. She had to go to town and have the tooth pulled. So much time stolen from the land—that was bad. But worse was to come. Following the extraction, the abscessed socket of the tooth refused to heal. Instead, the inflammation spread, and a nasty growth appeared on the inside of the mouth. It grew with frightening rapidity. Soon the whole left cheek was infected, and the left eye was threatened.

Dr. Dionis of Clermont-Ferrand operated. A brief improvement followed, but soon the growth began to spread again, involving the eye to a degree where it seemed she might lose it entirely.

She was sent to a clinic, where Dr. Gildard recorded her affliction as "a swollen tumor completely closing the nasal cavity, bathed in a purulent and bloody liquid." A piece of the diseased tissue was sent for examination to the laboratory of

Dr. Laroche, who reported: "We have to deal with a malignant tumor beyond the help of surgery."

The patient was then sent to Dr. Dechambre for radiotherapy. Several treatments were given but the condition was in no way improved.

She returned home in a very bad state. Her pain increased daily, she was obliged to take to her bed. (Tragedy for a woman given to the land!) Morphine seemed the only thing that could help her, and the injections became more and more frequent. Her general condition grew quickly worse, strength failed rapidly, and beginning at the left nostril a red mass of tissue extended all over the left side of the face, forcing the eye out of its socket.

The disease was pronounced cancerous; declared incurable, and all treatments useless.

But Madame Gardelle had a niece who possessed an immense faith in Notre Dame de Lourdes. She persuaded the family to make a Novena to obtain the cure of their invalid. The first Novena was in vain; so was the second. But the niece redoubled her prayers, persisted in using compresses of water from the Grotto, and in spite of her aunt's desperate condition, never gave up hope.

The pain had become so great that it was necessary to give the patient eight morphine injections in twenty-four hours. Delirium was constant, and it was feared the end might come at any moment, especially during the days of March 13–16. During those days Madame Gardelle took no nourishment at all—just a few drops of Lourdes water.

Another Novena was begun, the parish priest and all the neighborhood joining in the urgent and earnest prayers. (As they say in Lourdes, "an assault on Heaven.") Unlike the preceding nights, the night of March 17 was calm and the patient slept—a deep sleep. When she awoke on the morning of the eighteenth, the pain had ceased, also the delirium. Madame Gardelle asked for something to eat. They brought her some soup, which she ate with relish.

Suddenly the niece who was straightening the bed noticed something that made her cry out. "Madeleine, Marie, look! Her face—the tumor—*her face!*"

Everybody came hurrying to the bedside stammering, incoherent at what they saw. *The tumor had almost entirely disappeared.* The eye had gone back into its socket and the nostril was free.

The patient's appetite became rapidly keener, her strength returned, her general condition was transformed. A few days later she took up her work again.

All this is set down methodically, paper by paper, in the record of the case at the Medical Bureau. For cancer of the face is a disease whose cure requires indisputable proof.*

Dr. Haddou, the family physician who had followed the case from the beginning, certified that "Madame Celestine Gardelle, 54 years old, suffering from facial sarcoma, is today completely cured. The diagnosis made in November, a year ago, after laboratory examination of a piece of the tumor." Dr. Dionis (surgeon) also records that "the cure is complete." Dr. Gildard notes that "the growth in the molar region has disappeared, the skin has regained its normal aspect." Dr. Dechambre writes, six months after the cure: "Madame Gardelle presented herself to me today in a state of apparent perfect health."

In August, Madame Gardelle was examined at the Medical Bureau, where the record concludes:

The examination permits us to record that the general condition of Madame Gardelle is perfectly normal and her visual apparatus intact. Her face shows, on the left side in the region of the sinus, a scar of 2 to 3 centimeters (about 1 inch) following surgical operation, and a slight depression due to the absence of the molars and

---

* The instantaneous or even very rapid cure of cancer by means of natural causes is impossible. For, as the doctors of the Medical Bureau point out, in this disease not merely the original cancerous organ is involved. The cancerous cells rapidly invade surrounding tissues, the disease gets into the blood and the lymphatic system, and swiftly penetrate the whole organism. It is thus *the entire body*, not merely the initial organ, which in a miraculous cure is instantly healed—an accomplishment medically and biologically impossible.

premolars. . . . Five doctors have observed the development of a malignant tumor proceeding beyond the help of surgery, and regarding the nature of which there can be no doubt. All declare that the cure is complete. All recognize that this cure, practically instantaneous, is scientifically inexplicable. We can thus attribute it only to a cause beyond the forces of nature.

16

"I Don't Believe It!"

The last resort of the skeptics, both lay and medical, is a flat, "I don't believe it! It's too fantastic. It couldn't happen. It just isn't so."

When I was a young reporter in Asia, people in remote Indian and Chinese villages did not believe in the New York skyline either. They would shake their heads and smile, and say, "But of course such a place does not exist. It is only a picture!"

Nothing I could say would change their conviction. They had never seen such a place. *It was something outside their experience.* Therefore it could not be true.

Thousands of people are like that about Lourdes. They have never seen it. They have never known these things—in their own town or their own experience. So they boldly announce: "Such things do not exist. I don't believe it. You are crazy— it cannot be!"

"In the medical world," says one physician who comes to Lourdes, "people go about denying what they themselves have not had opportunity to see. But things cannot be denied until they have been examined. That is the role of science. For long years doctors refused to study these cures seriously, though to say that something is not true without first having examined the facts, is to commit a grave scientific error."

"Before you enter into a discussion about Lourdes with any-body," says Dr. Smiley Blanton, "it will save lots of time and much useless argument if you find out, first, if the person you are talking to was ever there. More important, did he actually spend some time there? Breezing through Lourdes on a typical tourist schedule is often more misleading than no visit at all. Most critics of Lourdes are people who have never been inside the place. They sit snugly in their offices at home and write learned dissertations about a center they have never seen, and matters of which they know—from direct experience—absolutely nothing."

One thing you quickly notice: the difference in attitude of the rationalist physician *before* he has seen a cure, and *after*. Doctors who have actually seen a cure usually have nothing to say. They are no longer ready with glib explanations. They are completely bowled over.

Their vocabulary changes, too. Before they've seen a cure, they avoid the word miracle. Afterward, they use it freely—almost involuntarily. A miracle has happened within themselves, also. Their scientific cocksureness has been severely shaken.

Much depends on whether "*I* was there," before they will accept the proceedings as "scientific." If some other doctor reports an extraordinary cure, this is apt to be labeled "charlatanism." But if "I saw it with my own eyes," that's a different matter. Then, it's "scientifically accurate."

Here, as everywhere else, the human factor has to be taken into account. A scientist is a human being. However coolly impersonal he may consider himself, however calmly detached and impartial, he is influenced by personal considerations, prejudices—of background, of national and cultural bias— which manifest themselves in his appraisals, both in his professional and personal conversation.

This is very evident in the story of one self-styled "rationalist" doctor in whom a change of view took place after he actually saw a cure, and saw it occur "right there before his eyes." *

Doctor Carrel came to Lourdes in charge of certain patients

* This story, taken from the book *Voyage to Lourdes* by Alexis Carrel, is reprinted by kind permission of Harper & Brothers.

with the National Pilgrimage. He described himself as "a tolerant skeptic, a positivist—*interested* in Lourdes cures but not *credulous* regarding them." His religious ideas had long since been destroyed, in the course of his scientific studies.

On his first day at Lourdes he was discussing miracles with Dr. B. who was a strong believer as well as a scientist of note. Dr. C. goodnaturedly chaffed Dr. B. about his views, and especially about a supposed "cure" that had occurred that morning.

"Straight autosuggestion, my dear fellow. That good nun had been getting well gradually, right there in her own convent —but she *believed* that her arm would be cured at Lourdes, and so it was."

"What about the cases of Joachime Dehant and Pierre de Rudder?"

"Pious propaganda. Extremely interesting, but not valid. De Rudder's case is obviously incredible. If his story were really authentic, it would be an archetypical miracle—like the signature of God himself. But it is a duty to meet 'facts' of that kind with complete skepticism."

"Yet twenty-eight doctors in good standing examined de Rudder over a period of several years, and testified to the veracity of the testimony and the facts of his cure. Can you throw out their findings so lightly? And who is to decide which doctor's work is 'scientific' and which not?"

"Well," said the other more mildly, "I am the last to discredit any reputable colleague. Certainly there is an incredible power of suggestion in these pilgrimages, and at some sacred shrines, no doubt; but not for organic diseases. If de Rudder's cure were authentic, if it was methodically observed by scientists, I do not see how it could be explained except in terms of the supernatural. But such things must be seen to be believed."

"What kind of a disease would you have to see cured, to convince you that miracles exist?"

"An organic disease: a cancer disappearing, a bone regrown,

a congenital dislocation vanishing. If ever I should see such a phenomenon I would willingly throw overboard all the theories and hypotheses in the world. But this is not likely, among the patients I have to do with here."

He spoke of one patient, Marie Bailly, in whom he had become especially interested—a girl in the last stages of tuberculous peritonitis.

"I know her history," he said. "Her whole family died of tuberculosis. She has had tubercular sores, lesions of the lungs, and now, for the past few months, peritonitis diagnosed by both a general practitioner and the well-known Bordeaux surgeon, Bromilloux. Her condition is very grave. She may die right under my nose. If such a case were cured, it would indeed be a miracle. I would never doubt again."

When she actually *was* cured, and he fully realized it, he was completely overwhelmed.

He had examined the girl just an hour before as she lay on her bed in the Sept Douleurs Hospital: noted her white, emaciated face, her racing pulse—150 to the minute, the distended abdomen, her ears and nails already turning blue.

"She may last a few more days, but she is doomed," he told the Sisters. "Her heart is giving out. Death is very near."

A few minutes later, in front of the Grotto, where they had carried her in spite of his protests, he saw an extraordinary change take place: first in her face, which gradually seemed to be losing its ashen hue; then, more amazing still, in her swollen abdomen—which flattened out under the blanket, before his very eyes. Her pulse now was calm and regular. She drank a glass of milk. Her respiration had become completely normal.

The doctor walked back to his hotel, his mind in a tumult. A dying girl was recovering. It was, literally, the resurrection of the dead. *It was a miracle!*

At the hospital that evening he examined her again, along with three other doctors. They confirmed what he already knew: *She was cured.* In the span of a few hours, a girl with a face already turning blue, a distended abdomen, and a fatally racing heart, had been restored to health.

The sweat broke out on his forehead. He felt as though someone had struck him on the head. His own heart began to pump furiously. It was the most momentous thing he had ever seen. It was both frightening and wonderful to see life come pouring back into an organism almost totally destroyed by years of illness. Here was an indisputable fact—yet a fact impossible to reconcile with science: a girl dying with an advanced organic disease, had recovered—was sitting there on her bed, smiling, eating, talking in a firm quiet voice. Radiant.

"And what will you do now?" he asked her.

"I shall join the Sisters of St. Vincent de Paul and nurse the sick!" she said, eyes shining.

He fell silent. He no longer knew what to think or what to say. He had no explanation to offer. He said good night briefly and went out into the street, and so into the Domaine and toward the Sanctuaries.

As he made his way past thousands of fervent, rapt pilgrims, he no longer wanted to smile at their childlike hopes. All he had ever believed was turned upside down. The wildly improbable had become a simple fact. The dying were cured in a few hours—a few minutes. These pilgrimages had a power of their own, and brought results. Above all, they brought humility.

It was disconcerting, to say the least, to have declared after careful examination that a patient would die, and then watch her recover. He might have doubted his own diagnosis, or his own memory, if he had not kept a written record of the case. But there it was—he reviewed it again: her tuberculous family, her own gradual deterioration, all the classic symptoms, and finally the diagnosis of the physicians and surgeons who had had her under their care.

No, there was no doubt of its having been a true case of tuberculous peritonitis. At the hospital that afternoon he had said she was about to die. Now, tonight, he was unable to offer any explanation for the incredible fact that she was alive and appeared to be cured. On the point of death at noon, and well by seven in the evening!

"When one reads about such things," he said to his friend Dr. B. later, "one cannot help suspecting some kind of charlatanism. But here is a cure I have seen with my own eyes. I have seen an apparently chronic invalid restored to health and normal life. These facts must be recorded, they must be conscientiously studied.

"Of course," he added, "facts are not the whole answer. Such cures cannot be brought about by natural means. Autosuggestion is not the final answer—nor the Lourdes water either, for cures have taken place without it."

What then? Was it in truth the Virgin, or God Himself who works the miracles? He could prove neither the existence or nonexistence of God. He was alone in the night, a solitary human being, wrestling with his doubts and questionings. Was the phenomenon he had seen a new fact in the tangible world of science, or did it belong to the realm of the supernatural? This was the vital point. It was not a question of accepting some abstract theorem. It was a question of accepting facts that might change the conception of life itself.

In his restless searchings for an explanation, for an answer to the tremendous event he had seen, one thing came back to him over and over again: that girl's face, after her cure; the joy that flowed from her, shining out to everybody in the room. They all felt it. Peace and serenity seemed to flood the place.

He had never beheld such joy or peace, following an ordinary cure, in his experience as a physician.

It was not an emotional joy, but a deep and quiet calm, "a profound sense of well-being" which, he remembered now, is recorded many times of Lourdes cures. It is not recorded of natural cures in a hospital, nor of cures by hypnotism or auto-suggestion. This in itself would seem to tell something about the cause: the Power from which the cure proceeds.

Doubts and questionings faded away beside this girl's happiness. Intellectual systems no longer seemed to count. In the face of life and death, mere theories were void. One thing he saw clearly: it was not science that nourishes the inner life of man. It was the faith of the soul.

17

Two Famous Cures

One Sunday afternoon I was chatting with one of the doctors at the Bureau—an old-timer who had been coming every year for twenty years to Lourdes to study the cures.

"Tell me," I asked him, "when you look back over the years, the hundreds of cases you've seen, the thousands of patients you've studied, what are some of the most remarkable cures you've witnessed or known about during these years?"

"Oh," he said, "any number. Hard to select. But—well, there was Madame Augault. That was a very remarkable case—fibroid tumor. I lived near her town, Craon. I knew both the surgeons who attended her. I know her parish priest who has known her all her life. So I know from my own personal standpoint that her cure was genuine. But the official medical documents are all here on file, and it is a thoroughly clear case medically, too."

This woman had been ill for twelve years, with a tumor of the uterus which had grown to enormous proportions. These growths often weigh ten to twenty pounds. "I don't know how much hers weighed," said the doctor, "but it was tremendous." X-rays confirmed the diagnosis of the family physician, Dr. Faligant, who certified, "Madame Augault is suffering from a voluminous fibroid tumor which produces intestinal compression and a state of intractable constipation."

Because of a heart condition she could not undergo surgery. Two surgeons whom she consulted, Dr. Martin and Dr. Le Basser, both advised against an operation.

Dr. Loiseleur of Laval, who did her X-rays, suggested possible X-ray treatments but Madame Augault decided she could not afford these.* She grew steadily weaker—could take only liquid food and that only two cups a day. Finally, through weakness, even lost her voice. Because of pressure on the intestine, gastric troubles became a major feature of the general condition. Vomiting was continual. The case had reached a desperate and apparently hopeless stage.

As a last resort Madame Augault decided to go to Lourdes. Dr. Faligant strongly opposed this. He told her it was "a last imprudence" and that she would never come back alive. But Madame Augault persisted.

She had a double reason for wanting to make the pilgrimage. She had a neighbor, a retired railroad employee, who was a complete unbeliever and who laughed at the idea of a cure through divine intervention. Especially a cure for such a malignity as Madame Augault's tumor.

"If Madame Augault is cured at Lourdes, I will become a believer myself," he vowed, "and I will walk barefoot through the streets of Craon, carrying a penitential candle!"

Madame Augault heard this, and was deeply stirred. A profound believer, she became more eager for the conversion of her neighbor than for her own cure. "I *must* go," she said. "Perhaps the Blessed Virgin will cure *him!*"

She made the journey on a mattress—at the limit of her strength and very close to death. Four injections were necessary to help her heart during the trip. Dr. Bucquet of Laval, who visited her on the train, told the doctors at the Medical Bureau later that he "had been startled by the dimensions of her abdomen."

Madame Augault arrived at Lourdes on the twentieth of

* Dr. Loiseleur subsequently reported to the Medical Bureau: "In September, 19—, I examined Madame Augault of Craon who came to me from Dr. Faligant. She showed: a fibroid tumor grown into the little basin (of the uterus), and extended over the pubic symphysis by about 8 centimeters (approximately 3 inches)."

August and was taken to the Hospital of the Sept Douleurs. From the time of her departure from Craon she had taken no nourishment and she took none until evening of the following day.

On the morning of August 21, she was taken to the piscine on a stretcher. During the brief instant of her immersion she felt excruciating pain, but then the pressure in her abdomen seemed to disappear. She felt no distress—all pain had ceased. Very tired, she was taken back to the hospital. She took no nourishment at noon, either solid or liquid.

Again, at 4 P.M., she was carried on her stretcher to the Procession. Lined up with her companions in misery, she suffered terribly while waiting for the passing of the Blessed Sacrament. But at that precise moment, as the Host was raised above her, her sufferings vanished. It seemed that her energies were reborn, and she could get up and walk!

She stayed on her cot, however, said nothing to anyone as to how she felt, and was brought back as usual to the hospital. Arriving there, she began to walk a little. That night she was hungry, but she ate only dry bread—which she had not tasted in four years. The following night was an excellent one.

Next day, August 22, she returned to the piscine. The attendants who had bathed her before observed with amazement that her abdomen was entirely flat and apparently normal. Besides, she had recovered her voice.

After this bath she presented herself at the Medical Bureau where, within a few minutes, some thirty doctors had gathered to investigate this extraordinary cure. Dr. Juge, surgeon of Marseilles, conducted the examination. The official record at the Bureau reads:

The abdomen, on examination, was found to be perfectly supple. The skin was "pleated," like that of a woman who has had a child. The abdomen is easily depressable and entirely painless. It is thin— no pain on palpation.

The belt which the invalid wore on her arrival at Lourdes is now 20 centimeters (7 inches) too large. The measure of her bloomers belt also shows a decrease of 18 centimeters (from 90 to 72). The coat which she wore shows the marks of the stretching of the buttonholes from the distension of the abdomen. This garment has become much too big and its sides now overlap considerably.

Results of the gynecological examination are given in detail: vagina supple to the touch; neck of uterus easily accessible; volume and consistency normal, etc. The heart was also normal, pulse regular and well marked. Everyone noticed how easily the patient lent herself to the examination.

After some discussion of the doctors' certificates, X-rays and so on, which attested the existence of the tumor over a period of years, the President of the Medical Bureau concludes:

The cure of Madame Augault, instantaneous and without convalescence as above related, astonished a number of our colleagues who observed it. The day after her deliverance, August 23, she ate without inconvenience the regular diet served at the common table at the Hospital, went up without fatigue the steep steps of the Rosary Church and the hard climb of the Way of Calvary. (A very hilly path of half a mile.) . . . The opinion of the doctors present is that such a cure can find no place in what we are accustomed to observe in our habitual medical practice and is definitely outside the range of biological laws—that is to say, it cannot be attributed to natural processes.

To complete the record, let us add that the cure of Madame Augault has been steadily maintained. Her attending physician informs us that he visited Madame Augault on her return from Lourdes and several times since. He says she feels well, eats well, has normal stools. The heart is normal. She has gained 2 kilos (4 pounds) this week. Within a month she had gained 16 pounds.

Madame Augault continued in excellent health, according to doctors who visited her in 1951.

And the neighbor fulfilled his vow. He walked barefoot through the streets of their little town, carrying a candle like any sincere penitent, and became a firm practicing Christian. Madame Augault's joy was then complete.

In the files of the Medical Bureau are to be found a number of cases headed: "Cured on the train going home" or

"Cured on the point of departure." One of the most interesting of these is the case of Lydia Brosse.

This young woman suffered for years from intestinal tuberculosis and later from tuberculous abscesses on her back and thighs. At the Hospital of St. Raphael in the south of France, she underwent one operation after another to be rid of these abscesses. Instead, she seemed to grow constantly worse. In September, 1930, Dr. Clement, surgeon at St. Raphael, was about to perform additional incisions; but the patient, weary of suffering and at the end of her resources, asked to be admitted to the Rosary Pilgrimage which was about to go to Lourdes.

For her admission to the Pilgrimage Dr. Clement gave her the following certificate: "I the undersigned, Dr. Clement, Surgeon of the Hospital of St. Raphael, declare that Mlle. Lydia Brosse, suffering from repeated multiple abscesses, affections of bone and skin, and of tubercular nature, is in a condition to be admitted to the hospital at Lourdes." (Signed, Dr. Clement, St. Raphael, September 26, 1930.)

Lydia departed on the Pilgrimage on October 7. By this time she was suffering from a large abscess extending to both buttocks and had to lie on her stomach during the whole journey. She weighed only 78 pounds, and the doctor who helped her to the train declared that the poor girl would never live to reach Toulon, the next station.

The trip to Lourdes was one long agony. Arrived there, she was so exhausted that the nurses felt great concern for her. She was bathed twice in the piscine (October 9 and 10) but on the latter day she was so weak she was merely lotioned with Lourdes water. Her sores discharged abundantly, the dressings having to be renewed twice during the day.

Her suffering was greater than ever that morning, as she recounted. She could not even pray. The nurses were filled with compassion at seeing her getting ready to depart "in the same corpselike condition as when she came."

The train left at 2 P.M. Before arriving at Toulouse, four

hours later, she felt suddenly better. She managed to raise herself on her elbows and declared that she no longer felt pain. The nurses took advantage of the interval to change the dressings. The compresses and the cotton were just as soiled as on preceding occasions. They made a new dressing.

At Carcassone, the Sister-nurse brought Dr. de Vernejoul, surgeon of Marseilles and physician of the train, to change the dressing. To their utter amazement, they found the compress only faintly reddish and the wounds almost closed.

At Narbonne, it was seen that the sores were definitely healed; Lydia, on her feet now, could walk about the train. The rest of the journey she accomplished in a sitting position. Hospital orderlies at St. Raphael had come with ambulance and stretcher to meet the invalid. Open-mouthed, they saw her jump lightly from train to platform and walk along with the greatest of ease.

Although it was raining, she insisted on walking—in her slippers—to the Hospital ("So happy I was to *walk!*" she said) and was received by the Superior and the Sisters, who were quite overcome at sight of this "literally resurrected one."

That same day, which was the twelfth of October, Mlle. Brosse was seen again by Dr. Clement. He later certified:

I, the undersigned, Dr. Clement, surgeon at the Hospital of St. Raphael, declare that I have had under my care since the month of January, 1929, Mlle. Lydia Brosse for repeated abscesses and phlegmons, most of these very voluminous, the inflammation situated mainly in the buttocks and lower part of the abdominal wall. Incised and drained, these purulent collections cicatrized very slowly and much sloughing off of tissue resulted. On October 12, I found complete cicatrization of various incisions previously made, as well as complete disappearance of a voluminous collection of pus in the left buttock. All trace of inflammation has disappeared and Mlle. Brosse has at this moment all the appearances of good health. (Signed, Dr. L. Clement, October 17, 1930.)

A letter from another physician at the St. Raphael Hospital, Dr. Chabal, noted that when Mlle. Brosse entered the Hospital

(April 12, 1929) she had pus in her urine and very troublesome nasal and intestinal hemorrhages. He described various operations the patient had undergone on account of tuberculous disease of the bones and recalled her condition when she departed for Lourdes. He, too, observed the amazing change in the patient on her return, and confirmed everything Dr. Clement had found: "Her wounds entirely filled up, and she has now only her scars, enormous but healthy—and an increase of weight to 104 pounds."

Dr. Chabal, an agnostic, adds: "Personally, without denying their possibility, I did not believe at all in miraculous cures. I must acknowledge that this cure, in a patient whose case I had followed, astonished me extremely. Certainly the gravest lesions may be healed, when they are tuberculous, as was the case here, but I do not believe that a natural cure can take place with such extreme rapidity."

On October 8, 1931, one year after her cure, Mlle. Brosse again came to Lourdes in the Rosary Pilgrimage, but in a very different condition from the year before. The account of her examination at the Medical Bureau records that she "appeared to be in excellent health," that "there remained no spot in the once diseased areas which was not completely healed," and that she "has gained 48 pounds in the space of one year."

The record describes in detail the various scars which bore witness to the former disease: on the left arm, right arm, right leg, abdomen, in addition to two great scars in the region of the thighs—"the principal wound in evolution at the time of the cure"—and notes that Mlle. Brosse had been anesthetized *twenty times* in vain attempts through surgical means to effect the cure of these abscesses which had miraculously disappeared within a few hours of her visit to Lourdes.

The President of the Bureau, summing up, and calling attention to the testimony of the various eye-witnesses of the cure, on the spot, as well as that of the patient's physicians at home, concludes:

"It is impossible that 'suggestion,' either personal or collective, could force various microbes to neutralize each other and disappear, cause large collections of pus to be absorbed, fill up gaps made by sloughing tissue, and form scars with a rapidity that amazed the surgeon concerned. Such healing surpasses all biological laws."

A nurses' aid who had helped care for Lydia at Lourdes, writing to her Chief of Service, added a few personal details to the case:

I remember very well this poor log of a human, lying on her stomach for eighteen months, whose back and thighs were freshly cut and whose wounds went all along her hips! Accompanying my friend at the station (for the return journey) I saw the poor invalid going back in the same corpselike condition in which she came. By the time they reached Narbonne, of course she was well . . . A week later she went to Toulon to assist at the ceremony of Thanksgiving of the Pilgrimage and publicly to thank the Blessed Mother. Since then she has taken service in the Hospital.

The letter goes on to say:

The doctor who had cared for Mlle. Brosse during her nasal hemorrhages (Dr. Chabal) had told the Superior: "Don't bother me any more, the poor girl is reeking with tubercle bacilli, and there is nothing more to be done for her."

I went to St. Raphael to see her. I saw her scars. Naturally the flesh that had been removed by several operations has not come back; but the skin is supple, there is no pain, and the patient moved around in lively fashion on her chair to show us, who had seen her in such agony, how she felt nothing whatever now, and all positions seemed comfortable for her. . . . One of the doctors said that even if she had been cured (by natural processes) she would never have been able to sit down without pain.

I expect to see her again and I will keep you posted on the developments of this remarkable cure. (Signed, G. La Croix, nurses' aid. Juan-les-Pins, Dec. 2, 1930.)

According to last accounts, Lydia Brosse is still well and vigorous. She leads an active life as a practical nurse.

18

Relapses, Frauds, and Conversions

The cure of diseases logically poses the question of their possible recurrence or relapse. Relapses are extremely rare in Lourdes cures—I found less than ten in records covering seventy-five years. They seldom occur; and in such cases, the doctors point out, a relapse after several years, or death by a malady other than the one miraculously cured, cannot be used as an argument against the miracle. It is still not possible to explain the original cure.

Among the exceptional cases may be mentioned that of Madame Rouchel of Metz, cured of lupus (tuberculosis of the skin), but after two years seized again with the same illness. She died in a hospital nine years after her cure at Lourdes.

A case of relapse, interesting from several angles, is that of Elie Auclair. Auclair, an ex-soldier, developed Pott's Disease after his war service. A complete atheist and violent foe of religion, he had married a devout Catholic girl to whom he was deeply attached. But he scoffed at her faith and said he would rid their children of "all that nonsense" just as soon as they were old enough to reason.

Then this terrible illness came upon him. His wife spoke of Lourdes. Auclair hooted at the idea. He, a freethinker, go to Lourdes! "I forbid you ever to bring a priest to me!" he thundered. "If I know of it, and have strength enough, I will drive him away."

Some time later, he happened to see Paul Merat, a young

boy who had been cured of his same malady at Lourdes, a couple of months before. Auclair was deeply impressed. He thought perhaps the Lourdes waters did have some curative quality. He consented to go. Once there, he was moved by the simplicity and faith of those about him. He saw that there was more to it than just some curative water. Wondering at himself, he began to pray.

Two days later, his abscesses had dried up, mobility returned to the spine, his wounds healed. Auclair, who had come to Lourdes on a stretcher, returned home walking and free from pain. Within a month he resumed his work as a blacksmith.

He was a changed man—a radiant Christian, *living* his faith, and overwhelmed by what God had done for him. But he kept saying, "My past is terribly stained. I was an enemy of God. What have I done that He should grant me such grace?"

He was intensely conscious of his black past and his guilt.

In a few months his pain began again. "It is only just that God should try my faith," he said, "since I have been such a great sinner and have denied His existence."

He returned twice to Lourdes—but did not improve. He developed new abscesses and grew worse. He accepted whatever came as God's will, as suffering visited upon him "because of his faults." He "had increased Christ's sufferings on the Cross." He was overwhelmed by his guilt-consciousness; but was ready to accept cheerfully any amount of suffering as retribution for his "evil past." During the last seven months of his life he suffered intolerably but never complained.

"Our Blessed Lady showed me the right road," he said. "That was sufficient. I shall never forget it." He died holding his Lourdes medal and his crucifix, and with an expression of joy on his face.

&ent; *The question of fraud* has been a burning issue at Lourdes from the very beginning. There have been violent attacks by

Lourdes adversaries on the veracity of both *miraculés* and witnesses; also accusations that the medical men of France are in secret agreement with the Church in the proclamation of miracles. There have been assertions that the whole story of the cures is just a huge piece of Catholic propaganda.

But many of the certifying doctors are not Catholic, and some have no religious belief whatever: such as Dr. Pellé who certified the cure of Jeanne Fretel, Dr. Chabal who certified the cure of Lydia Brosse, and Dr. Bardol who certified the cure of Marie Borel.

In the end, it comes down to the word of the examining doctors and the doctors in attendance at the patient's homes. Are they telling the truth or are they lying? The integrity and prestige of the doctors in charge of the Medical Bureau, the noted specialists and Chief Surgeons of the Paris Hospitals— Oberlin, Grenet, Mauriac, etc.—can hardly be challenged; nor can one doubt the large and very distinguished membership of AMIL. Five thousand doctors in good standing can't all be fools—or fakes. Nor can they be parties to what would be— were Lourdes *not* "on the level"—one of the most gigantic frauds in history. This would be practically impossible, even if morally conceivable. If a fraud, Lourdes would have blown up long ago instead of increasing in dignity and winning the respect of the medical profession steadily, every year.

The severity of the examining physicians at the Medical Bureau, their tendency to reject rather than accept alleged cures, and to subject each cure to merciless (and year-long) scrutiny, is the best guarantee against any fraudulent cases slipping through.

Attempted frauds against the Medical Bureau are not infrequent; some inspired by vanity, some by greed, some by definite animosity and the desire to injure or destroy.

For example, one day a young girl of about twenty, with a quiet voice and an air of complete innocence, presented herself at the Bureau. "Doctor," she said tremulously, "I believe I have been cured! For three years I have been in bed unable to walk, and since this morning I can walk perfectly! Isn't that wonderful?"

The doctor looked her over. "What was the matter with you, my child?"

"Oh, that I don't know, Doctor."

"Where is your medical certificate?"

"I have none."

"And why not?"

"Oh, I did not think I was going to be cured."

The secretary got out his notebook and the doctors prepared to take the record. . . . Lucie M—twenty-one years old . . . Pilgrimage of the North, etc. . . . Then they began the examination.

For one who had not walked for three years, she had muscles like marble. They told her to take off her shoes. "But why?" the girl objected. "My feet do not hurt!"

They wanted to see the way she planted her feet—which naturally is not the same for a normal person as for one who has been in bed for some time. She planted her feet like one who uses them every day. The doctors told her severely: "You are lying. You have been walking straight along. What is all this trumped-up history?"

Then she broke down, burst into tears, and between sobs told her true story. "You see, Doctor, in the village next to mine, last year, one of my little friends became a *miraculée*. When she came home she was greeted with flowers, triumphal arches, the rector blessed her and the mayor kissed her. I want people to do all that for me, too!"

There are half a dozen Lucies every year. Sometimes they can do real harm to the reputation of the Bureau and to the genuine cures.

Another time, one of the brancardiers came running to the Bureau, his face radiant with joy. "Doctor! What do you think?

A magnificent miracle! A boy, deaf and dumb from his birth, and the son of deaf-mutes also. He began to speak at the baths this morning. Isn't that *marvelous?*"

"We shall see. Send him along to me."

Some minutes later the young boy of the supposed miracle walked in. Blond, curly-headed, about fifteen, with rather a childish air, he was escorted by an extraordinary individual of about thirty—black as jet, long whiskers, cavernous jowls—in brief, a person one would not like to meet on a dark street at two in the morning.

"You two are relatives?" asked the doctor.

"Oh, no," said the escort. "I have known the boy only three days." He had asked for help, it seemed, in the train.

"When did he begin to speak?"

"This morning, at the baths."

"And what did he say?"

"He said: 'I fervently thank the Blessed Virgin Mary.' "

"But that is magnificent," said the doctor; "that is not a miracle, that is two miracles. First, he has acquired the gift of speech; second, he has instantly learned grammar!"

The escort saw that he had made a blunder. "But doctor, you must understand—for four years now he has been in an institution for deaf-mutes."

"Well, well! And he could not by chance have learned to speak in that institution?" The doctor turned to the boy. "Now look here, my son, tell me the truth: how long is it since you have been able to talk?"

"Since two years, doctor," said the youngster.

The escort, in considerable confusion, hustled him out of the Bureau. But the two were not through yet. They bought two thousand post cards and spent the rest of the day writing on them: "Souvenir from a deaf-mute miraculously cured at the piscine on this very day." They sold the cards for ten francs each to gullible pilgrims, the escort pocketing the proceeds—

which amounted to about 18,000 francs, (fifty-odd dollars) before the police caught up with them.

The worst type of all frauds is the intentionally malicious. One morning a woman came rushing into the Bureau with disheveled hair and in great excitement, crying: "I am cured —I am cured! Come at once—a real miracle!"

Her malady, the woman declared, had been an anal fistula. Now, thanks to the Blessed Virgin and glorious St. Bernadette, she was "freed—delivered!"

The doctors brought her into the office and began to take the record: personal antecedents, family history, history of the illness, history of the cure. The patient answered all questions readily, even volubly. When she had finished, she rose to leave.

The doctors detained her. "Wait, madame, we have not finished. We must now examine you."

"Examine me—but why?"

"In order to verify your cure, madame."

"And all that I have been telling you—that is for nothing?"

"For nothing, madame, if we do not examine you."

"But I do not wish to be examined."

"Then you should not have come here and made us waste thirty-five minutes. Why *did* you come here?"

"I came to have myself verified."

"Very well, in order to verify a cure we must examine the patient. If you do not consent, we shall tear up the record."

"Then I shall not be verified?"

"No, madame."

After much protesting and objecting, finally she yielded, and the examination took place. Five or six doctors assisted. There was nothing whatever the matter with the woman, and never had been—certainly not of the malady she described. When the doctors asked her to show them where the anal fistula was, she pointed to a little white scar (vestige of an old cyst operation) quite high up on the back and in a spot where certainly no one ever had an anus!

The doctors' annoyance was evident. The President said to her firmly: "Madame, you have lied to us. What *is* all this story?"

She looked much embarrassed, finally said she would tell it "to the Chief of the Bureau, but not to all these people."

The President took her into his office and there, in bits and pieces, the truth came out. She had been purposely sent, by an antireligious organization of one of the big *départements* in the middle of France, to bring back a personal document showing that at the Medical Bureau of Lourdes they recognized miracles *without examining the patients.*

The enemies of Lourdes were clever, but not clever enough. If the Bureau had not acted with its usual severity, if the doctors had said, "Well, madame, we will verify this next year," they would have been immediately involved in a press campaign, perhaps national, which they could never have lived down, whatever proofs they might have produced. The result might have been catastrophic.*

One of the worst frauds against Lourdes was perpetrated by Zola who, by his own confession, in his novel *Lourdes* deliberately altered the facts in accounts of three cures and made their story come out to suit himself—i.e., in death, not health as actually occurred.

"My characters are my own," Zola wrote to Dr. Boissarie grandly. "I shall do whatever I like with them."

But they were *not* his characters. They were living persons—Lourdes characters—whose stories he had purloined and abused; using enough of the truth to leave no doubt as to *who* they were, but changing the ends of the stories so as to make the

---

* These three stories are taken from official records in the book *Guérisons Miraculeuses Modernes* by Drs. Leuret and Bon and are reproduced by kind permission of the Presses Universitaires of Paris.

conclusion entirely false. When his ruse became known, he secretly visited the cured persons and offered them comfortable sums of money to leave Paris and live in a foreign country. They indignantly refused.

ఎక్ *On the positive side,* a strong impetus to moral living and active religious faith is given by Lourdes cures, both in their immediate circle and farther afield. We find many examples of this among the letters and personal notes filed with case histories.

John Traynor records "a large number of conversions" in Liverpool after his cure. His return, whole and well, made a tremendous impression. And there was the family chauffeur of Marie-Louise Arnaud, so moved by her cure that he was converted and became "a good Christian." There was the atheist neighbor of Madame Augault, who kept his vow and walked through the streets carrying his penitential candle, following her astonishing cure. Mademoiselle Delot, also, tells of her neighbor who, though dying, had refused all religious consolations. She went to visit him.

"Mademoiselle," said the patient, "I saw you before you went to Lourdes, and the contrast I see in you now makes it impossible for me to doubt the power of God, about Whom I never learned much." He asked to be permitted to make his confession and receive the Last Rites and died happy, "in religion."

There was the whole Belhache family, who "had lived as pagans" till the cure of Lucien, and then came into the Church all together; they have been fervent and active Christians ever since. And Elie Auclair, and Gargam, and Madeleine Guinot, and Madame Pouxvieille, and many others. It is safe to say that every Lourdes cure brings a score of converts into active Christian faith—in addition to reviving in their own families a faith that had sometimes lapsed into apathy. Multiply this by ten thousand and you get the nucleus of a substantial religious revival.

A striking aspect of this spiritual renaissance is its impact upon the medical profession. Dr. Vallet wrote in 1944:

No one can ignore the revival of religious faith during the past forty years; the medical world not excluded. The physician who is of a positive mind has found in the Fact of Lourdes a solid rock on which to reconstruct the shattered temple of his faith. . . . And it is not only a few isolated cases among the doctors who have thus come back to God, but a majority . . . among them some of the greatest names in French medicine, and those you would least expect to find.

He is referring here to a majority of the medical men who have visited Lourdes—some 30,000, he says, since 1890.

The thing that incited this medical army to come to Lourdes for some of course was a tremendous and quite legitimate curiosity; but for others also . . . the desire (confused and a bit melancholy) to find again the reasons for belief which their studies and life itself had rendered dim and obscure—until a state of complete darkness had been reached.

What confidences have I not heard!—until a recognized confessor could be found to clear the consciences weighed down by years and years of abandonment, and lead these wanderers back to spiritual security again.*

And not only the doctors. Evidence for the fact of miracles has a powerful effect upon the belief of people generally. Whereas miracles have been, for many, a primary reason for doubting the truth of large portions of the Bible, proof of their occurrence here and now gives new foundation for faith in the Scriptures as a whole.

"If miracles occur, then God exists!" is the basic theme of this revival of religious belief through Lourdes.

* From Dr. Vallet's *La Vérité sur Lourdes,* with kind permission of the author and of Flammarion and Co.

19

The Big Pilgrimages

*

No *story of Lourdes* is complete without some account, however brief, of the big pilgrimages, for there is nothing like them anywhere else in the world. They bring anywhere from 20,000 to 100,000 people together in this one place, at this one Shrine, to pray, to give thanks, to meditate . . . to "recollect" in times of joy and gratitude, or after periods of strife and disaster.

The two historic yearly pilgrimages—the French National and the Rosary—have been going on since the very early days of the Shrine—1871 and 1872 respectively; the National under the direction of the Assumptionist Fathers, the Rosary Pilgrimage under the Dominicans. They bring pilgrims from every diocese in France, from French territories, and other countries also. The priests of these Orders organize them locally in the various dioceses.

Then there are special pilgrimages such as that of the French Army—25,000 in 1954; the Men's Pilgrimage—20,000; the Pax Christi—an international pilgrimage of the Catholic Peace Movement; the Pilgrimage of Deported Persons—60,000; and the War Veterans Pilgrimage topping them all with 100,000 soldiers from twenty nations.

The French National (last week of August, each year) brings a large number of sick, usually around 1,200, and is famous for its many cures. The Rosary is a pilgrimage of prayer and devotion. It is the last big event of the year and highly prized by Lourdes devotees.

Each pilgrimage follows the classic pattern: Prayer at the Grotto—then up along the Way of Calvary. Welcome by the Archbishop; the Baths, the Procession and Blessing of the Sick; prayers at the different altars; visits to the churches and museums, and to the homes of Bernadette; confessions—Masses— the Torchlight. For the well, sometimes excursions to the mountains or the sea (Biarritz is only thirty miles away). For the sick, additional prayers and "recollection," the cherished Communion at the Grotto or at the altar of Bernadette. Finally the farewell—always a time of sadness. Nobody likes to leave Lourdes.

In some of our accounts of Cures we have followed a pilgrim from the time he leaves home until his return: his preparation —prayers and confession; sometimes, through the Hospitallers, meetings with other sick who will be traveling with him. On the train more prayers, hymns, and joyful anticipation. A Lourdes train leaves the home station with a rousing *Magnificat*; the *Ave Maria*, the *Song of Bernadette* and other hymns are heard throughout the length of the train, and at each station along the way.

The departure of the White Train from Paris at the time of the French National Pilgrimage is a remarkable sight. For days in advance, trains filled with pilgrims and invalids have been starting for Lourdes, from the north, south, east and west of France. The White Train carries the *"grands malades,"* the utterly helpless and hopeless cases whom science has declared itself powerless to relieve.*

On the day of departure the Austerlitz Station in Paris looks like a vast hospital. Rows of stretchers are lined up—on them men, women, children, all so white, so wan, so visibly sick unto death as to make one's heart ache. The train, its white pennon

---

* Parts of this account are from an article in the *Rosary Magazine* of New York with kind permission of the editors.

flying from the engine, is in readiness; one of the carriages is fitted up as a pharmacy, where the Sisters of the Assumption dispense food and medicine during the journey. The Sisters are at their post.

The priests who direct the pilgrimage move to and fro among the sick, speaking words of comfort. It is wonderful how these patients, practically all of whom belong to the working classes, rise to the occasion. They long to be cured, certainly, but there is no impatience in them; and they enter into the spirit of the pilgrimage with a sense of acceptance and humility which, considering their condition, is infinitely touching.

The Cardinal Archbishop of Paris never fails to visit the *grands malades* at the station, passing from one to the other, speaking a cheering word.

Then the business of carrying the sick into the trains begins. The brancardiers handle them so gently, so carefully. It is no easy matter to lay the invalids down in their appointed places without adding to their suffering, causing them additional pain. The train is an ordinary one and, though all precautions are taken to make the journey as easy as possible, much unavoidable discomfort must be faced.

All the available places are given to the sick. The volunteer workers—men and women—who look after them snatch a few minutes rest on camp stools they have brought. People who think of the French upper classes as completely light and frivolous would be surprised to find the nobility and wealth of the country largely represented in the plainly dressed women and devoted brancardiers who serve their patients so untiringly. Usually they are standing all day and all night.

Most of their charges are actually dying. Several have received the Last Rites, just before leaving home. But whatever their condition, every one of the *grands malades* is a willing traveler and often a cheerful one. It is the onlookers who shed tears as they watch one stretcher after the other carried into the train.

At last all is ready, and, at the end of two hours' hard work, priests, nuns, infirmarians, brancardiers—everyone is at his post. The railway men close the doors, the *Magnificat* goes up with a great shout, and the White Train with its freight of suffering humanity slowly steams out of the station.

Arrived at Lourdes, these sixty thousand people who have poured in from all over France "for the National," with their twelve or fifteen hundred sick drawn up in eager, waiting ranks along the Esplanade, make a never-to-be-forgotten spectacle. Father Robert Hugh Benson tells how they look, seen from the Basilica above, during the Procession:

The crowd was beyond describing. Here about us was a vast concourse of men; and as far as the eye could reach down the huge oval and far beyond the crowned statue and on either side—stretched an inconceivable "pavement of heads."

Above us too, on every terrace and step, back to the doors of the great Basilica . . . was one seething, singing mob. A great space was kept open on the level ground beneath us . . . and the inside fringe of this was composed of the sick, in litters, in chairs, standing, sitting, lying, and kneeling . . .

After perhaps half an hour's waiting—during which a constant gust of singing rolled this way and that through the crowd . . . the Procession appeared . . . the singing ceased . . . a priest standing solitary in the great space began to pray aloud in a voice like a silver trumpet . . . the crowd with one passionate voice repeating:

"Lord we adore Thee! Lord we worship Thee. Lord we love Thee. Save us, Jesus, or we perish!"

The Archbishop left the dais—advanced with the monstrance. One after another of these taut quiet figures received the blessing. Overhead the quiet summer air was aquiver with the power of those passionate entreaties, charged with feeling as a thunder cloud with electricity. And then—all of a sudden it came.

I saw a sudden swirl in the mass of heads beneath the church steps, then a great shaking ran through the crowd . . . A cry broke out and it rang through the whole square, waxing in volume as it rang . . . Hands clapped, voices shouted: "A miracle! A miracle!"

Just as suddenly the shaking ceased and the shouting died to a murmur.

The canopy moved on and again the voice of the priest rose high and clear with triumphant thankfulness: "*You are the Resurrection and the Life!*" And again, with entreaty once more—since there still were two thousand sick untouched by that Power, and time pressed —that infinitely moving plea: "*Lord, he whom You love is ill. . . . Lord, that I may see. . . . Lord, that I may hear. . . . Lord, that I may walk!*"

And then again the finger of God flashed down—and again, and again; and each time a sick and broken body sprang from its bed of pain and stood upright. . . . Five times I saw that swirl and rush— the last when the *Te Deum* pealed forth from the church steps as . . . the Sacrament came home again.*

Yes—there are great cures and grand events at the National. There have been as many as a hundred cures at a single Procession, in the fervent early days.

⚜ *The military pilgrimages* are no less remarkable, though in a different way. Lourdes will never forget the great War Veterans' Pilgrimage, when soldiers of twenty countries—including recent enemies—came together in three days of prayer for peace. Nearly a hundred thousand of them there were—Scots in their kilts, Bretons in their big hats, Belgians, Canadians, Irish, Italians, French, Dutch, and many others, most of them wearing decorations, many of them wounded.

Group by group they marched to the Grotto—a magnificent caravan. The Abbé Bergey—Director of the Pilgrimage and himself a famous veteran—made the opening address, asking his comrades to give an example of Christian brotherliness in a

* From the book *Lourdes* by Robert Hugh Benson, with kind permission of his executors.

world which seemed to have forgotten it. "All of us have fought for our countries. Now we must say to the world that we have had enough of fighting and that the time has come to love one another."

Immediately after the Benediction, four German veterans wearing their decorations entered the Grotto. Two of them took up their position on either side of the altar. Two others, seated near the grille, remained ready to relieve them; and all four began the prayer—continuous and fervent—which throughout the three days of the Pilgrimage would be offered day and night on this spot; the British following the Germans, then the Irish, the French, the Scotch, the Canadians, the Belgians, the Italians, and so on.

Masses go on continuously at the Grotto. At the end of each service, the soldiers of that group depart to climb the Way of the Cross. A moving sight, this endless defile of men who had climbed their own Calvary many times during the terrible war years, now completely absorbed in the sufferings of their Master.

The Mass for the Dead brings them all together on the steps and Esplanade in front of the Sanctuaries: the great Requiem chant sung by a "choir" of one hundred thousand voices. Then the Procession, with its crowds of sick and wounded of many nations.

Many touching glimpses: Thousands of men praying in the different churches and altars. Confessions being heard all day and through the night. Toward midnight of Saturday, 354 priests were counted, up and down the Domaine, hearing confessions in the open air, on the benches of the Esplanade, and along the river. All these sturdy soldiers on their knees, asking forgiveness and praying for help to do better in the future.

Then the grand Pontifical Mass of Sunday—the crowd augmented by people from all over the country. At ten, the bells of the Basilica ring out in joyful welcome. Every inch of space as far as you can see is packed with people.

Down the left rampe comes a dazzling sea of flags—flags of

twenty nations, allied and enemy—more than three hundred of them; new flags of proud silken beauty, others in tatters, the companions of stormy days and zero hours. Immediately behind them, the splendid procession of Cardinals and Bishops in their gorgeous red and purple.

And now the veterans—row upon row, line upon line, a slow, majestic, irresistible mass, thousands upon thousands—slowly advance, singing the *Ave Maria* of Lourdes, the "Song of Bernadette."

Slowly they move down the Esplanade, slowly they turn and come to a halt in front of the benches where the mutilated and the "big wounded" are seated; stand before them, heads bowed, in silent recognition. This simple gesture, performed in absolute quiet, brings the vast crowd to tears. This, everyone says afterward, is the real and fitting climax to the Pilgrimage of the War Veterans.

✎§ *The Pilgrimage of Prisoners and the Deported* in 1946 had a somber splendor all its own. Here 60,000 persons brought their gratitude for the past and their promise of Christian fidelity for the future. In the filth and wretchedness of German concentration camps they had prayed to Notre Dame de Lourdes, and had vowed, these miserable thousands, that "if ever we get out, we will go to Lourdes on a pilgrimage of thanksgiving." Now here they were, fulfilling that pledge.

To accommodate these swarming thousands, the big field at the right of the Domaine was turned into a "Camp of Return"; the different groups finding their place under the old labels: Dachau—Belsen—Buchenwald. Here the companions of the evil days found one another again with joyful cries, or more often embraced without a word, unable to speak. People dart across the path suddenly recognizing friends they had thought dead; handshakes, exclamations, shaky laughter. The Minister of the Armies, Monsieur Michelet—himself an old Dachau "graduate"—throws his arm around his old *copains*, sharing those poignant reminiscences.

From early morning a vast stream of people winds endlessly toward the Camp of Return and to the Sanctuaries. In the Square on the Esplanade an enormous podium has been erected, seventy feet high, with eighteen altars, visible from all parts of the Domaine. In front, on the open space of the Rosary Church, three funeral biers draped with the Tricolor and surmounted by a Cross—homage to those dead in captivity. The living, passing before them, stop, kneel and pray, choked with emotion. Here at night, after the great Torchlight, 60,000 men give forth the death-defying cry: "You are the Resurrection and the Life!"

R. P. Robert, Dominican Religious, escaped from the camp of Rava-Ruskaia, gives the opening address. He recalls to his comrades the memory of the Mass in the camps, where the most indifferent found comfort in a faith reborn—where they had promised Notre Dame de Lourdes if ever they were freed, to come here and thank her. "Today we keep that vow. Free of the German jails, we begin now a task perhaps more difficult than the tests of imprisonment: to bring our Christian faith into the difficult life of the postwar years, taking up our big burdens in the confusions of these days."

A spirit of deep quiet and "recollection" pervades the Pilgrimage. From three o'clock in the morning Masses are celebrated at the various altars. All day long the men make their confessions. The body has been freed—now one must free one's soul. Communions follow, one upon the other, without ceasing, while the Grotto and the Basilica are jammed with kneeling people.

At the Procession in the afternoon, a vast reunion of former prisoners and deported. General Giraud, the Prince of Bourbon-Parma, and other famous personages, are lost in the mass, intent only on joining their thanks with those of their companions of the bitter days, at this fraternal meeting place where all are equal: An endless file of men marching in rows of four on each side, a spectacle of moving grandeur.

Many touching incidents marked this Pilgrimage. On the first morning across the Esplanade came six women—knapsacks and canteens strapped to their shoulders, faces tired but joyous. "They have done thirty-two days *on foot* here to Lourdes, from Chartres," said a brancardier. "Without stopping, they have come to bring their thanks to Notre Dame de Lourdes."

People watched them wonderingly. Impatient to accomplish their mission, they hurry to the Grotto. The brancardier fills in details.

"The Chief of this remarkable caravan, Madame Ayle, is fifty-three; the youngest member, twenty-five. Madame Ayle's husband was shot by the Germans. She was a valiant Resistance worker and an ardent Christian. Deported, she made herself an apostle of Notre Dame de Lourdes to her companions in the concentration camp. They pledged themselves to make this pilgrimage if they should emerge alive from the Nazi hell. You see they have fulfilled their promise."

Another group—unusual visitors for Notre Dame de Lourdes, certainly—were twenty coal miners from Pas-de-Calais, brought by their local curate. A *kermesse* (country fair) which he had successfully organized permitted the little priest to offer this bounty to his old comrades in captivity. All of them were Communists, and thus, in principle, not pilgrims. But this fraternal gesture touched them. It was made with a generous heart, and accepted in the same spirit. After all, a trip to Lourdes, if it is not a pilgrimage, is always a "poem for the eye," not to be refused. Anyhow, a meeting place for former brothers in misery. As to the prayers, processions, Masses, and so on, "We will be tolerant spectators," they said, "not actors."

And yet, once arrived, these independent fellows would not leave their little curé. They followed him everywhere. With him they looked, marveled, listened, sang, and—responded to the prayers. Next morning, two of them went to Communion; the following day, six. Lourdes—the Camp of Return!

᰿§ A *pilgrimage of peace and calm*—but also of great spiritual strength—is the Rosary; organized by the Dominican Fathers and arriving each year at Lourdes the first week in October. I had the privilege of being present at the 1953 Rosary—40,000 people from all over France—1,200 sick: a spirit of extraordinary quiet and devotion.

I was down at the station from six in the morning, watching the trains come in—twenty-two of them that day, from Lille, Nancy, Grenoble, Bordeaux, Lyon, Avignon, Tours, Nice, Dijon, and many other places; thirteen or fourteen cars in each train—the very sick in the last carriage. One marveled again at the skill with which stretcher cases are handed through the window—three brancardiers inside the train, four or five outside, receiving the patients with utmost care and gentleness. Tall men are needed to reach up and receive the stretcher.

Then the sick are wheeled out and placed in the big autobuses waiting outside, and carried to the hospitals. They roll off singing the *Ave Maria*. A big moment for them—almost at the Grotto now, after their long, difficult journey.

The Rosary is a pilgrimage of prayer and recollection. There are the usual crowds, the usual processions and Masses and addresses—but with a difference. People on this pilgrimage come primarily because they earnestly seek spiritual strength and sustenance; though as we know, many of the big "cures" have occurred at the Rosary too.

The sick join in all the ceremonies, to a remarkable degree. I remember especially the morning when, lined up on the Esplanade in the form of a huge Cross, they recited the Stations of the Cross in unison. Twelve hundred of them, lying there in the clear October sunshine in their little carriages, the big crowd of the well pilgrims a human wall around them.

Come for the most part from poor homes, some out of drab little sickrooms—prisons of pain for months or years—what these few days at Lourdes must mean to them! What a tremendous impression these great gatherings and processions, these rituals and ceremonies shared together, must make on them: this great Fraternity of the sick and suffering, drawn up there in their little carriages, watching and participating. The sunlight, the great peaks, the towering trees, the beauty of the countryside; the combination of imposing sanctuaries, statues, fields and rivers—beauties of nature and of religion, all around them. It might be almost too much for a sick person.

As I look on, standing quite close to that living Cross, my eye meets that of a sick pilgrim, who smiles at me suddenly, spontaneously. Without removing her gaze she starts praying, her eyes still upon me. I am reminded of a thought that has come to me more than once at the Grotto, watching these inert forms, these constantly moving lips: *the sick praying for the well.* Who knows how many prayers have gone up for *me,* here; prayers offered by generous sick folk I never saw before, of whose altruism and help I have been totally unconscious—I and hundreds of others who have been the beneficiaries of their earnest and unselfish supplications.

"But yes, madame," said the brancardier to whom I spoke of this. "The gift of the sick to the well, here at Lourdes, is perhaps greater than the gift of the well to the sick. We brancardiers are constantly aware of it!"

⋅⋅§ *Pilgrimages not so large* have yet their own significance. A clipping from a recent Lourdes newspaper reminds me of some of them: the Pilgrimage of Italian Farmers, the Pilgrimage of French Railway Workers, the Miners of the North, the Poor of Pau, the German Swiss, the Cadettes of Mary (2,000 young girls from many dioceses); the Pilgrimage of the Deaf and Dumb, the Scouts of Paris, the Young Basques, the English Schools

(400 boys, 800 girls), the Children of Bigorre—3,500 of them, come to walk proudly in the Procession. And the Pilgrimage of the Employees of the Hotels and Stores of Lourdes, which seems to me one of the most interesting, as the business people of Lourdes are often censured for their alleged unspiritual qualities. Here, at the beginning of the season, several hundred young men and women are excused from work to come and listen to the Christian counsels of Monseigneur the Rector, to pray at the Grotto, "do" the Way of the Cross, walk in the Procession, make their confession and attend their Mass—to follow the entire pilgrimage program, "with true piety and devotion," according to the Rector.

Many small-group pilgrimages are listed: sixty Ukrainian refugee pilgrims coming from England; thirty-six from Ottawa and Quebec; eighteen pilgrims from Ceylon; one hundred from Bilbao, Spain; thirty-six from Chicago; eighty from Malta; seventeen from Finland; forty-two from Alexandria, Egypt; fifty from Dunkerque: All these arriving during the one week of August 8, 1954.

In addition, that week: the Pilgrimage of the League of Belgian Workers—bringing 3,000, and 500 sick; the Pilgrimage of American Soldiers (only a few, but tremendously enthusiastic); the National Council of Catholic Women of Canada; students from the College of Wald on Lake Constance; 450 students and professors from universities and high schools of the Argentine; 1,800 German Catholics from Cologne, under the direction of the Knights of the Order of Malta.

Finally, the Crusade of the Blind—1,300 of them, from all parts of France, led by their Almoner-General. What can such a pilgrimage have to offer this contingent, for whom miracles have been few and far between? What can this unseeing visit, after a long, hard journey, mean to them? What can the blind get out of a pilgrimage to Lourdes?

They get more out of it than many of us who see. They get the inner shades of meaning and atmosphere more acutely, perhaps, than other people who come here, and receive perhaps more benefit, with their highly sensitive perceptions as they join in the various prayers and ceremonies. They "take in" truly the pervading spirit of the place.

"Life is beautiful for those who have no fear," their preacher, Father Boury, tells them. "For anyone who has *an end* in life, and knows that it is a useful end, life is beautiful. A blind person can have a useful life the same as anybody else—can make of his life a service; so for him too, life is worthwhile."

And they begin their service there and then with the singing of great Gregorian chorals and monastic Offices, an art in which they are specially trained, and a glorious contribution to that day's pilgrimages.

Yes, there is much more to Lourdes than the curing of sick bodies. A new vision for the blind. . . . Girls deciding to replace exiled nuns in the schools. . . . The profound impression on large bodies of organized workers. . . . The great influence on the children who come here by the thousands with their spiritual preceptors. . . . The effect on the doctors and scientists of many lands. In brief: the work of Religion, of spiritual development and rehabilitation in a hundred different guises. Prayer and Penitence, as The Lady said—the greatest work of all.

⛫ *No pilgrimage has* greater popular appeal than the Pilgrimage of the French Army, particularly this last year (1954) when French fortunes were at a crucial point. For three days (June 12 to 14) twenty-five thousand soldiers came to pray for their comrades-in-arms and for the fulfillment of their own hopes and aspirations in a dangerous and uncertain world.

Many officers and military dignitaries accompanied them— the Chief of Staff of the Army, General Blanc; General Jousse, General Badre, General Descours, Commander Potter, and other distinguished personages. The Archbishop of Paris, Cardinal Feltin, *Ordinaire* of the Army, presided. But everyone's attention was focused during those three days on the vast assemblage of youth. As their Almoner said in opening the Pilgrimage:

Who can look upon this great company of young men, some just starting out, some seasoned men of battle, without profound emotion? Twenty-five thousand young men from all walks of life, all classes, all outlooks, representing their generation with its qualities, its faults, its hopes, its longings. Twenty-five thousand young men on the threshold of life, ready to take active part in it, to found a family, to accept responsibility, to choose. [These three days at Lourdes, he hoped, would help them] decide now to respond to Christ, to take His message seriously, to pledge their lives today in the interest of tomorrow—to take their generation in hand, to transform the world!

Are you capable of this transformation? Yes. Because you are princes of all the possibilities, because you have not yet the habits that chain and hold down the adults, because your youth brings you into a climate of the new—of discovery and sincerity.

All were deeply conscious of the men fighting 6,000 miles away, in Indo-China, and of the terrific problems that beset their country and the whole world. "All this," said Monseigneur Théas, in his talk to the men, "imposes on your pilgrimage a gravity and a significance of which you are entirely aware."

He spoke to them of the quality of some of France's military heroes—particularly Marshal Foch who led the Allied armies to victory in 1918. Everyone knows the deep religious faith of this great general, but not all are aware of his intense consciousness of personal weakness and his complete dependence on the Divine Power. We have proof of this in his personal letters.

On April 7, 1918, he wrote to his brother Germain: "Without the special help of God I would find myself *absolutely incapable* of assuming the heavy task which has been imposed upon me." And on June 22, also to his brother: "Your prayers . . . for me, *are all my strength.*"

Marshal Foch did not shift onto others his duty of prayer,

however. Twice daily he got down on his knees. "I pray when it is cold, and above all when things get hot." Each day he said his rosary, and each day he invoked the Holy Spirit and recited the *Veni Sancte Spiritus*. In the most tragic hours he begged for guidance from above.

On December 10, 1914 he said to his brother: "During great events we are the instruments of Providence. How else have I been able to make the decisions which alone could carry us to victory. . . . I cannot explain it otherwise. Continue then to pray; pray to the Blessed Virgin for us, and we shall arrive!"

This was also Monseigneur's message to the young soldiers in the crises and anxieties of today: *"Pray*—never stop praying and hoping and believing; and we shall arrive, no matter what the obstacles."

And they follow his counsel—crowds of them at the Grotto and in the Sanctuaries, all day. On Sunday, from early dawn, they go the Way of the Cross by groups, each group preceded by a great wooden cross carried by two soldiers.

"A service by command?" asked one of the foreign visitors.

"No, monsieur," came the immediate reply, "a free and voluntary service. We have come here on pilgrimage because we ourselves wanted to come, and in complete freedom to act according to our religious convictions!"

The High Mass finds them packed into the Square in front of the Rosary Church—in the first row the sick and wounded, and behind them the great assembly; calm and profoundly attentive. At the Procession in the afternoon, those thousands of young men are on their knees, ardently praying for their sick. At the Torchlight in the evening, they march through the Domaine for hours, singing the *"Ave Maria"* and then the Credo. Unforgettable spectacle for those who witnessed it: all that wonderful youth, proclaiming strong and clear, its Christian faith.

*　　　*　　　*

I have told you—a little—of some of the big Pilgrimages.
Every one of them might well have been concluded with the
words with which Monseigneur Théas closed the 1936 Pilgrimage of the War Veterans:

Do you know what I was thinking of, just now when we went up
and down these paths in this great Procession? I was thinking of
that little peasant of our Pyrenees, that little shepherdess without
beauty, without credit, without a complicated theology, without
human influence, without eloquence—who, on her knees seventy-
eight years ago, a few steps from here, received from The Lady,
to give them to us, the commands which have made Lourdes.

My friends, if Bernadette had not knelt with her rosary before
the Grotto seventy-eight years ago, *you* would not be here. And if
she was capable, this poor weak child, with that one arm to mobilize
the world; if she was capable of bringing here the princes of the
Church, Bishops, priests, immense crowds, Papal Legates; capable
of bringing upon Lourdes innumerable benedictions such as we have
just received—she who had only one secret—can we, today, do
better than to follow her?

She gave us that secret; she herself said it when her nurse re-
proached her for not knowing her catechism.

'Eh, yes,' she said, 'I don't know much, but I know how to say
my rosary and to love God with all my heart.'

Can we, today, find a better armor?

Part Three

RECENT CURES:
CAUSES AND CONCLUSIONS

In contrast with the highly dramatic scenes of the early days when a cure took place, procedure today is much quieter—more conservative and more scientific.

The cured patient comes directly to the Medical Bureau and is examined, unknown to the crowds. If his cure appears to be genuine, the long investigations into the case are set in motion. Today, with all the rigorous medical inquiries and Church procedure, it takes several years before a cure can be definitely and officially declared.

For this reason a person cured as a child may be in his teens before his case is proclaimed as a recognized official cure. Two of the cases recorded (Pascal and Leydet) were very young when their cure took place, but are now fourteen and nineteen years old respectively.

The war years shut Lourdes off from the usual pilgrimages, so that between 1939 and 1946 no cures were recorded, though some occurred and were investigated later. Between the years 1946 to 1954 a number of remarkable cures have taken place. Some of the most notable were interviewed by me—at Lourdes, or in their own homes—and are described in the following pages.

20

Three Canonical Cures

Seven o'clock on a crisp autumn evening. . . . The big gates of the Sept Douleurs Hospital are closing for the night. The last stretcher cases have been carried in, the last of the little carriages put away till morning. Nurses going off duty come hurrying out to meet their friends. Brancardiers take off their leather harness, rub their tired shoulders, joke with their pals.

I wait—near the door. Indeed, I have something to wait for. Here she comes, swinging along in her nurse's uniform, a slim girl with big dark eyes and a big smile: Jeanne Fretel, one of the most famous of recent Lourdes cures.*

She has been on duty since six o'clock this morning. Her ward is four flights up. She "does the stairs" each time her patients need something from the kitchen or the office. She has washed, fed, and dressed some twenty to thirty patients—given injections, done dressings all day long; got them ready for the baths, prayed with them, soothed them, encouraged them. She has been interrupted many times by visitors—families of the sick who wanted to see her, to touch her. Yet here she is, fresh and smiling and unfatigued.

Who would think, as she sits opposite me in the hotel restaurant a few minutes later, laughing and chatting over a good meal, that five years ago today this girl was herself carried from the hospital to the Grotto in a dying condition—unconscious,

* *Jeanne Fretel, tuberculous peritonitis, cured at Lourdes, October 8, 1948.*

given up. "I didn't even know I was in Lourdes," she said. "I was so far gone, I didn't know anything—till suddenly It Happened."

Jeanne Fretel had never in her life been well. In 1939, her illness became acute. Diagnosis: tuberculous peritonitis with additional meningeal symptoms. She had thirteen operations. Her case history—one of the most complete of all Lourdes cures—contains eighteen pages of fever charts, eighty pages of detailed hospital reports, laboratory analyses, X-ray records, etc.

Jeanne was born May 27, 1914, in the town of Sougeal, near Rennes. She came of simple people. She had her way to make. She was waitress, practical nurse, mother's helper. From childhood her health was precarious. In January, 1938, when she was twenty-four, she was operated on for appendicitis at the Hotel Dieu Hospital in Rennes. This was the beginning of a long series of operations and sufferings.

The abdomen gradually increased in size, became hard and thick, and intensely painful. Surgeons at the Hotel Dieu diagnosed her illness as tuberculous peritonitis, and performed a laparotomy. This brought no improvement; indeed she became worse.

The year 1946 she spent in various sanitoriums, going through more operations. After all this surgery she was extremely tired and weak. She grew very thin. On December 3, 1946, she came back to the Hotel Dieu, as she said, "to die there."

She had not left her bed for one year and was unable to get up. Her temperature was usually around 103–104 degrees. To calm her sufferings, she was given frequent morphine injections. Some time before, she had been granted a pension as an "incurable."

From August, 1948, to October, 1948, (records Dr. Pellé of Hotel Dieu Hospital) the patient became more and more exhausted. She could take only small quantities of liquid. Signs of meningitis appeared. The abdomen was very swollen and painful. Pus flowed abundantly in the stools, also in the vomit, accompanied by black blood. All hope seemed lost.

For the third time in five years, on September 20, 1948, the patient received the Last Rites. It was in full development of tuberculous peritonitis with meningeal symptoms that she departed for Lourdes on October 4, 1948, with the Rosary Pilgrimage. She was completely unconscious when put aboard the train at Rennes. Dr. Hylli of Landisviau, who helped her during the journey, gave her two injections of morphine.

Arriving at Lourdes Tuesday, the fifth of October, she was taken next day to Mass at the Grotto and to the baths; but no improvement could be noticed. On Friday morning, October 8, she was carried, dying, to the Mass for the Sick at the Altar of St. Bernadette. The priest hesitated to give her communion because of her constant vomiting and extreme weakness. But her stretcher-bearer insisted, and he gave her a bit of the consecrated wafer.

"It was then," said Jeanne Fretel later, "that suddenly I felt well and I became aware that I was at Lourdes. They asked me how I felt. I replied that I felt very well. My abdomen was still hard and swollen but I was not suffering at all. They gave me a cup of *café au lait* which I drank gratefully, and which I kept down.

"After Mass, they took me to the Grotto on my stretcher. Arrived there, at the end of some minutes, I had a sensation as if someone took me under the arms to help me sit down. I found myself in a sitting position. I looked around to see who had helped me, but could see no one. As soon as I was seated I had the feeling that the same hands that had helped me to sit down now took my hands to put them on my abdomen. I asked myself what could be happening to me—was I cured, or was I just coming out of a dream? I perceived that my abdomen had become normal. And then I was seized with an extraordinary hunger."

Taken back to the Hospital on her stretcher, she told the

Almoner of her ward that she felt very well and no longer had a swollen abdomen. He, too, noticed the change that had taken place. She asked for something to eat. Dr. Gurgan of St. Meen-le-Grand, after examining her, gave the authorization. Food was brought and she ate with very good appetite: veal with purée, and three pieces of bread. She had not enjoyed such a meal in ten years.

"When I had eaten it all, I still was hungry and asked for more. They brought me as much again, and still I wanted more. Then, for dessert, they gave me a dish of rice pudding. I felt fine!"

In the afternoon she got up without help, dressed herself, and went to the piscine. . . . "I had not walked for three years, and I walked then as well as I walk today. Having arrived at the piscine, I took a bath standing up and with no fatigue." That evening she dined with appetite and at night awoke once, at eleven o'clock, only to complain of being hungry. After she had eaten, she went to sleep again.

The next day, Saturday, October 9, she was taken on a stretcher to the Medical Bureau where she was examined by five doctors—one of them Dr. Guyon of Nantes. He, not knowing she had walked the day before, said: "Well, if you are cured as you say, get up! Try to walk, and we shall see!"

"They wanted to help me to get up" (Jeanne's story continues) "but I refused all help and began to walk. The doctor, seeing how thin I was—I hardly had legs at all!—came towards me, fearing I might fall; but I held firm. The doctor went quickly to the scales, wanting to weigh me. Even though he went fast, I followed him just as fast, and was weighed: 44 kg. (96 pounds). I was told then to return next year."

The journey home was accomplished without fatigue. . . . "On the way back in the train, I was on my feet a long time, tending other patients. The nurse wanted to give me morphine, to calm me. I refused, and was able to rest very well whenever I wanted. At home, I took up my work straightaway.

And since my cure at Lourdes I have remained always just as well as I am now. I have never taken even an aspirin since then."

Mlle. Fretel's story is confirmed by the testimony of the numerous physicians who examined her, at Lourdes at the Medical Bureau and at Rennes after her return. The verbatim report of her first examination at the Bureau confirms all the details above cited, and adds: "The abdominal perimeter which before the cure was 1 meter (39 inches) now is o.m 78 (32 inches). She walked for the first time since October 17, 1945. The abdomen has become flat and supple, not painful to palpation. Everything is perfectly normal except for muscular atrophy of the legs—very natural after such a long period of inactivity."

Her own physician, Dr. Pellé, who had treated her for so long, saw her on the day of her homecoming and at regular intervals thereafter. He declared in his certificate to the Medical Bureau:

The patient is completely cured, having no longer any of the pathological symptoms which she presented. We have followed her case regularly and have noted the continued improvement of her general state of health. Her weight, which was 44 kg. (96 pounds), has gone up to 58 kg. (128 pounds). During the first week she gained 1⅛ pounds each day. Her temperature is normal. Appetite and sleep are very good. From the very next day (of her return) Jeanne Fretel was able to undertake a very active life, which continues without any pathological incident. She has never felt any pain. Every day she gets up at five-thirty, goes to bed at eleven at night. She has the most tiring work in the whole house.

On October 23, 1948, an X-ray was taken at the Hospital Center of Rennes, Dr. Barbot reporting:

No organic lesions discoverable by X-ray study of the intestinal tract. The spasticity observed in preceding examinations and which seemed intense is now normal. The right and transverse colons take the barium washing very well and evacuate slowly.

On October 5, 1949—one year after her cure—Mlle. Fretel came before the doctors of the Medical Bureau for a second examination. Naturally this cure had caused a great stir. Twenty-two doctors were on hand, among them several who had examined her the year before. The examination went on for two hours. At the end the doctors declared their conviction that it was a genuine cure, that "the disease had been abruptly arrested in its course when there was no apparent tendency toward improvement. All morbid symptoms have disappeared. No medical explanation of this cure can be given. It is outside natural law." There follow the signatures of all the physicians.

The Medical Commission at Paris, after studying these various documents, reported (March 12, 1950):

> The impressive history of this illness, the importance of the dossier which includes thirty temperature charts (eighteen before the cure, twelve after), the calibre of the doctors who examined the patient, the meticulous details of the daily records during the period from April to October, 1948, the period just before the cure, compels our long and earnest attention, and leads us to conclude that this is an inexplicable cure.*

A Canonical Commission confirmed these findings, and on November 20, 1950, Cardinal Roques, Archbishop of Rennes, proclaimed the case of Jeanne Fretel a Miraculous Cure.

An interesting sidelight on this case reveals that the physician in charge, Dr. Pellé, was an agnostic and unbeliever—"hostile" to religion, the Medical Bureau report says. However, it was his precise records and certificates, before and after the cure, that established it as a miraculous case in the eyes of doctors and clergy.

I saw Jeanne Fretel on the evening of October 8, 1953; five years, to the day, after her cure. She comes each year as a nurse with the Rosary Pilgrimage: an attractive, slender young woman, animated, full of life. Sitting opposite me in the hotel after a long day's work at the hospital, she filled in the details of her story.

---

* The writer possesses a complete photostat file of the medical record of Jeanne Fretel, with temperature charts, daily hospital records, laboratory analyses, X-ray reports, etc. Eighty pages in all.

She had thirteen operations—three on the mouth ("there were great holes in my jaw"), several on the feet, the others on the abdomen. After she became so terribly ill, she was fed with serum only, and was given injections of morphine, four or five every twenty-four hours. Friends offered her the pilgrimage trip to Lourdes, and saw that she got on the train. "But being so far gone, I was not conscious of my departure or the trip or anything." The Dominican Fathers were very good to her. She was in a coma till that Friday morning when, brought to the altar of St. Bernadette in a dying condition, she came away cured.

When she got back home and reported to the hospital, one of the young doctors went running to Dr. Pellé.

"Jeanne Fretel," he gasped. "It is Jeanne Fretel!"

"Poor girl—she is dead?" asked Pellé.

"Come and see!"

When Dr. Pellé saw her he was speechless. He left the room, overcome. Back in a few minutes, he looked at her, the tears running down his cheeks. He spoke to the Sister who was there with them, then gave Jeanne the most rigorous examination. He could hardly believe his own findings, after having seen her so desperately ill for so long. "I have been for Dr. Pellé something terrible—a blow to his scientific self-respect!"

Even now she is incredible to him. Each time she comes to see him, he says: "So! You are feeling sick, *hein?* You aren't feeling so good?"

"But certainly, I am feeling fine! I'm always fine—couldn't be better."

He seems almost disappointed. But it was thanks to his fine records and thorough information on the case that Jeanne was declared a *miraculée*. He rendered her a tremendous service. He had served her devotedly all through her illness, and has always had a great affection for her.

Jeanne is in perfect health now. She works as a practical nurse. It is confining work, and the hours are very long; but this doesn't bother her at all.

At Lourdes, at the Hospital of the Sept Douleurs, she feeds the sick, changes their dressings, gives them all the regular nursing care. The trip from Rennes—6 P.M. to 10 A.M.—is very hard on the sick. Jeanne gives injections all night long, thinking of the time when *she* did that long and painful journey on a stretcher.

The life of a *miraculée* isn't easy, she says. Everyone wants to see you. It's a perpetual assault—on the street, at prayers in church, in the train, everywhere. "Last year I wore a blue sweater for the Pilgrimage. Everyone would point me out. 'You will know her, she's the one with the blue sweater.' So this year I wore a black one. But it's just the same."

Six persons came up and spoke to her during the brief time that I was with her, even at table in the hotel. "I can't refuse them," she said. "I can't refuse *anything*, after what has been done for me."

Her correspondence is tremendous. Letters come from all over the world—from doctors, from sick people, from unbelievers wanting to be reassured. If she sends typewritten replies, people are not satisfied. The letters must be in her own hand. She works far into the night, often writing those letters after her regular day's work is done. She gets invitations to lecture—to go to the ends of the earth—to exhibit herself. Once she had to take part in a film—a church film. "Never again!" She is going to stay at Rennes and do her work—visit the sick, give them consolation when she can.

An attractive, intelligent woman—lots of personality; sensitive insight, keen appreciation of life's values, both spiritual and human. Her great desire: to give her entire life in service to other sick people in gratitude of what has been done for her. "One asks oneself again and again: why was *I* chosen? Many others deserve it far more."

Many people have become believers because of her cure. The Cardinal often sends for her—the doctors too—to talk with skeptics, and sometimes to the dying.

"Were you very scared when you had to go before the Cardinal and the Canonical Commission—and before all those doctors at the Bureau?"

"Terribly!" she nodded vigorously. "All those eyes—and questions fired from all sides. Very confusing." She remembered having given a couple of inaccurate dates—she was so mixed up at the time—referring to the year 1937 instead of 1938. They had pulled her up sharp.

"It sounds more like a criminal investigation than that of a *miraculée*," I suggested.

"Very severe," said Jeanne.

But then, after all the examinations, inquiries, probings, and recapitulations, finally came the great moment: the solemn *Te Deum* Mass in Rennes Cathedral that Sunday, following the pronouncement by the Canonical Commission and the Archbishop that Jeanne Fretel was a Miraculous Lourdes Cure.

A long road—for the girl who had been carried on a stretcher dying and unconscious to the Grotto at Lourdes—now the radiant creature walking up the aisle in the Cathedral between Bishops and Archbishops, and crowds of lifelong friends to sing "My soul doth magnify the Lord!"

Jeanne Fretel's whole life is a Magnificat.

✍ *Two of the most striking* "Before and After" pictures at the Medical Bureau are those of Mlle. Gabrielle Clauzel.* The note under the pictures states that this lady comes from Oran, Algeria, that she was instantly cured of a long and almost fatal illness: spondylitis, or inflammation of the spinal vertebrae, with complications involving various organs.

I had the good luck to be at the Medical Bureau and to have a long talk with Mlle. Clauzel when she came for her yearly examination and check-up. Seven doctors were present. Two

* *Gabrielle Clauzel, rheumatic spondylitis, cured August 15, 1943.*

had known the patient for a long time. One, Dr. Zimmerman, was an actual eye-witness at the time of her cure. These doctors and the Oranian parish priest, Father Capparos, told the story.

Dr. Vincent, pilgrimage physician and old friend of the Clauzel family, was the first to speak: "I have known Mlle. Clauzel for many years. Her father, one of the great merchants and industrialists of North Africa, founded the Friends of Notre Dame de Lourdes Society in Oran, and was its first President. Mlle. Clauzel later became President and for years did all the organizing and management of the Oranian pilgrimages. She was a tireless worker—absolutely devoted. Imagine, then, everybody's concern when Mlle. Clauzel became ill—and gravely ill at that. Dr. Maurin was called, and he remained her attending physician.

"She was stricken first with articular rheumatism in her left wrist and with great pain along the spinal column. In March, 1938, after much pain on the lower right side, she had an appendicitis operation. Following this, the pain grew more severe, which seemed to indicate that, like all her other troubles, it came from the spinal condition.

"Recovery was slow after the operation. She had much difficulty in walking. To stand upright was painful; the body was bent forward; even a sitting position was extremely tiring. She could not hold her neck straight; her head would always fall forward."

As Mademoiselle Clauzel said, "I felt as though I were crawling, rather than walking. Then in January (1939), I had another acute attack, and could not stand up at all."

The pain now spread over the whole spinal column. After an X-ray on March 1, 1939, Dr. Maurin diagnosed the case as vertebral rheumatism. Dr. Porot of Algiers, called in consultation, agreed. The usual treatment for rheumatic disease was followed: regular doses of salicylate through the mouth and intravenous injections of potassium iodide.

The fine summer weather seemed to bring a slight improvement. To her great joy Mlle. Clauzel was able to go with the Pilgrimage to Lourdes, in August as usual—but this time she had to take part in the various ceremonies from her little carriage, for she could not stand or move by herself. War was declared while she was still in France. When she finally reached home, she seemed for a while somewhat better. But in January, 1940, she had a relapse; and again in November, 1940, she was stricken with a new attack more violent than ever before.

"Mlle. Clauzel then went to bed—where she remained," said Dr. Vincent. "The illness took on a very serious aspect. The patient could not raise herself in bed. The least movement caused terrible suffering. The principal organs became involved —first the kidneys, then the liver and intestines. Her heart was also seriously affected. She had continual severe headaches and her eyes could hardly bear the light of day.

"Nevertheless, during intervals of calm, she continued to interest herself in the Society of the Friends of Notre Dame de Lourdes. Strangely enough, she never thought of asking for her cure. People had asked for it for her, but she herself just didn't think about it."

"I knew very well," put in Mlle. Clauzel, "that Our Lady of Lourdes could do everything, but so many other things seemed to me more necessary than my cure, I asked for everything else but that!"

She thought she might be helped if the doctors would remove some small, pointed pieces of bone—"parrots' beaks," they called them (the medical term is osteophytes)—that had shown up in the X-ray picture of her spine. She begged Dr. Maurin to perform this operation. He did so, unwillingly, in October, 1941, only because he thought it might help her morale.

Benefit was nil. In June, 1943, a second extraction of parrots' beaks—again without good result. During all this time the disease was steadily growing worse. From the beginning of 1943 Mlle. Clauzel grew very thin. During June this loss of weight became frightening. The patient herself knew that now, only with great difficulty, could she climb back up again the road to health.

In August, they took her to the country, to the family home at Palissy. She suffered at this time from continual vomiting and was unable to take the least bit of food. Her heart was very bad, her pulse frighteningly rapid. Her family feared that the end was near.

She had gone to Palissy on August 6. The week that followed was a terrible one for her. She weighed, at that time, just seventy pounds. On August 11, Dr. Pamart, summoned from Sidi-bel-Abbés nearby, gave his opinion that the patient could not be saved. In the opinion of three physicians, Dr. Vincent among them, her death could be expected at any moment.

Then came the great day of August 15—the feast of the Assumption and the date when, usually, the Oran Pilgrimage was at Lourdes, also her own birthday. This being wartime, the journey was impossible, and the Oran pilgrims had to content themselves with prayers and supplications to Our Lady of Lourdes from a distance. They directed their prayers, especially that year, in behalf of Mlle. Clauzel, their beloved President and leader, who as everyone knew was at death's door.

A Novena on that day was being made to the Blessed Virgin. The Bishop at Oran and the Abbé Capparos at Santa Cruz were to say a Mass for her. To join with their prayers—though again more for France and for Lourdes than for her own cure—Mlle. Clauzel asked to be taken to Mass at the Palissy village church.

"I thought," she said, "that this Mass would surely be my last, and that very soon I should be leaving everything."

Her family considered her going to Mass absolute madness, for one in her condition. "But, poor girl, it is probably the last thing we can ever do for her," said her sister, weeping. "Let her go." They decided to carry her to the church on a stretcher.

"It was I who helped carry the stretcher," put in young Dr. Zimmerman. "I was a young medical student in the neighborhood at that time. Her brother and I carried her from her home to the church. She weighed almost nothing. We set her down in a corner of the church where we could keep an eye on her."

Some Italian war prisoners had been allowed to come to Mass that morning. The church was full. The Mass lasted an hour and a half—a long time for one in Mlle. Clauzel's condition. "At one point," said Dr. Zimmerman, "she showed signs of agitation. We were anxious, naturally, thinking she had been tired out by the ceremony. In reality, it was the cure which she felt —without daring to believe it."

"Suddenly, in the midst of the ceremony," said Mlle. Clauzel, "I had a sense of profound well-being—not of agitation, but of a wonderful force acting within me, renewing my entire self. I knew that I was cured." She received the Communion. "I wanted to get up at once, and go to the altar, but I remained on my stretcher till the church was cleared. I didn't want to make a scene or create a disturbance of any kind while the war prisoners were there. Later, when they had left, I told my brother what had happened.

"I am cured, I tell you—cured! Help me up."

He thought it was some temporary exaltation—begged her to be prudent and let him carry her home.

"But she insisted," said Dr. Zimmerman, and he and her brother helped her from the stretcher.

"Let me go now," she said calmly. "I can walk."

"And—she walked!" said the young doctor. "She who had not set foot on the floor for three years!"

She walked to the altar and offered her thanksgiving. "It seemed to me," she said, "that I *flew*—that my feet did not touch the ground."

She went home, dressed herself, ate lunch with the family. And what a lunch! Hors d'oeuvres, ham, *pâté*, vegetables, three cutlets, and a slice of cake—she who had hardly eaten anything for months—had not even lifted her head. It had caused her the most cruel agony just to have the nurse help her into a fresh nightgown. She suffered so much that they would wash one side of her face one day, the other the next day.

Now, when they told her doctor she was cured, that she was actually walking, he said: "Yes, but can she raise her head? I'll believe it when I see her raise her head!" Even in the days when she had been able to walk, at the beginning of her illness, she had carried her head downward because of the terrible pain it caused her to raise it.

The parish priest, Father Capparos, now took up the tale. "Never will I forget that Sunday. We had all been praying for her. There was a special Mass at Santa Cruz too, that day. I had just got back home and was sitting down to luncheon. Suddenly, a telephone call. 'Mademoiselle Clauzel is cured! Do you hear, Father? Mademoiselle Clauzel is cured!'" He couldn't believe it. But he notified the Bishop, as was his duty.

"Get a report from Dr. Maurin," said the Bishop. "See what he has to say."

They got the report—also reports from Dr. Pamart and Dr. Porot, other specialists who had been in attendance. Reports, X-rays, the pieces of bone that had been removed from the spine—all were collected, and eventually sent to Lourdes.

The cure was steadily maintained. Mlle. Clauzel gained weight—three pounds a week, until she reached 116 pounds. Her strength returned rapidly. Her energy and the way she moved about astonished her family, who had watched her dying for many months. Ten months after her cure, during a long procession of the *Fête-Dieu*, she carried the heavy banner of the Children of Mary. On August 15, 1944, one year after her cure, she herself carried a stretcher—one of those which supported a large statue of the Virgin.

"No work frightens her," said Dr. Vincent. "Every morning she helps at one of the big Oranian clinics. She has twice given her blood for urgent transfusions. No, there can be no doubt of the permanency of this cure!"

"And now to the official medical record," said Dr. Leuret,

producing a thick dossier. "Mademoiselle Clauzel presented herself at the Medical Bureau of Lourdes on April 19, 1945—her first opportunity after wartime obstacles. Testimonies of several witnesses, besides her own, established the facts of the illness and the cure. A full report from Dr. Maurin was read, describing the illness and the present excellent state of his former patient. X-rays and 'parrots' beaks' were examined, following upon a lengthy examination of the patient herself. Her spine, and all the organs that had been affected, were found to be in healthy and normal condition."

At a second examination, held December 12, 1945, further documentation from Dr. Maurin, and new X-rays of the vertebral column were studied. The twelve doctors present closed their report with the following statement: "We note the complete functional cure of Mlle. Clauzel, maintained for two years without relapse; it has produced in this one-time invalid a renewal of her being which makes her appear twenty years younger."

The Canonical Commission later appointed to study this cure called attention to the various extraordinary characteristics which placed it above and beyond the laws of nature: (1.) Absence of special medication which might explain the cure. (2.) Instantaneousness of the cure. (3.) Absence of all convalescence. Mlle. Clauzel, who on the morning of August 15 was still in a desperate condition, on the evening of that day and during the following days gave the impression of being a person in perfect health. Her diet, following her inability to tolerate food of any kind, gave proof of the perfect cure of the functional malady of the organs which at that time were seriously affected —especially the stomach and the liver.

This, however (the Commission stated) cannot be called a mere "functional" cure. It must be emphasized that the illness from which Mlle. Clauzel suffered was *an organic illness*—rheumatic spondylitis with compression of the spinal roots, which, like all organic illness, has as a consequence functional troubles more or less serious—very serious in this case, since they brought the invalid to the edge of the grave. The cure of these functional troubles before the cure of the organic cause (vertebral deformation, osteophytes) which produced them, makes the case all the more remarkable.

The most impressive evidence, however, is still to be found in those two photographs—"Before and After." When she went to Mass that August morning, she weighed 71 pounds; at the Bureau the day I saw her, 142.

"And you have never suffered since?" asked Dr. Leuret.

"Never! My health has been perfect—never an ache or a pain since that wonderful moment ten years ago today. There was no delay—no convalescence—nothing! In that instant I was well, and have been every minute of my life since."

Since 1945, at the end of the war, Mlle. Clauzel has come to Lourdes every year. It is she who helps Father Capparos to organize the Oran Pilgrimage—nine hundred pilgrims, many sick patients, brancardiers, nurses, doctors, and priests. She begins in February to get ready for the Pilgrimage in summer: rooms, transportation, all the details. At home she fills a very demanding post in a local clinic. A happy, healthy woman—the picture of good nature and well-being. As usual, with *miraculées* —no pretense, no pride or vainglory. Simplicity, humility, naturalness.

"What did you think," I asked her, "that first minute when it happened—when you *knew* you were cured? What was the first thing that came into your mind?"

Mlle. Clauzel gave her rich, hearty laugh. "Oh, madame, you are going to be disappointed! Nothing seraphic or uplifting. I thought, So! So I have to go on working! I can't have that good rest in heaven I was hoping for!"

Mlle. Clauzel, among those who know her and see her often, has a reputation for great good sense, good judgment, solid character—the very opposite of a neurotic or hysterical temperament. Far from self-suggesting or anticipating a cure, she had gone to Mass that morning expecting only death, and that this was to be her last attendance in any church. Suddenly she gets up, goes to the altar, and walks about the rest of the day, eats and acts like a normal person.

How explain that sudden energy and suppleness of limbs? An hour before, and for many months, she was unable to stand, or to lie in any but one position. How explain eating that meal, which should have "finished" a person so long condemned to fasting? All the digestive troubles from which Mlle. Clauzel suffered, and all the pain that she had endured, disappeared at the same time and with the same suddenness. She led henceforth the life of a well and active woman.

The Catholic Church considered that the circumstances surrounding this cure left no doubt as to the cause. In an Episcopal Proclamation made at Oran, March 18, 1948, the Bishop of Oran declared:

"We judge that in view of all the circumstances this healing is miraculous and must be attributed to a special intervention of God through the intercession of Notre Dame de Lourdes." (Signed, Bertrand Lacaste, Bishop of Oran.)

⋙ *Certainly no one would call* Colonel Pellegrin hysterical or easily suggestible. Solid, substantial soldier, fifty-one years old, veteran of many military campaigns in Africa and Indo-China as well as World Wars I and II, he was never wounded, never sick a day in his life until this illness that struck him down.*

At home in Toulon, all of a sudden one day (December 19, 1948) he felt severe pain in his right side, under the rib cage. A few weeks later, he entered the Maritime Hospital at Toulon. The doctors at first thought he might have a bit of pleurisy; they made various punctures. No improvement—in fact, the pain grew worse. Eventually the attending physician, Dr. Pierre, operated on a red spot in the painful area, "to find out what

* *Colonel Paul Pellegrin, chronic fistula resulting from abscess of the liver, cured at Lourdes, October 3, 1950.*

was going on." The wound did not heal. The patient had considerable fever, and increasing discharge from the wound, which finally became purulent. Diagnosis: abscess of the liver, with chronic fistula.

Colonel Pellegrin was in bed an entire year. Never ill before, he took it hard. He suffered constantly and ran a high fever. Despite various therapies, the wound refused to heal. It had to be dressed two or three times a day. The patient lost weight, was in a very depleted state and thoroughly discouraged.

"Lying in bed—drinking slops like an old woman!" said he disgustedly.

"He had always been so strong—so healthy," said Madame Pellegrin, when they were telling me the story at Lourdes last summer—"and then, just a shadow!"

"How did you happen to go to Lourdes?" I asked him. "What gave you the idea?"

"I was always a believer. All my family were believers—practicing Christians. But it was my own idea, going to Lourdes. I must admit that it came partly from an experience with our eldest child, years ago.

"We were living in Damascus at the time. The boy was only five. He was hit by infantile paralysis of the left side—couldn't move either his arm or leg. We were told that this would probably be for life and would get worse instead of better. My wife begged the Sisters at Damascus to make a Novena to Notre Dame de Lourdes for the boy. On the last day of the Novena the child moved his arm. You may imagine our delight. Gradually the use of both arm and leg returned. While the condition is not absolutely perfect, you would have to know the young man very well and look at him very closely to discover any imperfection.

"So," continued the Colonel, "when my own illness persisted in such a discouraging fashion, and remembering what had happened with the boy, I thought: well, I will go to Lourdes and pray for my cure. Maybe Our Lady will take pity on me.

"We arrived at Lourdes on the second of October. The first day, nothing happened. On the third of October I went to the piscine for my second bath. Then something extraordinary occurred."

His wound was still being dressed several times a day and was discharging abundantly. When he got back to the hotel after this second bath in Lourdes water, he told his wife: "You had better put a new dressing on the wound—they took everything off at the piscine."

He took off his coat and shirt. His wife came with the bandages. Then, when she saw the wound, she cried, "But it's *closed!* Paul! You've been *cured!*"

"I am not ashamed to tell you, madame, we threw our arms around each other and wept!"

"He had been ill for so long," his wife put in. "If you had seen him when he came to Lourdes—so thin and weak! He weighed only a hundred pounds. Now he weighs one hundred and forty."

They had made no great fuss about the matter—no sensational disclosures. They went home quietly. There, the Colonel showed himself to his own Dr. Pierre. The doctor gave a long whistle of astonishment when he saw the wound.

"Well!" he said. "Our Lady of Lourdes did better by you than your doctors did. You don't need dressings any more."

He'd been ill for so long, at first he couldn't believe it. When the skin grew over the wound and formed a permanent scar, he saw that it was truly a genuine cure.

He presented himself at the Medical Bureau (October, 1951) after the regulation interval of a year had gone by, bringing his medical reports—X-rays, and certificates from his doctors and from the hospitals and laboratories that had served him: reports from Dr. Paul Berny, Dr. Roger Bureau, and Dr. Charles Arnoux, in addition to those by Dr. Pierre; thirty pages of hospital charts, the fever charts especially being impressive. High fever had been one of his greatest difficulties.

The Medical Bureau report on the case reads:

Pellegrin, Paul. Chronic fistula since 1949. Cured October 3, 1950. Seen first at Bureau October 10, 1951. At the time of his cure, the patient had been going three times a week to the hospital for dressings, the flow of pus being abundant and resisting all therapies. In October, 1950, he departed for Lourdes, with his fistula continuing very active.

The patient, after his second bath at the piscine, observed the complete disappearance of the fistula which had given a purulent discharge sufficiently abundant to necessitate dressings two and sometimes three a day. He did not at first feel sure of a cure. But the nature of the scar and the continued absence of drainage led him to present himself at the Medical Bureau.

The physicians then present examined the scar, which was about three inches long, supple to the touch, and entirely painless, and noted that for one year it had remained healed. The patient was in excellent health. He was requested to return for further examination the following year. At the second inquiry (October 8, 1952) the twenty-nine doctors present considered that "while the cause of this fistula and the abscess related to it are unprecise, the practically instantaneous closing of a suppurating fistula which had lasted eighteen months, makes the case deserving of being retained as an extraordinary occurrence."

The Medical Commission, after a full investigation, confirmed the findings, and declared itself "of opinion that the case should be submitted to Ecclesiastical authority." On December 7, 1953, the Archbishop of Toulon proclaimed it a Miraculous Cure.

Colonel Pellegrin comes to Lourdes every year; serves as one of the *commissionaires* from Toulon, who keep order, direct the crowds, assist the brancardiers in policing the Processions, and help bathe people at the piscine.

"Naturally everyone who has been cured wants to be of some service to Lourdes," says the Colonel.

I used to see him running up and down the Esplanade carrying chairs and benches, helping with the sick, doing all sorts of odd jobs. One would never know he was top brass, with a chestful of decorations. A solid, well-set-up, splendid specimen of a man—the picture of health; fresh-faced, ruddy, quiet, friendly. Modest, like all the Cures. He has never known a day's illness since his miracle.

21

Cures of Children

Particularly appealing are the cures of children, and particularly interesting, since many of them are too young to be influenced either by religious faith or by suggestion—the favorite explanation by skeptics regarding Lourdes cures. A long list of children's cures is found in Lourdes records. One of the best known in recent years is that of Gerard Baillie.*

Gerard, a boy of eight, lived at the Institute for Blind Children at Arras, in the north of France. He had not had the use of his eyes since the age of two, and recognized people only by their voices. It was pitiful to see him, an energetic, otherwise normal child, groping his way about like a hesitating little old man, staring at his parents and friends with blank unseeing eyes.

He had lost his sight after an operation; a degeneration of the inner tunics of the eye had progressed until the optic nerves in both eyes were completely atrophied. This, as every doctor knows, means blindness.

His parents brought him to the institution at Arras with the following certificate from Dr. Biziaut, an oculist of Dunkerque: "Double optic atrophy. Blindness—*incurable*." (Underlined by Dr. Biziaut.)

Another physician, Dr. Viton of Arras, examined the boy

* *Gerard Baillie, chorioretinitis (bilateral) and double optic atrophy—an "incurable" disease—cured at Lourdes, September 27, 1947.*

and declared on January 26, 1945: "I, the undersigned, certify that I have today examined Gerard Baillie, aged seven and a half years. He is afflicted with bilateral chorioretinitis, double optic atrophy; blindness—incurable."

For five years Gerard had crept about among the other sightless children at the Arras Institute—feeling his way, fumbling, hesitating, often falling. His mother was heartbroken. She prayed earnestly and constantly that he "might be restored to a normal life." We must be careful what we pray for. Sometimes we are taken precisely at our word.

In September, 1947, a month after Dr. Biziaut had again pronounced the case incurable, his mother brought Gerard to Lourdes, as a member of their diocesan pilgrimage. Nothing happened at the first bath, or at the Procession. But the day after their arrival, while they were walking down the path of the Way of the Cross, all at once the child began to pick up pieces of wood from the ground and to offer them to his mother. Looking up into her face, he cried delightedly, "Oh mamma, how beautiful you are!"

The mother, completely overcome, rushed him back to the hostel. The next day, after his second bath at the piscine, she noticed that he really did see better. He remarked upon the curtains at the baths which, the day before, he had not seen at all.

That same day, September 27, she took him to be examined at the Medical Bureau. The seven doctors present recorded the case as follows:

The child has an external strabismus (squint) in the left eye. He sees two fingers at a distance of one meter (slightly over a yard), does not see at two meters. He shows a slight vertical nystagmus (oscillation of the eyeballs) more accentuated when tired. He reacts weakly to light. In walking around the room he guided himself by the edge of the table and ran against the chairs, which indicates a considerable limitation in the visual field. The next day, September 28, 1947, seen at the Hospital of the Sept Douleurs, he ran around the room without bumping into the beds, went into the hallway, ran to the elevator, could tell whether it was going up or coming down, and saw the elevator button. He recognized different colors and several objects near at hand.

They took him to an oculist at Tarbes—Dr. Camps, graduate of the National School of Ophthalmology of the Quinze-Vingts, Paris. He examined the boy at length, and declared: "This child has a bilateral chorioretinitis, with double optic atrophy. He cannot—or should not—see." Yet he saw—not very well, it is true; nevertheless he saw.

Coming back in the car on the road to Lourdes, he saw the mountains with a fresh snowfall on the peaks, and described their beauty. He saw other cars along the road, described their different stylings, and kept urging, "Let's pass them!"

The Bureau appointed two physicians in the boy's neighborhood—Drs. Domesant of Dunkerque and Dhellmes of Lille—to continue the study of the case and to make a report at the end of a year.

Naturally Gerard left the Institute for Blind Children, and began attending a boy's school at Dunkerque, where he proceeded to make an excellent record. He went to school alone, crossing several big highways at the busiest hours of the day. The tremendous changes that had come about for him can best be shown by two letters.

On September 4, 1948, Dr. Leuret, President of the Medical Bureau of Lourdes, wrote to the Directress of the Institute for Blind Children at Arras, asking various questions regarding Gerard's vision before and after his coming to Lourdes:

In particular, could he get about alone? Could he see an object at some distance away? What was the exact diagnosis for which he was being treated at your institute? During the two and a half years that he spent there was he examined by ophthalmologists— by whom and how many times? When he came back from Lourdes did you find a change in his vision? Did you make any tests to determine whether he could see clearly? Who made the decision that he should leave the Institute?

The reply from Sister Agnes, Directress of the Institute—a very fine letter—is given here only in part:

We didn't see Gerard immediately before his departure for Lourdes in September, 1947, because he was on vacation with his family. But when he left us in July he was what he had always been during his stay here: a blind person.

He was absolutely incapable of going about alone. When he came and went, indoors, he bumped into obstacles. No, he was not capable of seeing an object at any distance. He could not take a paper bag of candy offered to him, because he did not *see* it. (And if a child could see anything, he could certainly see candy!) On one occasion a whole roomful of deaf children was moved to compassion when he tried to find his shoes under his bed—his hesitation, his searching with both hands, his big eyes raised and fixed in the *opposite* direction.

When he returned from Lourdes, however, there could be no doubt in our minds: Gerard was no longer the little blind boy who had left us in July. He had regained his sight. He ran about the house freely, from one room to another, remarking on the dimensions of the apartment, making a world of discoveries, admiring the beauty of the little girls' courtyard which he had crossed so many times before without seeing anything.

We put him through a number of tests: to recognize objects by vision alone, without touching them: spectacles, thimble, scissors, penknife, ribbons, watch (of which we changed the hands at his direction); to locate a person in an unfamiliar room, moving from one area to another; to enumerate what he saw from a window, etc.

There is also the definite fact that the child is able to follow a normal school curriculum. This certainly would have been quite impossible last July.

She stated further that she hadn't the diagnosis of the ailment for which the boy was sent to the Institute; that during his stay there he was seen by no ophthalmologists at the Institute. His parents took him to Dr. Biziaut at Dunkerque, she said, referring to Dr. Biziaut's certificate which she enclosed with her reply.

In a later account, Sister Agnes related more fully the story of Gerard's visit to the Institute after his return from Lourdes:

Gerard arrived with his mother. When I came into the parlor he ran and threw his arms around my neck without a moment's hesitation, and kissed me. Then he looked at me—at my white headdress which he had never seen, touched the tip of my nose with an affectionate little gesture, then hugged me again.

To express in words anything so wonderful as the recovery of sight is impossible for him—being so young in years and younger still in experience. He expresses it as best he can. When, one by one, the Sisters come in, he gives their names as they greet him. He knew them all by their voices, though he had never seen them. "Ah," he said to one of them, "you have spectacles. I never knew you wore spectacles!"

His comrades gather round him. He wanted to embrace them all. Some of them blushed for joy, others smiled, some wept. Nothing so touching as those tears in those unseeing eyes.

So many questions. "So you really *see*, Gerard? What is it like—to see?" Evidently it is too difficult for him to put into words. This meeting of the children with their little "miraculous" friend is filled with emotion, both for them and for the onlookers.

A letter from another teacher, one year after his cure, states: "I have had the pleasure of having Gerard Baillie among my pupils during this entire school year of 1948–49. He is a good scholar and a good friend, and attends his classes regularly."

These letters and accounts from personal friends, written in their own hand, seem to me almost as important as the medical documents.

On July 14, 1948, Gerard was examined for the second time at the Medical Bureau. Dr. Smith, an oculist of Glasgow, made the examination. He repeated the diagnosis of Dr. Camps: "This child has chorioretinitis with double optic atrophy. He ought not to see." But, like Madame Biré, he saw.

The doctors, in their record of the second examination, noted:

The boy keeps up with his classes normally. He goes everywhere by himself. He goes unaccompanied from his home to the school—though this involves half an hour's walk and he has to cross four big avenues where numerous cars pass. It is very evident that Gerard sees. At a distance, and without touching them, he can name various objects placed on a desk: a watch, a fountain pen, a bell, a pencil, a crucifix, etc. He copied letters on a white page, he did small sums in arithmetic, he could see the hands of a watch and the Red Cross insignia of the Lourdes physicians. He could tell colors.

The ophthalmological examination shows that pupillary reactions to light are normal. He counts fingers twenty-five centimeters (about eight feet) away. The left eye is crossed. The back of the eye shows the papillae atrophied at both left and right, though incompletely. (Whereas in 1947 atrophy was complete.) Degeneration of the retina and of the choroid (middle membrane), with a little pigmentary degeneration.

Dr. Leuret and seven other physicians signed the statement. The case was sent on to the Medical Commission which reported on it at its session in Paris on April 1, 1949: "The case of a child afflicted with blindness, with choroiditis, atrophy and discoloration of the papillae. He was cured along the Chemin du Croix in 1947. The examination shows that this child, who was completely blind, now possesses sufficient vision, with re-colored papillae."

A year later, the Medical Commission pronounced the cure "inexplicable under natural law" and voted unanimously to recommend its being referred to a Canonical Commission.

The Canonical Commission refused to consider it a miracle because it was not instantaneous and because vision was still not perfect, though sufficient for the boy to lead a normal life. (Which was what his mother had prayed for—*and all she had asked.*)

However, the doctors of the Medical Bureau and of the Medical Commission are firmly of the opinion that the cure of Gerard Baillie is "beyond the laws of nature" and may therefore rationally be considered to have taken place under supernatural influence.

"His infirmity," they declared, "was technically incurable. Yet at Lourdes, in a few hours, and with no treatment whatsoever, *he saw.*" One doctor testified that in his entire experience as an eye specialist he had never known of a case like

it: the recovery of vision and re-coloring of the papillae following two years' atrophy of the optic nerve.

The cure has been in effect now for six years, and Gerard
comes to Lourdes every year with his North-of-France Pilgrimage. He is now a nice-looking boy of fifteen, wears glasses
—his vision is 6–10—which he says is a whole lot better than
being blind. According to him and his mother, Our Lady of
Lourdes certainly did perform a miracle.

❧ *Still more dramatic was the cure* of Francis Pascal,* whom I
recently visited at his own home.

Francis lives at Beaucaire, close to Avignon and the famous
Palace of the Popes. He was born October 3, 1934, and was a
happy, normal child until December, 1937, when he became
seriously ill.

He was seized with a high fever. Water streamed from his
eyes, which became acutely sensitive to light. A general stiffness set in throughout his body, and he was subject to constant
vomiting. Signs of meningitis increased. His temperature went
up to 104 degrees.

Finally the supreme blow: absolute blindness and complete
paralysis of both arms and legs.

The child's parents nearly went out of their minds. They
were poor people, small winegrowers in their region—but they
did everything they could for him. They had him examined by
five doctors—Dr. Darde of Beaucaire, Julian of Tarascon, Barre
of Avignon, Dufoix fils of Nîmes, Polge, an oculist at Arles
(all nearby cities). He was under Dr. Darde's constant care.
In March, 1938, a lumbar puncture was made in the spine,
and an analysis of the spinal fluid at the laboratory of Dr.
Lesbros in Avignon confirmed the diagnosis of meningitis.

In May, Dr. Polge wrote: "Following upon a meningitis the

* *Francis Pascal, paralysis and complete blindness following upon
infectious meningitis, cured at Lourdes, August 31, 1938.*

child Pascal was brought to me. He is paralyzed and no longer sees. The ophthalmological examination on the third of May shows: the pupils react very little to the light; a light passed before the eyes was never followed, nor any other object presented. At the back of the eyes, the veins congested and there is a certain degree of optic pallor. Prognosis: '*Very reserved.*'"

The doctors in charge saw the child regularly until June, 1938. By this time the paralysis of the arms and legs was complete; sight nil.

In June, Dr. Darde considered the case hopeless, and stopped all treatment. The parents were desperate. Every possible therapy had been tried. As a last hope, they decided to take Francis to Lourdes, with the Pilgrimage of Aix-en-Provence. In the train, the blind child, completely helpless in his little carriage, drew the sympathy of everyone.

To get him admitted to the pilgrimage, Dr. Darde, on July 19, made out the following certificate: "I, the undersigned, declare that Francis Pascal, aged four years, has been under my care for residuals of meningitis—with complete paralysis of the lower limbs. The lesions noted above have not changed during four months, and appear not to have been affected in any way by treatment." (Signed, Dr. Darde.)

Dr. Roman added to this report: "As physician on the Pilgrimage train, I can confirm the certificate of my confrere of Beaucaire. The child traveled in a recumbent position. He saw neither light nor objects presented to him."

The Pilgrimage of Aix arrived at Lourdes on August 23. Francis was utterly helpless at the time. At the Grotto, his mother prayed the Blessed Virgin to "heal him or let him die!" She could not bear to have him go on living in his present condition.

She carried him to the piscine. He was plunged into the water. The child cried out. His mother thought he had been seized with a convulsion. She kept hoping and praying.

"I had faith, madame—I had faith!"

On August 26, he was brought again to the bath. The water had no apparent effect. But a few minutes later something extraordinary happened. The mother was carrying him across the Esplanade, back to the Hospital. Suddenly the child spoke.

"Mama, Mama—look! The lady wheeling the little carriage— it's a tricycle. Mama, look—isn't it pretty?" He moved a finger, pointing toward a nurse who was wheeling a tricycle across the Square.

His mother raced with him back to the Hospital, half fainting with excitement. He *saw!* He moved his finger!

From this moment his sight came back—he became interested in objects around him. Before he left Lourdes, he began to move the arms and legs hitherto paralyzed. After his return to Beaucaire he began to walk—"teetering a bit at first," his mother said, "but after a little, quite normally."

On August 28, Dr. Darde saw the boy again, to his utter amazement, *walking*. The doctor later wrote the following report to the Medical Bureau:

I, the undersigned, declare that I have had under my care, from December 18, 1937, to June 14, 1938, the young Francis Pascal, aged four years. This child, who was seen in consultation with Drs. Julian of Tarascon, Barre of Avignon, Dufoix fils of Nîmes, Polge of Arles, has been suffering from lymphocytic meningitis (analysis by Dr. Lesbros of Avignon). At the end of July the patient was paralyzed in all four members. Visual acuity was nil. The child did not perceive even light and could not distinguish between day and night. An examination by Dr. Polge in May, 1938, was completely unfavorable.

About August 20, this child was to be taken to Lourdes with the Aix Pilgrimage. I was called to re-examine him. The condition recorded in June remained exactly the same: paralysis of the four limbs, vision nil. Returning from Lourdes (August 28), Madame Pascal brought the child to me, leading him by the hand. *He was walking!* I recorded the disappearance of the paralysis and the return of vision. The gait was normal except for a slight degree of unsteadiness.

From that date the improvement has been maintained. This new condition came about after immersion in the piscine at Lourdes. Medically, one cannot explain such a result. (Signed, Dr. Darde, November 9, 1938.)

Dr. Julian sent a similar certificate, adding that the condition of the child before going to Lourdes had been extremely serious.

Because of the war, Francis' case could not be brought before the Medical Bureau until 1946—at which time he was described by the doctors as a "sturdy boy, tall and well-muscled, who rides a bicycle and goes to his classes at school in normal fashion."

From the examination of the documents submitted to us (the Bureau report continues), it is evident that the boy suffered from an organic illness of infectious origin, involving the meninges and the spinal cord. The ocular lesions and the spinal-fluid analysis permit us to confirm the organic nature of the disease. The replies to the official five questions regarding a cure are as follows:

1. The illness certainly existed. It consisted of meningomyelitis with choked disk, flaccid paralysis of the lower limbs and stiffness of the upper limbs. Cerebellar disturbance.
2. There was abrupt cessation of symptoms at a time when the development of the malady left no hope of a tendency toward improvement. The child could distinguish a tricycle the day of his second bath, and on return home he walked.
3. There has been a definite cure, confirmed by the complete recovery of vision, of the ability to walk, and of all other functions.
4. No question of delay regarding a conclusion on this cure. It dates from ten years ago.
5. No explanation can be given medically for the instantaneous disappearance of the malady and its symptoms.

There follow the signatures of eleven physicians and finally that of Dr. Auguste Vallet, President of the Medical Bureau at that time. The document is dated October 2, 1946.

Further, in a postscript: "Patient re-examined in 1947. This child is in perfect health. Normal vision. Walk normal. Reflexes normal." (Signed, Dr. François Leuret, President [1947] of the Medical Bureau of Lourdes.)

The patient has been seen several times since then. The report is always the same. Francis comes each year to Lourdes on a pilgrimage of gratitude, serves as stretcher-bearer, and is seen regularly at the Bureau. He is now a fine, healthy boy of nineteen, with perfect eyesight, perfect use of his once paralyzed limbs.

"He can read until midnight, and be on the run for hours!" says his mother. "On his feet all day at Beaucaire with the vines, or carrying the stretchers all day at Lourdes—it's all one to Francis. One would never know he'd been sick a day of his life!"

Last October, I paid him a visit in his own home.

It was a blustery autumn afternoon, pouring rain. I drove the fifteen miles from Avignon to Beaucaire—a little town of 10,000 population. At the house in the Rue Camille Desmoulins they were waiting for me—smiling faces, kindliness, hospitality: Francis, his father and mother, his aunt, and his little brother who had just come home in his raincoat, dripping, from school.

The mother had a big pot of coffee ready and we sat drinking it in the living room and talking and laughing, while the rain streamed down the windowpane.

"What's it like, for a young man who has been cured at Lourdes, in this day and age?" I asked Francis. "Your friends— do they tease you? Do they make it difficult?"

"Not much. Once in a while, just one or two, you know."

"And these young people—do they believe in Lourdes and the miracles?"

"Most of them do. Even the ones who say they don't, do— really. People in a little town like this believe in them more than people in cities," said Francis. "Maybe that's why God favors them with more miracles."

"The people around here have been very good to Francis," said his mother. "They always give him a wonderful welcome."

"How could they help it?" asked the aunt. "Lots of them remember what he looked like when he went off to Lourdes—

blind, and stiff as a board, not able to move hand or foot, poor baby!"

"Every year, now, he carries the banner for the Aix pilgrimage," added the father proudly. "Everybody says Francis must be the one to carry the banner!"

"And the girls? Does it make any difference with the young ladies, this being a *miraculé?*"

Francis blushed. "Plenty of time for that," he said.

"He has to begin to earn his living first," said the father; "get himself established."

"What is he going to be?" I wondered if, perhaps, he might enter Religion, like so many of the *miraculés?*

"He is going to be a winegrower, like the rest of the people of his region," said his father. "He prefers the outdoor life."

"But Francis is a great reader," said his mother. "How that boys reads and writes! Many journalists came, after the cure. And Francis has lots of correspondents wanting letters from him, or just his signature."

"Oh, there's not so much of that now," Francis said deprecatingly. An attractive, unassuming boy—well-brought-up; good with his younger brother who obviously worships him. A close, affectionate family circle, pleasant to be with. Much the same atmosphere as in a Pennsylvania farm or a ranch in Texas or Montana.

Similar problems, too. Father Pascal told me they sell their wine for twenty-eight francs a liter. The buyer in town pays a hundred. Many middlemen, slim profits, taxes. Everything is very dear. During the war they had a bad time. Food was very expensive. Were they in occupied territory? Oh yes! Germans were quartered in the house. No, the Germans weren't bad to them—saw them only morning and night, coming and going. . . .

A warm, friendly afternoon, long to be remembered: the cozy little room, the comfortable armchairs, Aunt Melanie's luscious tartlets, the hot strong coffee, the farm animals close by. . . .

"We are peasants, madame," Father Pascal said again proudly.

They take their boy's cure simply, deeply grateful, but with no unction or sanctimony.

I was sorry to have to leave them—waving to me from the doorway. Francis took me under a big umbrella to the car.

"Come back again, madame! Anything we can do for Lourdes, you know—well, it's never enough."

His is one of the famous cures—recognized by the Medical Commission and by the Church.

The first medical examination took place at Lourdes on October 2, 1946, with eleven physicians present; the second was in July, 1947, when fifteen physicians confirmed the original conclusion. Again, on September 1, 1948, the case was once more discussed with twenty doctors approving the conclusions previously reached, and declaring that "the cure of Francis Pascal, humanly inexplicable and in effect for ten years, is beyond the realm of natural law."

The Canonical Commission appointed to investigate the case on behalf of the Church referred to the abundance of witnesses (five doctors who attended the child) and "the exceptional number of proofs attesting the existence of the illness and its absolute cure, humanly inexplicable."

The Commission stressed that "it was a serious illness, organic, refractory to all treatment, considered a hopeless case. The cure—which came suddenly, after a second bath in the piscine of Lourdes—was perfect, and still is, after ten years, and cannot be attributed to any natural cause."

The Church, in distinguishing between this cure and that of Gerard Baillie,* declared that the Pascal cure was instantaneous and perfect, and therefore pronounced it a Miraculous

---

* It is interesting to compare these two cases (Baillie and Pascal) which illustrate the severe requirements of the Church in proclaiming a miracle.

Cure. On May 31, 1949, the Archbishop of Aix-en-Provence issued the following Proclamation:

In view of the various medical certificates appearing in the dossier, especially those of Dr. Darde, dated July 19, 1938, November 9, 1938, June 5, 1939; and that of Dr. Julian, dated December 6, 1938:

In view of the verbatim reports of the Medical Bureau of Lourdes, dated October 2, 1946 and September 1, 1948:

In view of the reports of the Canonical Commission constituted by us under date of December 10 and 17, 1948:

The Holy Name of God being invoked: by virtue of the authority conferred upon us by the Holy Council of Trent, and while subordinating our decision to the authority of the Sovereign Pontiff:

We judge and declare that the cure of Francis Pascal, which occurred at Lourdes on August 26, 1938, is miraculous and must be attributed to a special intervention of the Most Blessed Virgin Mary Immaculate, Mother of God.

Proclaimed at Aix, May 31, 1949, on the fete of the Most Blessed Virgin Mary Mediatrix of all grace.

Charles,
Archbishop of Aix, Arles and Embrun

◆§ *From Avignon to Montmarte* is a long jump—but the two young men were not so different; not in the essentials, anyhow.

I came upon the case of Yves Joucan * while prowling through Lourdes histories, and pounced on it; the cure of a Parisian is so unusual, but there it was: "Yves Joucan, seven years old. Pott's Disease, cervical abscessed. Cured at the National Pilgrimage of 1933." I carefully noted the address.

It would be amazing if a family were still living in the same place after twenty years, in Paris or anywhere, these days. But there they were, the Joucan family—still living in the same pleasant little apartment in the same modest street not far from

---

* *Yves Joucan, Pott's Disease, cervical, abscessed, cured at Lourdes, August, 1933.*

the Place Clichy. Madame Joucan, an attractive, slender woman with dark eyes, was quite willing to tell me about her son's cure. She got out some pictures of the pathetic little boy in his plaster cast.

"He was just seven when he was taken ill, madame. Until that time he had always been perfectly well. First he had a growth behind the ear which soon became the size of an egg. Our family doctor, Dr. Cauhapé, had us take him to a specialist, who made an incision. Other doctors later said this should never have been done.

"The child did not improve; on the contrary, he rapidly grew worse. His head began to bend to the side. I would say to him, twenty times a day, 'Lift your head, dear!' He would lift it, but in five minutes it would drop back again. He had no appetite—he became very thin and weak. Of course my husband and I were frantic with anxiety. We had no money to spend for expensive treatments. Were we really going to lose our boy?

"We took him to the clinic at the hospital. And there the terrible truth came out. X-rays showed tuberculosis of the spine—several bones in the neck had already degenerated. They put him in a plaster cast. They told us he had Pott's Disease. He might be in the cast for two or three years—or he might become completely paralyzed.

"Well, madame, you may imagine! Our only child—our son! The doctors promised absolutely nothing, simply looked embarrassed and kept repeating: 'It is very serious, madame—we regret to say, *very* serious.'

"We decided to take him to Lourdes. One of the Sisters of the Assumption made out the papers and got him admitted to the National Pilgrimage in August.

"The day after we arrived at Lourdes he was bathed at the piscine, his plaster cast and all, but only up to the waist. Nothing happened. But after the Procession that day, back at the hostel, he began to move around, said he felt well, wanted to play, to eat, doing things he hadn't done for months! He began to move about, inside his cast. Well, you may imagine—we were in heaven right then, his father and I!

"We went home. The bones and tissues resumed their normal place. We had another X-ray made. Everything normal! The boy has been gloriously well from that day to this. What can we say—except eternal thanksgiving to Notre Dame de Lourdes? And the little Bernadette too—I have always felt that she had something to do with it."

On February 4, 1934, Dr. Cauhapé—intern of the Departmental Hospital of the Seine—sent the following certificate to the Medical Bureau at Lourdes:

I, the undersigned, Dr. Cauhapé, certify that I examined the child Yves Joucan twice during June, 1933, for localized pain behind the ear, and sent the young patient to Dr. Nectoux, specialist residing at _____. At the time the child departed for Lourdes, the wound was in a suppurating condition and he was in a plaster cast.

I saw the child during the past few days. All lesions have disappeared and an X-ray examination on January 22 shows an entirely normal condition of the vertebral column. (Signed, Dr. Cauhapé, 83 Avenue de Clichy, Paris.)

Another certificate was furnished by the Paris Hospital where the child had been treated:

République Française. Administration Générale de l'Assistance Publique à Paris. Hôpital Bretonne Consultation de Chirurgie—Dr. Leveuf. Dr. Leveuf, extern of the Paris Hospital, certifies that the child Yves Joucan, in July, 1933, had osteitis (inflammation of the bone) of the cervical column, abscessed, as shown by successive X-rays. In December, 1933, the X-rays no longer showed any lesions and the clinical aspect of the child is normal.

Today, twenty years later, Yves Joucan is a vigorous, attractive, healthy young man, working in the electrical services of the Government. He takes part in all kinds of sports—football, swimming, tennis, etc. "He is hardly ever home," said his mother. "Always out with his friends at some game or other, after work."

However, he stayed home on the occasion of my visit, and we spent a very agreeable evening in their cozy little apartment. Madame Joucan's mother was English. She was born a Protestant and became a Catholic when she married. They are devoted to Lourdes—as the families of the Cures always are. They go back every year with the National Pilgrimage.

We went through scrapbooks and albums of photographs showing Yves as a boy, and then as the young man of today: in his bathing suit, or with his tennis racquet, or on his bicycle at the finish of the local bicycle race. The same friendly, simple sort of visit as with the Pascal family. Paris instead of Beaucaire —but the hospitality and kindness just the same.

One of the delightful features of this work was going into French homes, getting in touch with French people again— hearing their stories, sitting with them round the lamp in the evening, listening to music, looking over the old snapshots, talking about similar homes and families in America. International relations would certainly improve if more people, all over the world, could drop in on each other in these little homes of an evening.

UNIQUE IN THE ANNALS OF LOURDES, said the newspaper headlines. THE CURE OF A CHILD WHO WAS AN IDIOT. PARALYZED IN ARMS AND LEGS.*

Today this child is sane and whole. I myself saw him well and happy, running off with his friends to play football.

Guy Leydet was a normal child till the age of five. Then he was stricken with acute meningo-encephalitis—a brain disease that can wreck a nervous system. He came out of it alive, but paralyzed in both arms and legs, and subject to frequent convulsions and epileptic fits. Worst of all, in a state of progressive mental breakdown which ended in complete idiocy.

* *Guy Leydet, infantile encephalopathy, with idiocy, quadriplegic, cured at Lourdes, October 6, 1946.*

"He didn't even recognize us," his mother told me. "He couldn't speak at all; he had lost all his happy little vocabulary that he had before his illness." He could not even call his mother—only uttered guttural sounds like those made by congenital idiots.

He forgot how to eat, and had to be fed, as he no longer was able to carry the food to his mouth. Thus he had degenerated even lower than an animal. He dirtied himself with no consciousness of what he was doing. And this condition had lasted for nearly two years.

His parents all but ruined themselves financially in their effort to cure him. They tried every treatment and therapy that offered the slightest hope—all in vain. The doctors told them it was useless and pronounced the dread word: "Incurable."

"Then (like thousands of others after exhausting all human possibilities)—we thought of Lourdes."

They arrived at Lourdes that bright fall morning with the child still in the same horrible state. How many idiot children have I seen thus arriving!—slobbering mouth, vacant eyes, incessant gibberish cries. Suppose, like many others, he should live like this for years and years!

Numb with anguish, they wheeled him to the piscine. "Notre Dame de Lourdes was our last desperate hope!"

I often think, as I write the stories of these cures, how casually we take them—we who read about them, we who set them down. "Now that was a rather interesting cure," we say; or "Let me tell you about this one—it made quite a stir." Casual, even a bit blasé, sometimes.

If we stop to think about it, any single one of these cures is staggering. Suppose it was your child who had become that slobbering idiot—your mother who had gone stone-blind or had cancer of the face. Suppose it was *you* and your husband or wife who went up to that mysterious fountain, carrying all you hold dear in the world—with all your trembling hopes and fears wrapped in that agonizing little bundle. How do you think *you'd* feel when something happened suddenly such as happened to Guy Leydet? I think the heavens would open, and—believer or unbeliever—you would sing glory to God!

They took him to the piscine. The father waited outside, on his knees, praying with the rest of the crowd. Inside the baths, compassionate nurses dipped the rigid little boy into the water. His mother stood near, fearing another convulsion—ready to grab him when he came out. They handed him back to her.

Then suddenly, sensationally, it happened.

Guy Leydet opened his eyes, looked about him with an *intelligent* glance, reached his arms toward his mother and in a clear, childish voice cried "Mama!" He then began to count his fingers, naming them over, as French children do.

Wild with joy, his mother snatched him up and ran with him out of the piscine to find his father. "He said 'Mama!'" she gasped. "He said 'Mama!'"

The father, longing to believe but skeptical, cautioned her against too much hope. "We have hoped so many times," he reminded, "only to be disappointed."

But in the days that followed they knew that this time it was true. The child's mind was rapidly reawakening. He began to talk. He moved his arms and legs perfectly. They called in their doctor, who gazed in stupefaction at his former patient, admitting he could not understand it at all. "Well—try to re-educate him," he said, still incredulous.

So the happy parents began to teach their boy all over again. It was easy. Within one year he recovered his normal mentality, could read and write and even draw a bit, as well as walk and play vigorously like other children.

On September 26, 1947—one year after his cure—he was examined by forty doctors at the Medical Bureau. Dr. Dailly, a children's specialist of Paris, for two hours put him through all the classic tests by which a physician judges the state of a child's mental development. At the end of his examination, the doctor announced simply: "This child is normal."

The case provoked long and heated discussion at the Medical Bureau. This was not a case of simple mental backwardness, as Dr. Leuret emphasized, but of total idiocy. And of quadriplegic paralysis which had resisted all treatment over a period of many months, and was given up by the attending physicians as definitely incurable. It was this idiot child, who had not spoken for two years, nor shown the least sign of intelligence, nor moved his arms or legs, who on that morning of October 6, in the piscine, suddenly opened his eyes, stretched his hitherto motionless arms toward his mother and said "Mama!" Since that moment, he has been in perfect health and full possession of his faculties. If this was not an instantaneous Lourdes cure, what was it?

The doctors nodded—or shrugged their shoulders, still unconvinced. One major question tantalized them all.

"With what brain does this child think?" Dr. M——— of Bordeaux put it bluntly. "What brain was he using when he stood up and suddenly called his mother and began to count his fingers, after two years of insensibility? Was it with a new brain, was it with a brain partially destroyed after an acute meningo-encephalitis?"

Another said: "Either he must be thinking with his brain such as it was when he was an idiot, and therefore—like Gerard Baillie seeing with eyes that could not see—he was thinking with a brain that could not think; or, he had been given an entirely new brain. In any case, the fact is absolutely contrary to all natural laws."

In the end, the forty doctors at the Bureau unanimously declared that the child had been supernaturally cured. One of the most eminent among them, Professor Lelong of Paris, clinched the matter by declaring finally:

"If there is a single one among you who has ever once in his whole career seen the cure of such a case—a postencephalitic idiot—I will pledge myself never again to sign a Lourdes dossier!"

He had no takers.

I visited Guy Leydet at his home in St. Etienne. He is now a tall, nice-looking lad of fourteen; very good in his classes, especially in English, geography, and history. I saw his notebooks—beautifully kept, almost no mistakes; fine, accurate drawings.

Guy came in from school, rosy-cheeked and the picture of health, dressed in red pull-over and tweed plus-fours, running up five flights of stairs to their apartment, so as to get back down again quickly to play with his pals.

His father is a professor in a local business college. His mother, a charming and very pretty woman, says they want to send the boy to England next year on an exchange basis with an English boy who would come to them. "He is crazy about learning English," she said, laughing, "and doing very well at it. They teach a lot by ear, and with records. He hasn't chosen his career yet, but I rather think it will be teaching."

I went into the details of the case with her, from the very beginning. After agonizing years—"heartrending," she called them—Notre Dame de Lourdes had had compassion on them. All three of them go every year to Lourdes on a pilgrimage of thanksgiving.

"No, the case was not proclaimed a miracle or a formal 'published' cure, because of lack of the necessary medical documents. The doctors who attended the boy before his visit to Lourdes have absolutely refused to submit any records or certificates. 'Lourdes! We're not interested!' is all they will say."

So, while there is ample evidence of the genuineness of the cure—testimony of neighbors, therapists, nurses, attendants at the piscine—it cannot be officially proclaimed.

"What do we care about that?" says the mother. "We have our boy—happy and well. Our *Te Deums* are sung right here at home, every day!"

I discussed this case with the President of the Medical Commission in Paris. He too was very much interested in Guy Leydet. He approved my including the account of his cure in my collection of Lourdes histories.

"It shows," he said, "how strict are the requirements of the doctors of the Medical Bureau and the Commission. It also shows what amazing things can and do happen at Lourdes: cures which cannot be officially and formally recognized but which have transformed the lives of families and brought joy and health where before there was anguish, despair, and only one prospect: death."

22

Celebrated Cures of Women

The young are not the only privileged ones among the cures at Lourdes. The old also are favored by the mysterious power which appears to act sometimes after the Sacred Name is invoked. Witness the cure of Sister Marie-Marguerite.*

Sister Marie-Marguerite, born April 13, 1872, was a nun at the convent of the Poor Clares at Rennes. She did all the shopping, errands, outside interviews, and running about for her Community. She was constantly on her feet.

She began to suffer from recurring heart attacks. Later she had a fall, followed by severe pain in the left kidney. Her condition grew steadily worse until 1936, when Dr. Branchard diagnosed her case as an abscess in the left kidney, inoperable because of the state of the heart.

During the same year, an edema (fluid in the tissues) of the legs also appeared, producing great swelling and discomfort: a condition popularly referred to as dropsy. Despite various treatments, the illness made dangerous progress and in the opinion of the doctors was "galloping" toward a fatal end. Sores on the legs discharged abundantly, and aggravated the Sister's sufferings. The heart crises increased. Staying in bed became impossible, and she had to remain sitting up day and night in an

* *Sister Marie-Marguerite, abscess of left kidney and edema of the legs, cured January 22, 1937, during a Novena to Our Lady of Lourdes.*

armchair. This terrible condition had lasted for months. It could not go on much longer.

On January 20, the entire Community began a Novena to Our Lady of Lourdes to ask for her cure. Prayers were continued in the chapel all day and all night, in perpetual vigil.

"On the morning of January 22," says Sister Marie-Marguerite, "suddenly I had an impulse to go to the altar at the second Mass." Moved by what seemed to her "a superhuman force," and "in spite of atrocious suffering, bathed in a cold sweat," she dragged herself from her chair. She managed to get to the chapel.

All of a sudden she found herself on her feet—without any support—a feeling of great tranquility flooding her whole being.

"Over my whole body I felt a gentle pressure. It seemed to me that a hand, both gentle and powerful at the same time, passed over my legs—which I felt had suddenly become deflated. New life flowed through them. The bandages, all at once too big, fell to the floor."

As soon as Mass ended, she went back to her room, walking with no difficulty, and was thrilled to find that the edema had disappeared. She put on her shoes, which she had not been able to wear for more than a year, went downstairs, and walked about all day, without feeling the slightest fatigue or the least tax on her heart. Next day she took up her duties again, and has remained well ever since.

In the official records, besides the report of the Sister herself, we find the testimony of the Abbess of the Order, that of the two Sisters who took care of the patient, also the deposition of the physician (Dr. Philouze), who for two years had seen her weekly and who was present the day after her cure. All gave their testimony under oath. To this was added the report of 1945 by three doctors under the Presidency of the Medical Bureau of Lourdes; their formal investigation of the case included the following note:

"Sister Marie-Marguerite, following upon renal and cardiac

symptoms from 1924 to 1934, suffered from acute inflammation of the kidney complicated by a generalized edema. This edema of the legs was aggravated by vesicles (blisters) which broke and discharged serous fluid. The Sister was cured suddenly on January 22, 1937, during a Novena to Notre Dame de Lourdes."

This was another cure which came to the attention of the medical and ecclesiastical authorities during wartime. A Commission of doctors appointed by the Cardinal Archbishop of Rennes examined Sister Marie-Marguerite in November, 1945, and reported that her state of health was excellent—heart normal, no pain in the kidneys, no edema, no painful condition of any sort. All trace of the disease had disappeared. The Sister immediately took up her arduous duties which, in spite of her advanced age, she was able to continue without any recurrence of her former trouble.

Because of the instantaneousness and absence of the convalescence in this case, the Archbishop declared that this cure could not be explained by natural causes. On May 26, 1946, he declared it to be a Miraculous Cure.

For the doctors, a particularly interesting thing about this cure was the immediate and complete disappearance of the large quantity of fluid (several liters) which had been present in the legs and was the cause of their tremendous swelling, plus the fact that no unusual amount of liquid was sloughed off through the normal channels. The Sister thought that the edema must have vanished through the sores on her legs and fallen onto the ground "in a lake." However, not a drop of fluid was discovered on the floor, and the linen was dry and clean, according to assurance given under oath at the Medical Bureau.

All this was astounding, the doctors said, "a material impossibility"—and yet a fact. The President of the Medical Bureau wrote a long article about it.

A Jewish physician, Dr. Koster, neurologist of Amsterdam,

gave a report of this case in a paper before the Netherlands Psychiatric and Neurological Association on March 22, 1952. In his paper Dr. Koster paid tribute to the physicians and to the methods of the Lourdes Medical Bureau. He said he was greatly impressed by the way in which information was most carefully and scrupulously gathered before any decisions were finally reached with regard to the cures at Lourdes.

Dr. Koster said he had become interested in Lourdes through the writings of Dr. Carrel. "I asked myself, Why should I not take Carrel's word about Lourdes as much as I would take it about the tissue of the heart of a chicken? * It was on the strength of his statements that I went to the Bureau to see for myself. I was not disappointed."

At last accounts Sister Marie-Marguerite was still in excellent health. I have never met her but I know a number of people who know her—among them Jeanne Fretel who lives in Rennes and who reported in autumn, 1953, that she was alive and well, and still "very active."

◄§ *Everyone in Lourdes knows* Mlle. Lacommère, the receptionist at the Bureau—brisk, helpful, efficient. She has helped me time and again, especially on one particular morning.

When I went into the Bureau that day, in the outer room sat a smiling little woman, middle-aged, modestly dressed and attractive, waiting for the doctors. I recognized her immediately from her picture, which I knew well. This was Madame Gestas,† one of the famous Cures of the past few years, and an official *miraculée.*

"Talk to her!" whispered Mlle. Lacommère. "I have told her about your book. Go on, she will be happy to talk with you."

* Referring to Dr. Carrel's famous experiments in connection with the heart.

† *Madame Jeanne Gestas, adhesive peritonitis, cured August 22, 1947, on Second Pilgrimage to Lourdes.*

Just then the doctors came in and proceeded with the examination—more exactly speaking, the yearly check-up which the Cures usually report for when they come with their local Pilgrimage.

Everybody filed into the examination room: seven doctors, two medical students. I was allowed to go in too.

A secretary turned the pages of the records. "When were you cured, madame?"

"August 22, 1947—seven years ago today!" She had come every years since then for her check-up, and to nurse the sick with the Bordeaux Pilgrimage. She undressed, lay down on the examination table.

Dr. Leuret began with a brief summary of the case, record book in hand. "Madame Jeanne Gestas, adhesive peritonitis. Patient of Dr. George and Dr. Dubourg of Bordeaux."

The doctor glanced benignly over his spectacles at the ex-patient. "Madame Gestas was fifty years old when she came to Lourdes for the cure which human aid had failed to give her. She had suffered for years from gastric and intestinal troubles, and had intense pain when taking even the smallest amount of food." He went on to give a résumé of the Bureau record.

In 1943 the case had been diagnosed as stomach ulcer, verified by X-rays. In December of that year the patient was operated on by Dr. Dubourg, the operation involving a large gastrectomy. But this had brought no improvement. Two more surgeries were performed (May, 1944, and January, 1946).

The third operation brought to light a web of adhesions so close-knit that on incision they would not permit a view of the abdominal organs. The operation was a lengthy one and the patient afterward remained in a prolonged state of shock, followed by pulmonary congestion and high temperature. For days her life was seriously in danger.

She had been obliged months before to give up all work, had become terribly thin, and her weight fell to ninety pounds.

After this third operation her condition became even worse. She had constant and violent spells of vomiting, and excruciating intestinal pain. In May, 1946, an especially severe crisis necessitated continuous aspiration for forty-eight hours. A fourth operation was considered but was put off because of the precarious condition of the patient. She suffered from frequent fainting fits after meals, vertigo in the street, and other morbid symptoms.

In August, 1946, she made her first pilgrimage to Lourdes. She came back definitely improved, as her surgeon Dr. Dubourg set down in his own record: "There is a definite amelioration . . . but the symptoms persist which indicate the existence of adhesive peritonitis at the subumbilical level. The general condition, while better, is still bad." The poor woman remained a victim of the same old agonies: digestive troubles, excessive constipation, and vertigo. She was very near despair.

On August 21, 1947, she went a second time to Lourdes with the National Pilgrimage. On Friday, August 22, while taking her bath in the piscine, she felt intense pain—"as though the whole intestine was being torn out." The pain ceased when she left the bath. She did not present herself at the Medical Bureau at this time but her nurses recorded that she took a light lunch at noon. On the morning of the twenty-third, she awoke with a sense of complete well-being. That day she ate anything she wanted, and had no trouble with her digestion.

Since her cure she follows a normal life, has no more pain, has regular stools, and can take up her work again. Seen on September 3, 1947, by her regular physician, Dr. George of Bordeaux, the latter noted that "she is completely transformed, suffers no more, and has regained a generally excellent condition."

The dossier contains certificates from Dr. George, Dr. Dubourg, and from the X-ray laboratory of Dr. Roger Guichard.

Madame Gestas was seen at the Medical Bureau in August, 1948, and each succeeding year. The cure is permanent. After her last examination, she talked to me for over an hour.

"This is a wonderful day for me, madame—I was cured just seven years ago today!" she said with a radiant smile. "I had been ill for four years—desperately ill; but I'd had this trouble really for twelve years. I was operated on three times. After the last operation, the doctor, when he came back next day, said to the nurse: 'She is dead?' "

He had expected her to die momentarily. Indeed, after the first operation he had told her husband there was no hope. "*Elle est perdue!* She is lost!" he said.

Now, she spoke of her first pilgrimage, in 1946. "At that time I had very little faith. I was *against* religion." A Sister at Bordeaux talked to her, helped to build up her faith. On that first pilgrimage she made some hesitant but sincere efforts.

"I made my prayer at the Grotto. I talked to the Blessed Virgin, very simply but very earnestly. I told her what she knew already, that I had not been much of a Christian. I promised her that from now on I would try—that I would go to Mass, receive the Communion, and try to be a good practicing Christian."

She kept her vow. It was hard, because her husband was a complete unbeliever. But she persisted. In 1947 she came back again to Lourdes.

"At the first bath I had a most agonizing pain, as though my whole insides were being torn out! I thought I was dying—and hoped I was. But when I got back to the Asile I felt better—ate something. I hadn't been able to eat for months—vomited everything." On the following day she ate more, ate things that usually would have caused her absolute anguish: beans, grapes, pears, peaches. She began to realize that something wonderful had happened to her.

"The Blessed Virgin had heard my prayer!"

She thought that she should go to the Medical Bureau to report her cure. The nurse at the hostel said no; if it was a real cure, it should be checked by the doctor at home. She had a comfortable trip back to Bordeaux, eating anything she pleased.

She had to smile at her husband's astonishment upon her return, when he saw her eating anything, walking, and doing everything like any healthy person.

"But I'm *cured!*" she told him jubilantly.

"*Tu penses!*" (The French equivalent for "You're telling me!") He came home each day expecting to see her ill again.

"And what did your doctor say?" I asked.

"Oh, at first he thought it was only temporary and that all the old troubles would return. But he was very happy when the cure held. No one was happier than he—except me!"

From the day of her cure to now she has been "absolutely well—feeling wonderful." She does all the housekeeping, cooking, and sewing for her family of seven—doesn't mind all the hard work. She comes every year to Lourdes to help with the sick—asks God to help her to understand why she was cured and what He wants her to do with the rest of her life.

One of her griefs is the irreligion of her family. Her husband and son don't believe at all in these things. *She* may come to Lourdes, go to Mass, do anything she likes. But for *them*, all that is nonsense. They make no attempt to account for her cure. "You believe in the Virgin—good. But don't ask us to have anything to do with that."

She leads her own life, goes to Mass, has her own friends who are believers, tries to help a bit with the poor and suffering, and thanks God daily for what has happened to her. A simple, smiling little woman, very modest and unpretentious, in spite of all the newspaper publicity and fuss that has surged around her.

On the occasion of Madame Gestas' visit to the Bureau in 1948, twenty-three doctors examined her and recorded the following conclusions: "From the clinical point of view we find no pathological symptoms, either physical or functional. The liver is a little low and the edge a bit hooked. Spleen not felt. No gas. No pains. Good abdominal wall. Heart normal, pulse normal. Functional amelioration giving impression of complete cure."

The Medical Commission two years later declared that time had confirmed this cure, that all the peritoneal lesions which for four years had tortured the patient had completely disappeared: that the case appeared to them beyond the laws of nature and "inexplicable."

The records were sent on to the Archbishop of Bordeaux for judgment by a Canonical Commission. On July 13, 1952, the cure was proclaimed according to the Canons of the Church as well as by the medical profession, and Jeanne Gestas took her place among the fifty-one official Miraculous Cures of Lourdes.

Madame Rose Martin—cancer of the uterus—
cured at Lourdes, July 3, 1947.

◄§ *People who say that Lourdes cures* consist of "a few neurotics who shed their nervous troubles under strong religious suggestion" get a shock when confronted with a pronouncement like the above taken out of an official medical report.

The first reaction is apt to be: "I don't believe it!" But twenty-two leading physicians and surgeons of Paris hospitals believed it, after rigorous examination of Madame Martin, a yearly check-up since her cure, the study of X-rays, surgeons' certificates and those of her local hospital.

I heard the story from Madame Martin herself, in her apartment at Nice not long ago. Here it is, as given in the report by her physician to the Medical Bureau at Lourdes.

From November, 1945, Madame Rose Martin showed symptoms of cancer of the uterus. In February, 1946, a hysterectomy was performed—she was operated on by Dr. Barraya of the Pasteur Hospital at Nice. Laboratory tests made evident a cancerous growth on the neck of the uterus.

Later complications necessitated two or more operations. In April, 1947, the patient was examined again, for digestive troubles: painful rectal crises, no bowel evacuation without enema, and a growth in the rectum the size of a small orange. One could feel this growth by abdominal palpation.

The unfortunate woman grew rapidly worse. She was confined to her bed for some months, continued to have constant vaginal discharges, no stools without enemas, and matter thus evacuated contained fetid debris.

The surgeons treating the case reported that the original cancer had spread to the rectum. They could offer no hope. Her pain was so great they had to give repeated injections of morphine.

On June 30, 1947, Madame Martin was taken to Lourdes in a grave condition. But after the third bath at the piscine (July 3, 1947) she asked to be bathed standing up, though for months past, to stand on her feet had been absolutely impossible for her. That same evening she got up alone, went to the toilet where she produced a normal stool, for the first time without enema. From that moment, never thereafter did she have any fetid or pathological evacuation. She felt no more pain, and had a "ferocious" appetite.

After her return to Nice, she was seen regularly by the doctor who had treated her—her home physician, Dr. Fay. He certified the complete disappearance of the rectal growth, besides the disappearance of functional symptoms. From the date of her cure there was total absence of pain, no vaginal discharge, daily stool, and steady gain in weight (34 pounds in ten months). "Housekeeper for a large family, she leads a very active and arduous life, but apparently thrives on it," added the doctor.

On July 6, 1948, one year after her cure, Rose Martin was examined at the Medical Bureau at Lourdes by a roomful of doctors. Her general condition was pronounced excellent. She had put on fifty pounds. A proctoscopy made by Dr. Leuret showed that the rectum was absolutely normal; the uterus and other organs were normal also. She has been periodically examined since then by Dr. Fay, who finds her in a flourishing state of health.

The case was sent to the Medical Commission—along with surgeons' certificates, X-ray and laboratory reports, and the complete hospital record. The Commission, at its meeting on February 27, 1949, "after a reading and discussion of the report by Dr. Oberlin on the case of Rose Martin, declares, in agreement with the *rapporteur*, that this case has no natural or scientific explanation, and unanimously considers that it should be submitted for examination by a Canonical Commission."

It was so ordered and on May 3, 1949, Monseigneur Rémond, Bishop of Nice, proclaimed Rose Martin a Miraculous Cure.

I had the good luck to hear Madame Martin's story from her own lips. I found her in her kitchen, cooking vegetables for the midday soup: a sturdy nice-looking woman of fifty, very energetic. Evidently she had been a very pretty girl.

In June, 1947, the doctors had given her three months to live. "I suffered the pains of hell, madame! My husband had to learn to give injections. I couldn't stand it at night, until the doctor came. I had more than 5,000 injections of morphine."

The Sisters down the street—Sisters of the Misericordia—took care of her. How good they were! They came eight times a day—think of that, *eight* times every day!—washed her, dressed her, combed her hair. They would never take any money. "No, no—use that for your own needs, madame. Put all that into getting well."

It was the Sisters who had said she must go to Lourdes, and who made all the arrangements. Her husband went with her. The doctor thought she would never make it. She weighed 70 pounds when she left on the Pilgrimage. Now she weights 154. When the Sisters saw her come back *cured*, they were overcome with happiness. The doctor didn't want her to go, but she had a presentiment that she would be cured at Lourdes. She insisted on making the effort.

At the moment of her cure, she felt "something moving, inside—through my whole being. Not painful—not tearing—but *moving.*" "It was your cure, madame," said the Sister who took care of her. "You will see, Madame Martin," they had kept telling her, "you will have your cure!"

The faith of the Sisters—how much it means to the patients! How often one is heard to say: "It was a *réligieuse* who took care of me—it was a Sister who came to see me. She talked to me—because of her I decided to go. I owe everything to those Sisters!"

Today Madame Martin is in the best of health. She does the family washing, cooking, cleaning and "feels fine"; she has felt absolutely well from the moment of her cure.

I talked with her physician, Dr. Fay. "Was there any doubt about its being cancer?"

"None whatever. You have seen the laboratory reports and hospital records. She had cancer, she was operated for cancer, but not cured by us doctors. On the contrary, the malignancy spread. This was a dying woman. Only after the bath at the piscine did she get well. She was cured at Lourdes—of cancer!" *

We have had a brief glance at some of the outstanding Lourdes Cures of recent years. Within the scope of the present book it is not possible to go into greater detail. I have given some idea of the documents and data available for on-the-spot study—though it must be remembered, all these papers and records are in French.

As I think about them—the Cures I talked with personally, and those I know most about—certain similarities, family likenesses one might call them, stand out very distinctly. While

---

* I have in my possession the complete medical record of this case: doctors' certificates, reports of the Medical Commission, of medical examinations, X-ray and laboratory reports, hospital records from Civil Hospital at Nice, from nurses in attendance, etc. Dr. Oberlin, surgeon of the Paris Hospitals and former President of the Commission, made the official investigation and wrote the history of the cure.

there is wide variety in the circumstances attending their cures, certain very definite likenesses appear in the people. When you have talked with eight or ten of them you begin to notice these common characteristics.

First, they are simple creatures: "Of the people," practically all of them. Not one that I heard of came from a rich or impressive family.

Second, they seem to be immune to illness after their cure: don't get sick at all, even with common colds or ordinary digestive troubles. They are in excellent health at all times.

Then—they are completely disinterested. They don't want any money, presents, or anything. Their desire is just to *give*, in gratitude for what has been done for them. They won't take money for any sort of help they may bestow.

Finally, they are calm. Though this tremendous thing has happened to them, though they have been bombarded by newspapers and well-meaning friends, they are never in a state of excitement. They come, most of them, from small towns, simple homes, where a great event like this might very easily turn a person's head. I have never seen a Lourdes Cure whose head was turned. They talk about their cure naturally, quietly, without commotion. They have, every one of them, a poise that comes from an inner dignity and the desire to be worthy of the great thing they have experienced.

I have never seen a Lourdes Cure flustered or upset. They are modest, but not unctuous; not a trace of sanctimoniousness or sentimentality in any one of them. They are happy people. They laugh a lot. They have fun.

But most unusual quality of all: they have no pride. Like Bernadette, their vanity seems "quite inaccessible." Let me add quickly, they are not plaster saints. They are human beings with human failings which no doubt are known to their families and friends, just as other people's are. But they are humble to the very bottom of their hearts—and they are pure hearts, with no selfish or ulterior motive.

"Every day," said Madame Gestas, "I ask God to show me *why* this great thing has happened to me and what He wants me to do with the life that He has saved."

Madame Gestas keeps house for seven people. Rose Martin is housekeeper for five. Jeanne Fretel is a nurse. Francis Pascal is a vinegrower, Fernand Legrand a cobbler, Colonel Pellegrin a soldier.

None of these people is sitting round looking pious, or setting himself up as something special, profiting in any way (as they easily might) from their spectacular experience. They are doing an honest, man-size job, wherever they happen to be. Not one of them is having an easy life, or would want it.

Whatever one may consider is the real source of their cure, however skeptical or "credulous" one may be regarding The Lady whom Bernadette so ardently believed in, there is no slightest doubt that a transcendental influence has laid its hand upon these people and has blessed them—not merely for a few moments with a physical cure, but for a lifetime, with deep joy, serenity, and peace. I count it a privilege to have known any one of them.

23

Causes and Conclusions:

*A*nd *over and again*, the crucial question: What is behind it all? What is the origin, the cause of all these cures? How do you explain them? More important, how does the medical profession explain them? If they are not miracles—that is, produced by some supernatural power, what are they? What power does produce them, and how?

We have seen the fallacy of many of the favorite theories: *The water*, which has no curative properties, either chemical or radioactive; *the climate*, some special quality in the atmosphere—but there is none. Lourdes has only the agreeable mountain air of many Pyrenees cities.

Errors of diagnosis—this occurs naturally and immediately to a physician. And in the early years, when the system of medical examinations and verifications was less severe, this might justifiably have been brought forward as an explanation of certain cures. Errors certainly occur in every doctor's practice. But today, pilgrimage certificates for patients coming to Lourdes are required to be exact, supported by case histories, clinical data, and doctors' day-by-day notations, which leave little loophole for mistaken diagnoses. A very substantial number of Lourdes cures, as shown in the accounts in these pages, are backed by "Before-and-After" X-rays, hospital charts, and biological analyses. These documents do not lie. They show, objectively and unmistakably, the condition of the patient before and after the alleged cure.

Again, as Dr. Blanton has observed, the percentage of these cures are certainly too great to be laid to coincidence. Doctors today are more apt to consider psychological causes as a probable explanation for such cures.

Emotional shock . . . suggestion . . . psychic factors . . . these are among the most popular of the tentative "solutions." People often speak of the "abnormal emotionalism and suggestibility" of the patients. That such a condition can bring about improvement or sudden cure of neurotics has been observed in various hospitals as well as at places of pilgrimage.

But in many Lourdes cures this element has been lacking: in the cures of the incredulous, of unbelievers, and of young children; in cures that have occurred at home, or on the return journey after all hope was given up; in cures elsewhere than at the baths or at the Processions in Lourdes; and in cures that have occurred after two or more pilgrimages.

Some people insist that miraculous cures are produced by "chants and incantations" that stimulate the patient into a state of exaltation: "That generous breath," as Zola says, "which emanates from the crowds in the acute climax of faith."

As I have repeatedly stressed, the atmosphere of constant prayer and faith must certainly have a tremendous effect upon sick and receptive persons. Undoubtedly suggestion is a powerful force. But can one contend (as Dr. Guinier asks) "that suggestion thus created can awaken vital energies asleep for months and years, and cause to disappear *instantly* local vascular troubles, muscular atrophy, and articular stiffness which disease brought about?

"Is it possible that 'suggestion,' either personal or collective, could force various microorganisms to neutralize each other and disappear, large collections of pus to be absorbed, gaps made by sloughing tissue to be filled up, and scars to form in a few hours or minutes which ordinarily require months or years? (As in the case of Lydia Brosse.)

"Experience proves," Dr. Guinier continues, "that therapeutic suggestion has never been able to cure, either rapidly or slowly, organic lesions.* The regeneration of tissues diseased for a long time or destroyed can only be accomplished by the multiplication of cells, engendered by pre-existing elements and adding to themselves new cells; thus succeeding in re-forming skin, muscles, fat, bones. . . . In such a succession of physiological operations *time* is indispensable. No organ rebuilds itself outside of the conditions of time necessary to the growth of tissues." No moral shaking or nervous crisis, he adds, can alter this fact or produce an instant creation of cells.

Dr. Vallet makes another interesting point on this question of suggestion. "If," he says, "as certain schools contend, Lourdes is the prime rendezvous for nervous and hysterical patients only, and if we have means of suggestion unlimited in their power, why are not more nervous patients cured here? How is it that our cures reckon especially affections of the lungs and organic lesions, caries, tumors, cancer, diabetes, diseases in which suggestion plays no part?

"When a cure of cancer or tuberculosis in the last stages occurs, as it has numbers of times, at the passing of the Blessed Sacrament, there are at the same time in front of the Basilica hundreds of patients suffering from nervous afflictions. Why do they not get up?"

Some of the National Pilgrimages have been the occasion of very remarkable cures. He describes one of the most memorable:

"Thousands of spectators. Fifteen hundred sick in long double rows on the Esplanade—a large number of instantaneous cures. Among the sick who then arose from their stretchers and

---

* Bernheim, chief of the Nancy school of therapists who specialized in suggestion, officially stated that "suggestion cannot do away with a lesion, set a dislocated limb, or restore destroyed substance; neither does it kill microbes or cicatrize tuberculous wounds." He declares: "Suggestion is a means which acts only with nervous or functional troubles; it has no effect on organic diseases." He thus places most Lourdes cures outside the reach of suggestive influence. For the cures at Lourdes are chiefly of organic diseases.

followed the Procession were Fanny Pepper, a consumptive in the last stages; Helene Duval, tubercular peritonitis; Philimene Albrecht, Pott's Disease; Josephine Grosset, tuberculous peritonitis; Irma Jacquart, cerebral affection complicated by paralysis; Felicie Serreau, another peritonitis victim; J. Lacome, Pott's Disease. . . .

"Now such diseases cannot be cured by suggestion. On the other hand, nervous diseases could disappear under this irresistible impulse. In this double row of litters that filled the Esplanade that day there were fully three hundred nervous patients. *Why did they not get up?*

"The secret of our cures is not to be found in the water in our pools. It is not to be found in the religious excitement which surrounds us at Lourdes. Wherein, then, does lie the secret?"

Many people ascribe it to *prayer.* One of the great experts on tissue building puts forward his own conviction on this point. Dr. Carrel writes:

Certain spiritual activities may cause anatomical as well as functional modifications of the tissues and organs. These organic phenomena are observed in various circumstances—among them being the state of prayer. Prayer should be understood not as a mere mechanical recitation of formulas, but as . . . an absorption of consciousness in a principle both permeating and transcending our world.

Our present conception of the influence of prayer upon pathological lesions is based upon the observation of patients who have been cured almost instantaneously of various affections such as peritoneal or bone tuberculosis, abscesses, osteitis, suppurating wounds, lupus, cancer, etc. . . . In a few seconds, a few minutes, at the most a few hours, wounds are cicatrized, pathological symptoms disappear, appetite returns . . . The miracle is characterized by an extreme acceleration of the processes of organic repair . . . The only condition indispensable for the occurrence of the phenomena is Prayer. The patient does not need himself to pray or to have any religious faith; but someone around him must be in a state of prayer.

Such facts are of profound significance. They show *the reality of certain relations of still unknown nature between psychological and organic processes. They prove the objective importance of spiritual activities* which hygienists, physicians, educators, and sociologists have almost always neglected to study. They open to man a new world.

Elsewhere Carrel stated his conviction that "the power of prayer is the greatest power in the world." Another great scientist, Charles Steinmetz of General Electric, asked by his colleagues what was the most important line of research for them to follow from here on, answered without a moment's hesitation: "Prayer. Find out about prayer!"

Dr. Vallet does not agree completely with the prayer theory as interpreted by Carrel, or with prayer as a complete and final explanation of miraculous cures, capable in itself of releasing the process of healing. Prayer is necessary for healing to be obtained, yes, says Vallet, "but it is not sufficient . . . *it is necessary that God agree to it*, and ratify the execution by His own intentions!"

And here we find ourselves confronted by that knotty problem that has plagued theologians and philosophers from time immemorial: the Will of God.

Vallet writes again:

These cures are not the result of accident but of an all-powerful will which hears this prayer and whom nothing resists—neither sickness nor death . . . And this will is none other than the will of God. The healings at Lourdes, so varied in their conditions, so different in their method of realization, proceed nevertheless from one unique antecedent: the imploring of God. These cures being obtained, it is He who heals.*

The Church declares the cause of these cures to be "a special intervention of the Blessed Virgin Mary Immaculate Mother of God" or "a special intervention of God through the intercession

---

* In this chapter again I am much indebted to Dr. Vallet and his publishers Flammarion & Co. for material drawn from his valuable book, *La Vérité Sur Lourdes*.

of Notre Dame de Lourdes." Such a declaration is made in every proclamation by the Church of a Miraculous Cure.

Many Catholic doctors, such as Vallet and Leuret, agree with this. Other doctors say that there are phases and functions of human personality of which we have as yet very little knowledge —they prefer to wait before pronouncing judgment. Orthodox medical men of today tend to believe that these mysterious cures are due to errors of diagnosis in some cases, in others to psychological therapy of one kind or another.

Dr. Blanton suggests that the cause of the cures may be a transference by the patient to the Virgin Mary—a complete surrender to the power and compassion of the Blessed Mother, who, he feels, has the power and the will to intercede for him with the Creator Himself. Dr. Blanton puts an interesting argument for this viewpoint, stressing the influence of motherworship on the race, the cohesiveness of the group at Lourdes around this worship, and so on. "It is only when they (the patients) have reached this state of complete surrender that they can be cured by such transference."

But however thorough the transference, however complete the surrender, transference—this mental and emotional shifting —can't build cells or join nerves and arteries in the twinkling of an eye. This, as doctors remind us over and again, is a *slow* and *progressive* process. No mere swift emotional change could accomplish it.

One of the favorite explanations of Lourdes cures by rationalist doctors is that they are produced by "unknown natural forces"—unknown today, but whose laws science may uncover tomorrow. I have heard interesting discussions on this by groups of doctors at the Medical Bureau.

Most of them appeared to discount this theory—because of the *irregularity of method* which, as we have seen, is one of the outstanding characteristics of Lourdes cures. They would point out that the action of the forces of nature is always general, universal, permanent and unchanging. The law of gravity, for example, works just the same for the learned scientist who falls from the seven-story window of his Paris apartment as for the savage in Africa who falls from the top of his coconut tree; for the Eskimo in Iceland, the tea-planter in Ceylon, or for any man any time, anywhere in the world.

So would it have to be with the "unknown natural forces" alleged to be responsible for Lourdes cures. They would have to act the same for all persons under similar conditions. Though their formulas are still unknown, their operation would have to show the characteristics of *generality*, *universality*, *permanence* and *changelessness*: the undeviating marks of the forces of nature.

But with Lourdes cures we see the exact opposite. Here, these "unknown forces" act neither constantly nor uniformly. They act today, but not tomorrow; for some people, but not for others. They have their privileged persons. They show a special fondness for the pilgrimage season. They appear less active during the winter.

Can we reasonably say, the AMIL doctors ask, that these are characteristics giving evidence of the action of natural forces?

Here, then, are various theories and hypotheses—probably none of them acceptable to both the religious and the scientific-minded, certainly none of them satisfactory to all. The reader must decide for himself, or delay decision if he thinks that further evidence is necessary. But before leaving this question of causes, there is a point worth noting—a point that we arrive at through the facts of our experience.

Our physicists, in their accounts of the recent discoveries of physical science, speak of forms of energy so fine that they can be known and described only through their effects. A Lourdes cure, as we have repeatedly seen, involves a profound spiritual as well as physical experience, and a profound and permanent spiritual transformation. These being the effects, we logically infer that the producing cause behind them must partake of the same qualities—in even larger measure: that the force which produces such profound spiritual transformation must be a force of tremendous spiritual power.

To bring about both physical and spiritual transformation, revolutionizing the whole being in an instant, it must be a magnificent force indeed.

24

First-hand Statements by "The Cures"

No *scientific hypothesis* up to the present accounts for the phenomena," says Dr. Carrel.

For myself, I have been interested in putting together first-hand statements by the Cures—comments made to me and to others about their sensations and subjective experiences at the moment of the cure and after. Similarities and repetitions among these, reports of the same sort of feelings among people of widely different types and ages, backgrounds and regions, may stimulate the reader's conjecture and further inquiry, as they have mine.

The two principal spots where cures occur are the baths and the Procession. At the baths, especially, many Cures speak of temporary but agonizing pain.

Elizabeth Delot (cancer of the stomach), cured at her first bath, felt "intolerable pain—a terrible burning and stabbing in the stomach and abdomen—as though they were holding her under the blows of a fiendish hammer." On coming out of the water, all this gave place to "a remarkable sense of well-being—a sense of vigor and appetite." She is cured!

Madame Gestas, cured at her second bath, of adhesive peritonitis—felt "diabolical pain, as though my whole insides were being torn out." Back at the Asile she felt better—began to eat. The cure made itself evident from that time on.

Fernand Legrand "felt as though his arms and legs were being broken to pieces"—a moment of utter agony. Only a moment, though—then he sat up and began to help the brancardiers to dress him.

Joachime Dehant, whole ulcered leg was cured at the second bath, felt "terrible pain, followed by a feeling of ease and disappearance of pain." She went home wearing the boots she had brought as an act of faith.

Francis Pascal uttered loud cries. His mother thought he had a convulsion.

John Traynor: At his ninth and last bath his legs became violently agitated—almost emptied the whole bath of its water. On his way to the baths, earlier during his visit, he "felt something burst in my chest, and blood flowed freely from my mouth." After that, "some change had taken place in me which marked the end of my epileptic fits. I never had another."

Madame Augault, partially cured at first bath, felt excruciating pain for the brief instant of her immersion in the water. "Sensation of being put in boiling oil." But the compression in her abdomen seemed to disappear. Calmed down on her return to the hospital. In the afternoon at the Procession, again great pain—"as though my insides were being torn out" (like Gestas). Everything quieted down at the passing of the Blessed Sacrament. From that precise moment as the Host was raised above her, "as though by enchantment," her sufferings vanished. Her energies had a rebirth—she could get up and walk!

Achille Billet, cured at the baths of a suppurating wound in the foot, of four years—felt "agonizing pain in affected foot and leg" at the moment of his cure. "Fine," afterwards.

Abbé Fiamma, cured at first bath of varicose veins with ulcerations—felt intense pain, "like the insertion of a red-hot iron under the skin." Francois Macary, cured of the same disease, felt no pain at all but woke up in the middle of the night cured, having simply put Lourdes water on his legs.

Patients do not always feel pain but it seems that in a great many cases they do. Constance Piquet, cured at the third bath of cancer of the breast, felt no attendant pain or disturbance. Swelling disappeared, everything normal.

Rose Martin (cancer of the uterus) "felt something moving inside—through my whole being. Not painful, not tearing—but moving." "It was your cure, madame!" said the Sister.

Madame Pouxvieille (stomach ulcer) at the second bath felt something extraordinary taking place within her, and then felt considerably better. From that time on, she was cured; felt "as though a current were running through her body."

Many accounts of spiritual healing speak of an "electric current" running through the body. Charles McDonald called it "a glow." The first bath had no effect as regards his illness. But at the second bath he "felt the first glow of health." "When leaving the baths I felt more fit than I had ever felt in my life."

Both McDonald and Joachime Dehant brought clothes with them to wear home for the return trip—as normal persons. In these cases, a psychiatrist might say that a powerful suggestion was conveyed to the subconscious, impressing it with the complete acceptance of a perfect cure; no complexes, no inhibitions. And the cure was accomplished.

Another striking case was that of Monsieur Vion-Dury, totally blind for seven years, afflicted with two detached retinas. Dipping a finger in Lourdes water, he passed it over his eyes; then felt a violent pain "as though someone had thrust a knife into his eyes." He thought the Sister had made a mistake and given him the ammonia bottle. But on that instant his sight was completely recovered. The case was the subject of a paper by Dr. Dor of Lyon, who had treated him, at the Congress of Ophthalmology in Paris.

Madame Pierson, suffering from contraction of the arms and legs with palsy, following encephalitis, took a partial bath in the piscine. Violent pain—"as though her right arm were being torn off." Immediately afterward the arm and hand could move with ease. Next day recuperation was complete.

Mademoiselle Maria Raedt, afflicted for several years with pyelonephritis and cystitis, the day before her departure from Lourdes felt a sensation of "tearing" in the lower abdomen, and of intolerable pain. Her illness was finished.

I have not heard any similar reports on this pain question from healing centers other than Lourdes, though they may of course exist. At Lourdes, especially at the baths, intense pain seems to be a very common characteristic.

While many cures occur at the baths, many others—and some of the most notable—have occurred at the Procession of the Blessed Sacrament. Sometimes peacefully, sometimes, as at the baths, accompanied by intense and painful sensations. "With the cures that take place at the passing of the Blessed Sacrament," says Dr. Vallet. "we observe similar phenomena which seem to indicate the intervention of some superior force."

Nina Kin, a girl who had been horribly burned by the upsetting of a demijohn of sulfuric acid—nerves of the leg involved— had been unable to move for six months. She felt herself "lifted up by a violent impulse" and started to walk after the Procession.

Marguerite Savoye, twenty years old, a living corpse weighing forty pounds, had not left her bed or taken any solid nourishment for six years. As the Blessed Sacrament passed, "a violent and irresistible impulse" raised her on her bed and threw her abruptly to earth. She found herself at the foot of her litter on her knees. "I am cured!" she cried. "I am cured!"

Mademoiselle Guimard of Bordeaux, paralyzed seventeen years, at the moment when the Blessed Sacrament came near her, experienced an indefinable feeling and motion "like the sweep of waves" which raised her from her litter. "This sensation," she says, "I can neither forget nor explain—but it certainly proceeded from a force outside of and superior to my own nature." She said she "became conscious of a violent movement of the knee—a violent force which suddenly took possession of her and *flung* her from her litter."

Gargam, the atheist—"in pieces" after his terrible railway accident—also declared that he had the sensation of "being thrown from his litter to the ground." "Hurled" was the word he used.

John Traynor records that "his arm began to agitate violently" at the Procession, as his legs had at the baths. He burst his bandage and freed the arm—now active again after being paralyzed for eight years.

Here are other interesting comments:

Jeanne Fretel, cured at Communion and at the Grotto, said: "I had the sensation that someone took me under the arms to help me sit down. I found myself in a sitting position. Looking round, I could see no one. As soon as I was seated I had the feeling that the same hands that helped me to sit down took my hands to put them on my abdomen"—which, she discovered, had suddenly become flat and normal. She thought she was dreaming, but came back to full consciousness, cured.

Sister Marie-Marguerite, also cured at Communion and "moved to go there by what seemed a superhuman force," records that "it seemed to me that a hand, both gentle and powerful, passed over my legs, which suddenly became deflated. New life flowed through them. The bandages fell to the floor."

The reader will have noticed how many cures occur at, or or just after, the moment of Communion—at the Grotto, at the Altar of Bernadette, or when the Host is raised over the sick at the passing of the Sacrament at the Procession. That is, at the moment when emotional intensity and spiritual fervor (their own and others') is at its height: when the intense emotional force of the crowd, and the spiritual exaltation of the priests and bishops, of their own families and attendants, reaches its climax.

Marie-Louise Arnaud was cured at the moment when she was praying for her dead brother, at the Grotto. She had just taken Communion. She did so, "completely absorbed in the thought of my brother and oblivious of myself and my illness." Turning her face on the pillow to hide her tears, she suddenly discovered that her limbs and sight were normal. She was cured!

Madame Charette (tumor of the liver) was cured while lying in front of the Grotto after a particularly painful "crisis." Cured just after Communion—she has been in flourishing health ever since.

Ernestine Guilloteau, a skeleton weighing forty-six pounds, dying of tuberculous peritonitis and supposedly on the very verge of death, got up and followed the Blessed Sacrament up the steps to the Rosary Church. She did this in a state of semiconsciousness, at the moment when, believing herself dying, she was thanking the Blessed Virgin for the great happiness of dying there before Her wonderful Grotto. Suddenly she found herself walking and following the Sacrament into the Church.

Many *miraculés* speak of this state of "unawareness" of what was going on in the physical world, of being transported, in spite of and "beyond" themselves and their normal consciousness.

Mademoiselle Clauzel was cured at Mass, between the Elevation and the Communion. At this moment her family noticed "signs of agitation" in the invalid which they took to be the result of the very long ritual. In reality it was her cure, which at first she did not dare believe. She records "a sense of profound well-being"—not of agitation but of "a wonderful force acting within her, renewing her entire being." She knew beyond the shadow of a doubt that she was cured. She went to the altar and offered her thanksgiving. "It seemed to me," she said, "that I was no longer touching the ground."

Jeanne Fretel said she never knew how she got to the Grotto from the Altar of Bernadette where she was cured. She felt as though she "must have flown there."

Mrs. Feely, cured at the baths of a diseased lung, knew "a supreme joy and peace—breath-taking! The next thing I knew, I was at the Grotto. Never knew how I got there. I felt as though I were floating—flying." She looked around to see if people were noticing her—afraid they would think her "queer." She knelt down and gave thanks; afterwards she ran all the way up the steep steps to the top of the Basilica. Her pilgrimage doctor, meeting her, gazed at her astounded.

John Traynor appears to have been in a detached subjective state for some twenty-four hours after his cure. He ran to the Grotto and prayed, came back to the Asile and dressed himself, went into chapel, and served Mass for the officiating priest. Then he had breakfast, went through a long series of interviews and events during a crowded day, still not fully conscious of what had happened to him. "Although I knew I had received a great favor from Our Lady, I had no recollection of all the illness that had gone before."

In the train on the way home, he was "still in a sort of daze" —until one of the bishops came in and talked to him. "John, do you realize how ill you were, and that you have been miraculously cured?"

"Then," said Traynor, "everything came back to me, the memory of my years of illness, the sufferings of the journey, and how ill I had been in Lourdes too . . . Suddenly I realized fully what had happened."

The repeated references by the Cures to "hands" helping them, "a violent force" hurling them to the ground, and so on, will interest those who believe in the influence upon human beings of beings in another world. Early man—and men of modern times also—have believed that spirits "gone before" could help mortals in their physical as well as moral need. According to Catholic doctrine, God may sometimes use the saints, angels, and other beings to assist in a work of spiritual or physical transformation. Prayer, ritual, the lifting of the heart in meditation—all are regarded as aids. But these are all considered preparatory disciplines, essential to a cure but not to be confused with the final Cause and Creator.

Our American Indians have some interesting beliefs in the matter of preparatory prayers and rituals. Mary Austin, who spent much of her life among them, quotes the words of an old Indian chief who offered prayers for the cure of her servant:

"He said you couldn't get help from the Friend simply by asking. You had first to get to Him. You had to make a veritable motion of your own soul—*here*. (He moved his hand over his solar plexus.) When you had climbed up to the Friend by rhythmic motions and sounds, then you came close to Him, and the thing you wanted happened."

Mrs. Austin added: "I discovered that the value of sustained rhythmic movements and sounds, so much used by the Indians, lay in their power to break the tension of immediate circumstances and their hold upon the attention . . . a completely integrated movement, persisted in until all the rhythms of the physical body are gathered together in it to the exclusion of all bodily sensations." *

A completely integrated movement: the prayer and faith at Lourdes perpetually going up as with one voice, certainly produces such a movement and constitutes a tremendous living force of which even the most callous and indifferent must be aware.

Apropos of relaxing tension and "letting go," we note that patients at Lourdes are often cured (1) when they are not thinking about themselves and their cure; (2) when they are praying for someone else; (3) when they have stopped hoping and have given up altogether—as with Ernestine Guilloteau and her mother.

Lydia Brosse was completely unconscious of her cure when it came. Nothing (apparently) had happened, at the baths or during her stay at Lourdes. Greatly depressed, she was on her way home. When she had stopped hoping, given up, *let go*, the cure came. Lydia, unaware of it, had to be told by another patient of her change in looks.

Cures often occur when the recipient is absorbed in the thought of God or of some absent loved one. In such cases the

* From Mrs. Austin's *Can Prayer Be Answered?* with kind permissions of Rinehart & Company, Inc.

person praying forgets all about himself—his personal problems, tensions, fears and anxieties—and becomes single-pointed, overwhelmed by a great, impersonal, selfless feeling for his neighbor, and by faith and reliance on a Higher Being or God. His own being is permeated with the consciousness of this Higher Being. Then the "miracle" of transformed physical structure takes place.

We have reviewed a series of facts—and some speculations—with regard to Lourdes cures. My own deepest impression has to do with the atmosphere of the place. *Prayer* is the essence and heart of that atmosphere. Constant prayer, constant repetition of certain liturgies, hymns, responses—the Rosary, the Stations, the Hail Marys—over and over, thousands of times, creates a spiritual and mental atmosphere surrounding the patient; opening his whole being to spiritual forces of renewal and transformation. The very air he breathes conveys this to him.

Faith too plays a major part. "I had tremendous faith," said Madame Pellegrin. "Well, madame, I had great faith!" declared the mother of little Francis Pascal. "How much the faith of those Sisters meant to me!" said Rose Martin, and Jeanne Gestas, and half a dozen others. "It did something to me, madame—it seemed to roll a stone away!" (Probably unlocked certain inner resistances and long-standing psychological blocks and disbeliefs.) The nurses, the brancardiers, the priests and everybody around them, are sending out this strong faith all day and every minute.

Last but by no means least, that ever-present spirit of *devotion:* the great wave of love and compassion pouring out over those rows upon rows of sick, every hour and every second throughout the Domaine. Thousands of people moving together as one being, acting in unison in faith and prayer and overflowing love and service; thousands of lives moving in concentrated purpose in one direction—a single motion, a single intent. What a rhythm *this* must produce! What an effect it must have on those receptive eager souls.

It may be that the wavelength brought about by constant prayer, constant spiritual "recollection" by people at the highest level of thinking and giving, produces a psychological condition that has a definite effect upon the patient. His own psychic and spiritual state, and that of his relatives, nurses, and others around him, may play an important part too in opening the way for a cure. The presence or absence of moral or psychological blocks must also have something to do with it.

All these are contributing *conditions*—but none of them can be a *cause*. No one of them can create new bone or tissue instantaneously. That, Catholics say, can be done only by a Divine Creator—God.

25

The End of the Road

Now, *what does it all* add up to? What stays with you? What is most important? And why is it important to *me*—asks the everyday normal person leading a healthy normal existence here at home. What significance has all this in relation to *my* everyday life and affairs?

Each of us must make his own appraisal. But for me personally, this is the core of it and the summing up:

Lourdes is important because it offers the thing most needed by every human being: spiritual assurance, solid ground to stand on. In a recent Town Hall poll, the major anxiety of modern men and women was found to be not money, or health, or even war. More than twenty thousand men and women gave as their major worry, *spiritual insecurity:* "The need for some solid spiritual and moral basis of life," "Something to believe in, to hang on to," "Something I can really be sure of, something I *know* is there."

Swept away from the old moorings, buffeted about between science and psychiatry, Kinsey and Comte, the menace of the guided missile and the super-bomb, now in the panic science has laid upon them, they desperately search for something to hold on to, some inner haven, since no physical refuge can be relied on.

For me, Lourdes gives that solid rock, that inner fortress; takes us back to the lost spiritual foundations so many thousands and millions are longing to find again.

Lourdes is one of the wonders of the world today, yes; from a scientific point of view, from a psychological point of view, from a human-interest point of view. But more than this—far more—Lourdes holds the answer to the problems of a sick humanity. Here is healing not only for a few thousand suffering individuals: here is the answer, the key, to the healing of a sick world.

Time and again a *miraculé* will say: "Well, we had tried everything else—doctors, medicines, hot springs, therapies. They all failed. There was nothing left. So we had to go to Lourdes. We *had* to try God!"

I heard the same thing at one of the big international conferences in Geneva. Going in to see the Chief of one of the top Commissions, I found him reading the Bible. In the midst of all the hubbub and confusion—telegrams, visitors, special messengers, transatlantic telephone calls—there he sat, with the Book in his hand, quietly reading.

"Well! Isn't this rather unusual?" (He was anything but a religious man.)

"Well," he said, with a tired smile across his littered table, "we've tried everything else. I guess you have to come back to it, don't you? You have to come to it, sooner or later."

A sick person—or a sick world. Sooner or later.

Today we are told, not only by the Communists but by many supposedly intelligent people in our own communities, that God and the Scriptures are myth and foolishness; that the idea of a superhuman power is "mediaeval superstition"—old wives' tales. The "rational intelligent" modern man is "old-fashioned" and "behind the times" if he believes in such things.

He is behind the times if he doesn't. The position of the non-believer, a Nobel-prize-winning physician has assured us, can no longer be sustained. Facts prove that there *is* a superhuman power. For at Lourdes—and at other healing centers—we see a superhuman power in action, doing what human power has repeatedly proved unable to do.

"That is actual which acts," says Dr. Carl Jung.

"It Acts—therefore It Exists," is the quiet assertion that rules this Domaine.

So Lourdes offers first this great message: *The fact of a higher-than-human Power* which we see here, undeniable and in actual operation. "If miracles occur, then God exists," as more than one skeptic has admitted. The fact of the existence of that Power, that man may have access to it, receive help from it, be healed of his ills and woes through it—this fact has been proved at Lourdes not once but hundreds and thousands of times. Sometimes physically, sometimes spiritually, or both.

The cures at Lourdes come about (as Dr. Blanton says) through surrender to a Higher Power—through complete dependence and reliance upon that Power. This is the process with Lourdes cures and the cures at other healing centers. It is the same with the cures that occur at Alcoholics Anonymous—where "surrender to a power greater than ourselves" is the keystone of the entire program; * with the "conversions" of the orthodox churches, and with practically every form of spiritual healing and transformation.

This Power exists (all teach). It can do what I cannot do. If I turn to it in faith and trust, it will help me. It will deliver me from my ills and problems, heal my iniquities, cure my diseases.

"Is there really such a Higher Power?" people ask doubtfully.

If there isn't, what cause is producing all these effects? Certainly no man or group of men is producing them. That is actual which acts. Here is a Power which we see in daily operation before our eyes, in concrete physical conditions.

Of the nature of the Power we are as yet woefully ignorant. We shall learn more about it when we seek further, try hard enough to find out more; when we try as hard to discover the

---

* Dr. Harry Tiebout says the root disease of the alcoholic is his idea of his own omnipotence. If you can get him to give *that* up, he has a chance for a cure. It is true of every disease—and of the world's illness also.

secrets of Life as men have tried to discover those of death and destruction.

But we do know this much: It Acts; therefore It Exists. There is a higher-than-human Power. Man is in contact with it—blurred, only partial thus far, perhaps—*but* contact. He can approach the Power by asking humbly, sincerely—and it responds to him.

This we know from actual facts of human experience, from tens of thousands of cases, not only at Lourdes but in many other places. And it is the most important knowledge in the world for every living being in it. God—not the hydrogen bomb —is the greatest Fact of present-day existence. This is the Fact of Lourdes.

So, the first great Lourdes declaration: *God is true.* And the second: *The Miracles are true.* The man with the palsy, the boy with the deaf and dumb spirit, the woman with the infirmity of twelve years, the soldier's son, the man with the withered arm, and many with much worse, are there before our very eyes.

These are no longer "quaint stories" of olden time, to be glossed over, "interpreted," glibly explained away in the light of the "higher criticism." They are facts of present-day experience: facts to be honestly acknowledged and respected.

Robert Hugh Benson, son of an Archbishop of Canterbury, puts it like this after his own visit to Lourdes:

For over thirty years I had been accustomed to repeat the accepted formula—that "the age of miracles is past," that "they were necessary for the establishment of Christianity but that they are no longer necessary now, except on rare occasions perhaps"—and in my heart I knew my foolishness . . . As for Lourdes, I spoke of hysteria and autosuggestion and French imaginativeness and the rest of it.

As a child on Sunday afternoons I used to walk with my father and listen to his discourse. As an Anglican clergyman I used to teach in Sunday schools or preach to children. As a Catholic priest I used occasionally to attend a catechism. At all these times the miraculous seemed singularly far away. We looked at it across twenty centuries.

It was something from which a lesson might be drawn, upon which the imagination might feed, but it was a state of affairs as remote as the life of prehistoric man; one assented to it, and that was all.

Here at Lourdes it was a present vivid event. I sat at an ordinary glass window, in a cassock made by an English tailor, with an Englishman beside me, and saw the miraculous happen. (Five times in one afternoon, he said, "the finger of God flashed down" and one of those dying figures rose and walked victoriously up the steps into the Church.) Time and space disappeared, the centuries shrank and vanished, and behold we saw that which prophets and kings have desired to see, and have not seen.*

The Miracles are true. The Scriptures are true.

The longer one stays at Lourdes, the more one is impressed with the literal truth of many passages in the Bible that, of late years, learned critics have insisted we should consider purely allegorical.

And this has a direct bearing on the spiritual insecurity of the present generation. One of the chief causes of moral breakdown during the past half century has been increasing disbelief in the Scriptures and in a Supreme Being whose moral law is the blueprint for sane human behavior. Without such belief we have no moral yardstick, no universal gauge of reference.

Our forefathers went through their terrific problems, wars, privations, sacrifices, because they had an unshakable faith in God and His divinely inspired Revelation, giving the laws of life by which they were meant to live.

How do we know that these laws given in the Bible truly are the basic moral law for us? Again, for the pragmatist, by effects. Because when we break them, we and our world know chaos. When we break the laws laid down for a moral human nature, we rapidly revert (as in recent years) to the state of the jungle.

There are some things in the Scriptures, no doubt, that directly apply to the times in which they were written; some that

* From "*Lourdes*" by Robert Hugh Benson. By kind permissions of the literary Executors of the late Mgr. Benson and of the Manresa Press.

do not apply today. But—and here is the never-to-be-forgotten point: there is much in them that is everlasting and eternal. Scientific theory changes every twenty-four hours. The great spiritual principles taught us by Christ and the Prophets and seers have stood unchanged for centuries. No modern psychiatrist has invented any substitute for them. On the contrary, the psychiatrists are going back to them, and preaching these principles themselves now, more and more emphatically.

The Fact of God—the Miracles—the truth of the Scriptures: these are great lessons, great gifts of Lourdes. But these are not all. There is still the innermost core of it, the thing that makes Lourdes take hold of you, never to let you go.

When I have these discussions with myself, trying to push through to the innermost secret—seeing those restless throngs, those eager, seeking faces—a certain text in the Bible comes back to me again and again:

"They looked for a city . . . a city which hath foundations" —foundations of love and devotion and unselfishness, just genuine friendship, *caring for people*—"whose builder and maker is God."

To my mind, that is the secret of Lourdes.

Here the homesick millions find what they are looking for, what they have been searching for, hungering after, ever since they were born.

The greatest thing at Lourdes is not the cures. It is not the rediscovery of the Scriptures. It is not the rediscovery of God, vital as that is. That is only half of it. The other half is putting God into actual everyday living.

The greatest thing about Lourdes is the spirit in which life is lived there: the Brotherhood of Man in actual performance, the Beloved Community, *the human dream come true.*

"You can't run any community today on the principles laid down by Christ," we are told. "It isn't practical. It isn't normal. It won't work. It just can't be done!"

At Lourdes you see it *being* done—joyfully, successfully—

every minute of the day. You yourself are part of its being done. That's why it seems "home" to the homesick hearts of men and women from all over creation. The way we were meant to live. A life based on Love instead of Power—of helping one another, serving the weak, sharing among the strong. No wonder thousands of practical people yearn for the few precious days or weeks each year when they can return to it—the most normal of all atmospheres.

Lourdes says the way to happiness is to give, not grab. It is every man's nature to give. Economic systems, exploitations, and tyrannies have forced him into the false position of fighting his brother, fighting *to get*. The modern human being is a mass of frustrations, conflicts and diseases, in consequence.

Lourdes releases him—to be himself: furnishes him an outlet for self-giving. So it seems like heaven. The one way to peace and bliss, every great prophet has told us, is to give yourself away. From the human standpoint, to give yourself to your fellow men; from the superhuman, to give yourself to God: to the Highest. We are all trying to find our way back—into that one normal and natural condition.

We set out on Pilgrimage the minute we are born: out into the glittering world of our own omnipotence, our arrogant self-sufficiency; and some of us wander into a very far country indeed before finally we "come to ourselves" and make the swing-around, back to the place whence we came forth.

Every race, every religion, tells of this eternal quest, this perennial journey. The Chinese call it "the Old Road"; the Hindus "the Path of Return"; in Christianity we read of it in the story of the Prodigal Son.

Everybody knows it is there—that Road of Return. Everybody knows that sooner or later he has to take it. Even the people who are yelling loudest about "sentimental eyewash" and "mediaeval superstition": even they, the self-styled atheists and agnostics know it, deep down in their hearts. The more loudly they howl, the less sure they are of themselves.

Every man is born with that picture—the image of the Goal —deep within him; and never loses it, no matter how low he may fall. The folklore of every people sings of it.

The road to Lourdes is the Road Back Home. Every man must take it, for in the end (as all us sick find out) there is nowhere else to go. In the end, everyone must "come to Lourdes"—the shining city, the beloved community, the city of brothers—the Father's House: the end of the long road where we pilgrims of all faiths and races come Home.

Acknowledgments

Thanks are due primarily to Monseigneur Théas, Bishop of Lourdes, for his gracious approval of this undertaking, and for permitting access to the records and all facilities at Lourdes. Also to the Rector of the Sanctuaries, Monseigneur Ricaud, and to the President of the Hospitallers, the Count de Beauchamp, for help with much valuable material.

I am especially indebted to Dr. Oberlin and Dr. Grenet of the International Medical Commission of Lourdes for their kind counsel and assistance in connection with medical records and appraisals. To Dr. François Leuret, President of the Medical Bureau during my stay in Lourdes, and to Mademoiselle Leuret, then Secretary of the Bureau and curator of the dossiers, my debt is incalculable. Also to Dr. Pelissier, Dr. Olivieri, and Dr. Niewdan—most kind advisers.

Among Catholic friends and leaders in America, besides those already mentioned, I am particularly grateful to the Reverend David McAstocker, S.J., and to Mrs. Fulton Oursler for initial help and suggestions; to the Reverend Michael O'Sullivan and Dr. A. E. Gourdeau for much valuable advice and checking of facts and figures; and to the Maryknoll Sisters for precious books and for their constant prayers and inspiration.

Deep appreciation goes also to Ruth and to Maxwell Aley, who occupied from the first a central place in the project; to

Marguerite Bowman for months of devoted and tireless secretarial service; and to Winifred Feely for special research and assistance along many different lines.

When it comes to acknowledging quoted material, one is in real difficulty. Lourdes material has been quoted and requoted so many times, it is hard to know where some of it actually originated. I have done my best to acknowledge original sources, and to give proper credit to the authors and publishers who have kindly allowed me to quote from their publications.

Foremost among these, thanks go to Dr. Auguste Vallet and Dr. Henri Guinier for the use of substantial portions of their very important writings: Dr. Vallet who as President of the Medical Bureau from 1927–1947 gave such wonderful service, and whose writings are among the most valuable on the cures and on Bureau procedure.

I am much indebted also to M. Louis Abadie of the *Journal de la Grotte* for permission to use material from former issues of the paper—especially stories of the cures and of the Big Pilgrimages. And to the Maison Viron and Maison Lacaze for similar generous help with pictures, old and new. Most of the photographs in this volume come from their files.

Special thanks are due Dr. Smiley Blanton for permission to use portions of his paper before the American Psycho-Analytic and Psychiatric Associations on the cure of Charles McDonald; and to Mr. McDonald himself and his publishers for their very kind cooperation in furnishing material from his personal account of his cure. Also to the Catholic Truth Society for permission to reprint substantial portions of Mr. John Traynor's writings from their booklet *I Met a Miracle.*

To the Cures themselves and their relatives, I am indebted for much generous help with personal material and photographs —especially to Jeanne Fretel, Fernand Legrand, Francis Pascal, Madame Leydet, and Madame Joucan.

In conclusion, I am well aware of some of the dissatisfactions that will be felt in regard to this book. Catholics no doubt will miss certain Catholic overtones and cherished references. But there are many Catholic books in which they will find them; and I believe they will agree that the important thing with a book like this is to get the Lourdes story over to the general public as simply and concisely as possible.

Protestants, on the other hand, may object that the writer —though a Protestant—repeatedly uses Catholic terms, such as the Blessed Sacrament, the Last Rites, the Blessed Virgin, and so forth. The reason for this is obvious. Lourdes is a Catholic shrine, and its religious ceremonies and observances are Catholic. It is therefore not only courteous but inevitable to use Catholic terms in describing them.

Many people will urge that I should have written more about Bernadette. I have not done so for two reasons: first, limitation as to time, and the great amount of research that would be necessary to write of her at all adequately; second, many writers have written volumes about her, and very beautifully—far better than anything I might add. The reader is referred to these books, in which he will find detailed and fascinating stories of this beloved and remarkable person. The present book has to do especially with accounts of Lourdes cures and the Pilgrimages.

Again referring to time limitations, I would ask my readers —especially doctors—to have in mind the enormous amount of material that had to be gone over, translated, and abridged in connection with these accounts. Any apparent gaps or omissions should be put down not to a lack in Lourdes records but to my own physical limitations of time and energy. The complete records are there for anyone who cares to take the time and trouble to read them.

In the midst of preparing this manuscript, word has come of the death of Dr. Leuret, from 1947 to 1954 President of the Medical Bureau. His passing is a terrible loss to all friends of Lourdes, myself among them.

Here was an ideal combination of exacting man of science

and unassuming follower of religion. Dr. Leuret never "talked religion." But he himself was such a humble and honest Christian, he gave one great respect for his faith. Every day before morning office hours I saw him trudging across the Square to Mass. Every day, broiling sun or slashing rain, I saw him walk the long mile down and back along the Esplanade, in the Procession—and always at the very end; after all the priests and bishops, nuns and organizations, all the pilgrims, came Dr. Leuret —last in line.

Something tremendously touching about that modest figure, so unobtrusive, so vitally important—for his sharp probing eye watched constantly for some significant move or sign of possible cure among the sick—even while his devout knee bent in earnest and sincere worship.

Without his unending kindness and help, this book would never have been written. It is dedicated to him especially— together with the other "valiant and devoted men" who have served Lourdes and the Bureau so faithfully.

Thanks are tendered to the following publishers through whose courtesy quotations and reprints appear in this volume: The Bruce Publishing Company for *After Bernadette* by Don Sharkey, 1945; Burns, Oates & Washburne, Ltd., for *The Crowds of Lourdes* by J. K. Huysmans, 1925; The Catholic Truth Society, for "I Met a Miracle" by Rev. Patrick O'Connor, 1951; Clonmore and Reynolds, Dublin, for *Miracle at Lourdes* by Charles McDonald, 1953; *Commonweal Magazine*; Flammarion, for *La Vérité sur Lourdes* by Augustin Vallet, 1944; Harper & Brothers, for *Man, the Unknown*, 1939, and *Voyage to Lourdes* by Alexis Carrel, 1950; Manresa Press, for *Lourdes* by Mons. Robert Hugh Benson, 1921; Presses Universitaires, for *Guérisons Miraculeuses Modernes* by Drs. Leuret and Bon, 1950; Ratisbone Publishing Company, for *Heaven's Recent Wonders* by P. G. Boissarie, 1909; Rinehart & Company, Inc., for *Can Prayer Be Answered* by Mary Austin, 1934; and *The Rosary Magazine*, for *The National Pilgrimage* by Comtesse de Courson, 1912.

Readers wanting further information about Lourdes should address their local Catholic authorities. The author is not qualified, medically or ecclesiastically, to deal with personal problems regarding health, Pilgrimages, etc.

A reminder should be added, again stressing the very small percentage of physical cures *at this shrine. The journey to Lourdes is a deep spiritual experience and blessing, and should be so undertaken. Only one out of ten thousand of the sick is physically cured. True, you might be that one. The chances are 9,999 that you would not be. So if you go, go with the hope of getting the spiritual strength and inspiration—and leave the rest with God.*

Ruth Cranston was literally born into religion. Her father was a minister, and her earliest memories were associated with his preaching. When she was a child, her father took his family to China where he was in charge of a number of missions. The family lived in China for several years, traveling extensively throughout the country. Upon their return, they settled in Washington, and Mrs. Cranston entered Goucher College. While still in college she began to write. Her stories and articles brought her to the attention of H. L. Mencken, then Sunday editor of the Baltimore Sun, and Theodore Dreiser, who was at that time on the staff of the Delineator. Both men commissioned her to write articles for them after her graduation.

Mrs. Cranston's travels after World War I to religious centers in many countries culminated in her appointment to the World Conference of Religions at Geneva. She served on that and other world bodies for ten years until the outbreak of World War II.

Mrs. Cranston has been interested in the subject of spiritual healing for twenty-five years. She began her study of Lourdes after reading accounts of the place in French newspapers and books. In the summer and autumn of 1953 she visited Lourdes, her interest grew, and The Miracle of Lourdes is the result.